THE
PAINE-FRENCH
GENEALOGY

THE
PAINE-FRENCH
GENEALOGY

Beverly Marion (Paine) Martinoli

Order this book online at www.trafford.com
or email orders@trafford.com

Most Trafford titles are also available at major online book retailers.

Print information available on the last page.

ISBN: 978-1-4251-4137-0 (sc)

Trafford rev. 01/15/2021

North America & international
toll-free: 844-688-6899 (USA & Canada)
fax: 812 355 4082

TABLE OF CONTENTS

INTRODUCTION

This book will record the descendants of Merton Kingsley Paine and Ella Gordon (French) Paine. **MERTON K. PAINE** is listed as **(GEN. IX, No.407)** in the Paine-Shepard Genealogy of 1463-1913, compiled by Clara Paine Ohler of Ohio and first printed in 1938. Copies of her book are available through the Higginson Book Company located in Salem, MA.

Clara Ohler's introduction in her book gives a summary of the probable origins of the Paine name. I will include here quotes and excerpts so that the family will be aware of information leading up to our Paine name. "Believed to begin originally with the spelling **PAGANUS** the following explanation is quoted from her book: The surname of Paine however spelled indicates a Norman origin. Rollo or Rolf, Duke of Normandy in the Ninth Century became a convert to Christianity. The people of his Dukedom, however, outside of the larger places, resisted the new religion as is usually the case in all innovations, which first find favor in the cities. The word PAGANUS **meant originally and solely, a dweller in the country as distinguished from one who dwells in the city.** So general was the refusal at first of the inhabitants of the country to accept the Christian religion, that to be a COUNTRYMAN came to mean an UNBELIEVER and the word PAGANUS to express a double meaning, and the name, coming to be thus generally adopted, applied to all who refused the Christian baptism." The dictionary of today gives the meaning of PAGAN as a heathen, one having no religious beliefs.

"When William the Conqueror went from Normandy to England he was accompanied by many of this class of people: and so the term became incorporated in the English language with its new meaning. About this time the habit of using surnames became prevalent, and as people usually chose something with which they had previous connection, the name of **PAGANUS** came into common use as a family designation. It gradually changed its form however to **PAGAN, PAGEN, PAYEN, PAYNE, PAYN** and **PAINE.**

The name is found wherever the Norman exodus pervaded. In **ITALY** it assumed the form of **PAGANINI or PAGANI."**

Her introduction continues with the inclusion of Pagen of Domesday 1041-1086 and Hugh de Payen, as crusader and founder of the Order of Knights Templar. Previous writers of Paine genealogy believe that we are descended from these people.

Mrs. Ohler goes on to say that the English ancestry and place of emigration of Moses Paine of Braintree, MA were discovered in 1912. The discovery was made by Miss Elizabeth French, a genealogist connected with the New England Genealogical and Historical Society. So far as has been determined, Miss French was not an ancestor of Ella G. French.

Thus the line was established back to "John Payn of Frythenden," (England) whose will is dated April 12, 1463. By means of their wills the line is traced through six generations. County Kent and the townships of Frittenden and Tenterden appear to be the areas where these ancestors resided. Moses Paine referred to as the 6th generation in England immigrated to New England. Clara Ohler included the following extract from the New England Historical and Genealogical Register, Vol. 65, pages 290-291.

Among the emigrants from Kent County, England, who came to New England with the company in "The Castle" in 1638, was Moses Paine (with his children Elizabeth, Moses and Stephen), whose forebears had long resided in Frittenden and vicinity, ------. This would appear to establish Moses arrival here in 1638." The foregoing reference can be found on page 36 of Ohler's Paine-Shepard Genealogy.

Therefore Moses Paine **(GENERATION VI)** in England became **(GENERATION I, No.1)** in America. We travel through Mrs. Ohler's book to **(GENERATION VIII),** Henry A. Paine and his wife Louise Stockwell then to **(GENERATION IX),** Merton K. Paine and his wife, Ella

Gordon (French) Paine, thus to their children **(GEN. X)** Mildred L, Gladys, Albert I., Madeleine, Mattie, Mabel and Archie W. Paine.

Further, this book will report as much information as I can locate on the ancestry of the parents of Ella Gordon French, namely William Henry French and Mary H. Dugan.

Many aspects of William H. French's interesting life were chronicled in a Springfield, MA newspaper article published Sunday, Sept. l6, 1924, a second article not dated, and again in his obituary as published by The Springfield Daily Republic on January 8, 1932. Some facts can be documented, others are hearsay. But all, I believe, proven or unproven will be of interest to us as his descendants. It is my understanding that Great Grandpa French loved to spin a good tale.

My sister Nancy and I found the articles and obituary in correspondence Dad, Archie W. Paine, received from his cousin William R. Cole, a grandchild of William H. French, and nephew of our grandmother Ella G. (French) Paine. To date I have been unable to correspond with him or any of his family.

The death of Madeleine (Paine) Seibert in April, 1998 at the age of 98, brought to a close a significant chapter in the Paine Ancestry since Mrs. Seibert was the last living child of Merton K. and Ella G. (French) Paine. I was fortunate to be able to speak with her regarding some of our family records.

This book will also include what we have been led to believe to be our Peregrine White connection (not proven) through Louise L. Stockwell, mother of Merton K. Paine. Peregrine White is believed to be the first white child born in New England, his parents having come over on the Mayflower. A chapter on the White family will show the information, which my research has been able to discover.

Where I have found vital records that pertain, I have obtained certified copies and so noted. Sources from which I obtained information on individual branches of the clan have come mainly from the clan members themselves.

Information was also obtained from the Family Bible of Archie W. and Eldora V. Paine, from cemetery records and gravestones, as well as obituaries, and newspaper articles.

Two World Wars were expected to bring peace to the world, but have not. We have watched many changes in the fields of science and medicine. Scientists still search for cures to the many diseases that kill or disable so many people.

Science can never find a cure for the peace problem. Only we can do that by becoming kinder and gentler, by treating each other as fellow human beings, not by looking at color, race or religious beliefs

Many of our forefathers came to this country over the past two hundred years hoping to leave behind that bigotry and prejudice. Our country fought a Civil War for freedom and equality, and yet over a hundred years after that war, bigotry and prejudice still exist in both our country and throughout the world. We *have* made progress but we still have so far to go.

Peace can only be attained, by allowing each individual the opportunity to become an integral part of society, living and working together as one Human Race. Perhaps the 21st Century will accomplish that goal.

ACKNOWLEDGMENTS

My thanks go to all of the Paine cousins who have contributed information to help put this family tree together, in particular to Rachel (Ferrante) Brown, who gave me a journal of Ella G. (French) Paine to copy, as well as a wedding picture of Merton K. and Ella Gordon French; to Bob August who wrote of memories of the Grandparents Merton K. and Ella G. French Paine and others; to Bertha and Lois (Weed) who wrote of family and traveling across the country when the family moved to Colorado, along with memories of the home in Simsbury and other families in Simsbury. Lois also speaks of her life in Attica, Kansas and their final move to the State of Washington. My thanks also go to Fred Weed who gave me excerpts from his Biographical Sketch of his first wife Jo Donna Berry Weed. Fred remarried and he and his lovely wife Ruth reside in Arizona. Many thanks too, to my cousin Bill Seibert who supplied me with a number of the pictures which will appear in this book.

Grateful thanks also go to Dr. Keith C. Alderman who remembers well my father, Archie W. Paine and our second mother Florence B. Paine when he helped them do some of the building at 4 Cemetery Rd, and also to my son, Jack for allowing me to print his Eulogy to his Grandmother, Florence and to my sister, Candy, for allowing me to print here her Memories of a Sister.

I've included verbatim several articles from the Springfield Republican, Springfield, MA dated 1924, circa 1930-31, and an obituary in January 1932 all in reference to our Great Grandfather William H. French.

My thanks and appreciation go to folks connected to the USS Constellation Museum, namely Chris Rowsom, Executive Director and John Pentangelo, Curator and Development Coordinator, for their suggestions and aid in editing the chapter on *Constellation*.

I must also mention authors of *Constellation*'s history for allowing me to use excerpts from the following:
"USS Constellation A Short History of the Last All-Sail Warship Built by the U. S. Navy" by Glenn F. William; and
"USS Constellation an Illustrated History" by Stephen B. Bockmuller and Lawrence J. Bopp, which is a part of "The Civil War Series." Both books contain a photo of William H. French and also include some of remarks.

I also must acknowledge a book entitled "Passenger Arrivals at the Port of New York 1830-1832" by Elizabeth P. Bentley which allowed me to find the record of the ship upon which the John French Family arrived in this country.

I cannot conclude this page without acknowledging and thanking Paul Sweeney, the great-grandson of William A. Leonard, who I lately discovered served aboard *Constellation* during the same time period as William H. French. Mr. Leonard kept a marvelous journal which has been made available to the USS Constellation Museum. Mr. Sweeney has graciously allowed me to make mention of excerpts from the journal.

My love and thanks to my own family, who have so generously helped in many aspects of the book including taking me to see *Constellation* in its various stages of restoration. I will be eternally grateful for their putting up with me in my research and listening endlessly to my excitement about my discoveries.

Lastly, heartfelt thanks to Kate Ladyko who so ably assisted me in proofreading this book.

CHAPTER ONE

GENERATIONS VIII, IX, and X

The Paine Ancestors and descendants as listed in the Paine-Shepard Genealogy compiled by Clara Paine Ohler, published in 1938 and listed here, pertain to Merton Kingsley Paine.

Copies of Ohler's "Paine-Shepard Genealogy" are available through the Higginson Book Co. in Salem, MA, which contains a more complete ancestral reference.

HENRY ALBERT PAINE (GEN. VIII, Paine Family)
   b. Apr. l, 1846 at Ludlow, MA
   d. Jan. 13, 1919 at Belchertown, MA
   bur. Mt. Hope Cem., Belchertown, MA
   m. Mar. 30, 1869 at Belchertown, MA to
LYDIA (LOUISE) LAVINA STOCKWELL
   b. Jul. 31, 1848 at So. Amherst, MA.
   d. Mar. 29, 1922 at Enfield, MA,
   bur. Mt. Hope Cem., Belchertown, MA

Authority: Certified Copies of Vital Records from Archives Div., Commonwealth of MA: Marriage and Deaths (Note) Marriage record shows Louise as Louiza.

In an excerpt from the Stockwell Genealogy by Mabel Stockwell Kennedy, I find reference to Louise's name as Lydia Lavina with same birth date and marriage date to Henry A. Paine. Further reference to names both given and surname of this family will be found in another chapter on spouses and their ancestors

Henry A. Paine and Louise L. Stockwell

GENERATION IX
Child number two of Henry A. and Louise (Stockwell) Paine

Merton K. Paine
Age 18

MERTON KINGSLEY PAINE (GEN. IX, No.407, Paine Family)
   b. Jul. 6, 1870 at Belchertown, MA
   d. Aug. 14, 1937 at Hartford, CT
   bur. Curtiss Cem., Simsbury, CT
   m. Jan. 7, 1891 at Springfield, MA to

ELLA GORDON FRENCH
b. Jun. 14, 1868 at Harpers Ferry, W.VA
d. Mar. 28, 1957 at Avon, CT
bur. Curtiss Cem., Simsbury, CT

Authority: Certified Copies of Vital Records Birth for Merton, Belchertown, MA; Marriage—Springfield, MA; Deaths—for Merton, Hartford, CT; for Ella, Avon, CT

GENERATION X
Children of Merton K. & Ella G. (French) Paine

626	Mildred Louise	b. Nov. 12, 1891 at Springfield, MA
627	Gladys	b. Feb. 8, 1894 at Springfield, MA, d. Jul. 9, 1894
628	Albert Irving	b. Apr. 1, 1896 at Springfield, MA
629	Madeleine	b. Dec. 22, 1899 at Westfield, MA
630	Mattie	b. May 5, 1903 at Simsbury, CT
631	Mabel	b. May 5, 1903 at Simsbury, CT
632	Archie William	b. Mar. 9, 1905 at Simsbury, CT

The following is an article submitted by Merton K. Paine and published August 5, 1934 in a newspaper having a circulation in Simsbury, CT.

M. K. PAINE TELLS OF TRIP THROUGH WEST
M.K. Paine of Bushy Hill, who has recently returned from a trip to the west, writes of it in the following interesting way.

Missouri is great and has many interesting things but the great spaces of unimproved land struck us for a hundred miles north of Springfield, MO. The people are not plenty and the little cabins are fenced in to keep out the cattle and hogs that roam everywhere. We saw a good sized shoat beside the road, killed possibly by a passing auto. The next morning we saw a good sized steer in the same condition.

No fences, no telephone poles beside the road for miles and miles made us feel that it was not a good place to have auto trouble, but we also saw great possibilities.

On into old Kentucky where I saw watermelons by the two mile load, by the auto truckload and the freight car load. Here we visited cotton fields, sweet potato fields. One farm where we stopped, of 750 acres with 200 acres of corn made us feel rather small. Here is where we saw water and toll bridges until we thought we would go broke. The Mississippi, the Ohio, the Tennessee, Cumberland, and the Green Rivers all come in a bunch and are wonderful to look at. It would fill a book to tell all we saw in Kentucky so I will not try.

But want to pass on to the mountains in West Virginia and the crooked roads, short turns, and sharp valleys. Here we saw where there had recently been floods. People were still clearing the mud from their homes. These were all new to us.

Maryland and Virginia were more along the lines of prosperous farms. Then on to Philadelphia, through Trenton, the outskirts of New York, up to Yonkers, where we crossed on the ferry across the Hudson and home tired and happy, filled with the thought that a good car and good driver and good weather and one may gypsy with pleasure and see and learn a great deal.

JOURNAL OF ELLA GORDON FRENCH PAINE
January 1943 through December, 1947

JANUARY 1943
Jan.26th-Alice passed away this morning

Feb.3-Bill took me to the Doctor (Murphy) then I spent the rest of the day with Mattie.

Feb.6-Dr. Murphy came to see me this evening. Mildred and Fred called-also Archie called

Feb.10-Archie ran in for few minutes.

Feb.16-32 below zero at 7:30 A.M.

Feb.17-went to see Dr. Murphy

March 6-went with Mabel and Dim after groceries-Ice storm last night

March 8-Monday-washed today, nice drying day. I went with Mary and Irving and Mattie up to Archie's. His Birthday Party as that was his day off-had a nice time. Willie did not feel well so did not go.

Tuesday Mar. 9-8 below zero at 7:30 A.M.

March 14-Sunday-Irving and family came for dinner-Mildred, Fred, Dorothy, Mildred Louise, Doris Brown (Elkhart), husband and baby also called in the afternoon. What a nice visit we all had.

March 20-evening went home with Mildred and Fred for a weeks visit.

March 21-Sunday-Dorothy, Mildred Louise, and I went to church at Bloomfield

March 22-Mildred washed and did the days work as usual.

March 23 Tuesday-Tony and little Jimmie came and stayed until (l) Friday 26. We all had such a nice visit.

March 27-Saturday-Mildred and Fred took me home-such a nice time and feel quite rested.

March 21-Willie's Birthday - gave her a party while I was away.

March 29-Monday and wash day

March 31-Wednesday-Madeleine and Harry came for a while. Mabel went home with them.

April 1st-Thursday - working out of doors today, what time I could, cleaning flower beds, trimming shrubs and etc.

April 4-Sunday-Bill Beine, Mr. and Mrs. Rice from Westfield called today

April 8-Thursday-snow last night-nice white world this morning.

April 10-Saturday-went with Mabel and Dim after groceries

April 11-Sunday-nice spring morning. Mabel and Dim went to see his mother. This has been a quiet Sabbath.

April 14-Wednesday Madeleine and Harry came for a few minutes today. It seemed so good to see them

April 23-Friday evening Ruth, Willie's friend and two of her friends came with her.

April 25-Easter Sunday-went up to Archie's for the day-found him sick in bed with Grippe. Mr. Bayette took us all down to church at Collinsville.

May 2-Sunday-Madeleine spent the day with us. Leonard and Donnie came for supper. Willie sick in Bed

May 3-Monday-washed and did the regular work-rainy day

May 10-Monday-Millie (French) and her brother came today.

May 14-Friday-Mildred and Fred came for a while

May 9th-Mother's Day-went to the hospital to see Uncle Arthur, with Archie and Dora.

May 26-Sunday-Irving came after Millie, Willie and I to have dinner with them-had a pleasant time.

May 16-Mabel's folks moved into their own house.

May 17-Millie went home today. Irving took her to Weatogue to get the bus to Hartford.

May 21-Friday-Rainy day and cold more like fall

.

May 23-Sunday-Dim, Shirley, Junior and I went to church-heard a fine Sermon by Mr. Pope.

May 26-Wednesday-raining this morning-lots of rain lately.

June 27-Julia and Bill came today

July 9-Julia and Bill returned home today-had a lovely visit.

July 12-Irving and Mary came this evening for my eggs. We do so enjoy having them for a little visit.

June 21-Millie's Aunt Jane died today

July 26-Fred Jr. and Mabel called this afternoon-so glad as he is leaving Aug.2nd for the service.

9

July 22-Martha, her two children and her two Aunts (visited)-was so glad to see them

July 27-Children had the telephone put in for me-so lovely of them.

July 25-Archie and family called this Sunday evening

July 17-went to see Dr. Murphy and said I must go to bed for a while and I am still there July 31 -am some better and hope I shall be around soon

July 29-Mr. and Mrs. DeCotean (?) called today

July 30-Herald Pierce and wife called today

Aug.17-Dorothy came to spend a few days with us

Aug.20-Willie and I went to Bill and Mattie's anniversary tonight

Sept.16-Archie came to take Willie and I up to their house for the day.

Sept.19-Mabel went with Mr. and Mrs. Hughes after apples this evening. This has been rather a lonely day as no one has been in.

Oct.2-Dim, Mabel, Junior and Buster went to the Stafford Fair today, Saturday.

Sept.29 –Irving, Mary, Mrs. Hadsell, Willie and I went up to Archie's for their 16th anniversary being tomorrow - had a very nice time.

Oct.1 -just heard that Merton Seibert has the Scarlet fever.

Oct.19-Mr. Geo. Case buried this afternoon. I went with Mabel and Mrs. Stumpf

Oct.4-Alfred Danforth married today

Nov.7-Sunday-Archie sent for Willie and I-to their home for supper and spent the evening. Dora's friends Dot and John and two children were there.

Nov.10-Went with Mabel and Dim after groceries-Mabel and Junior here for supper.

Nov.21-Sunday-7 A.M.-21 above zero.

Nov.22-Monday-our first snow storm of the winter

Nov.25-Thursday-Thanksgiving Day-Willie and I spent the day with Mildred. Mr. & Mrs. McLoughlin came for us and brought us home-had a very nice time-14 at dinner.

Nov.30-Tuesday-Arthur Pixley came this afternoon and stayed overnight with us.

Dec.1-Wednesday-Willie and I went to Hartford today with Bill and Mattie

Dec.12-Sunday-Archie and family came in for a few minutes—he did a little work at his house.

10

Dec.13-Mailed the last of my Christmas cards this a.m.-very cold-- high wind.

Dec.1-Wednesday-3 above zero at 8 A.M.-went after groceries

Dec.14-Mabel and I went to Hartford with Mattie-went in with Dim-came out with Bill

Dec.25-Saturday-Christmas-Willie and I spent the day with Mattie's family

Dec.27-Monday-Willie taken sick-hard cold

Dec.30-Thursday a.m.-4 above zero at 8 A.M.

JANUARY, 1944
Jan.1st 10 a.m. 35 above zero

Jan.2-Sunday-2 above zero at 8 A.M.

Jan.6-Thursday-our second snow storm last night and snow and rain
through the day-tonight the wind is blowing rather hard.

Jan.8th-Saturday-Mildred and Fred stopped on their way from getting groceries-the first time
since Mildred was sick.

Jan.9th-Sunday-20 above zero at 4 P.M. but just lovely and clear

Jan. 15-Sunday-went up to call on Mrs. Vining. Shirley started her job in the Finance Co.-starts
tomorrow-went to her boarding place today.

Jan.22-Sat.-Mildred and Fred stopped for a while on their way from getting groceries.

Jan.23-Sunday-Archie and Dora and the children came in this afternoon

Jan.25-Wednesday-raining tonight-Willie sick in bed over a week

Feb.14-Sister Millie came today to help care for Willie

Jan.16-Willie was taken sick in bed today

Feb.23-Took Willie to Private Hospital-Niles Hospital-60 Niles St. Hartford-took her in
William's car-Dim and Mabel went with us. I stayed with her all day. Roy came that evening.
Mildred came (on the) 22nd to help care for her.

Feb.24-Mildred went home today.

Feb.27 –Sunday-Archie and Dora came for Millie and I to go in to the hospital to see Willie. Roy
is going home on the 6 o'clock train

Feb.28-Monday-Mabel and Millie went to see Willie today.

Feb.29-Tuesday-Millie went with Mary and Irving and will stop to see Willie.

April 2-Sunday - went in to Hospital to see Willie today - went with Archie and Dora

April 9 -Easter Sunday-Dim and Mabel took me up to see Madeleine and Harry

Apr.11-Tuesday-Harry and Madeleine brought me home this a.m.-had a very nice visit.

Apr.14-Friday-went in to city to see Dr. Kilbourn-Eye Specialist about my eyes-also went to Hospital to see Willie-found her about the same

Apr.16-Sunday-Archie, Dora and Buster came this afternoon and stayed for supper

Apr.20-Thursday-Archie's garage burned down today

Apr.23-Sunday-Archie, Dora, Mildred and I went in to Hospital to see Willie

Apr.24-Monday went in to get my new glasses and then went to see Willie-found her not quite so well

Apr.30-went in to Hospital with Archie and Dora
May 19-Friday heavy frost last night-went in to Hospital

May 20-Saturday-frost last night

May 21-Sunday went to Hospital to see Willie

May 14-Mother's Day-Fred came and took me down to church-spent the day at Mildred's-Dot brought me home at 6 P.M.

June 6-Tuesday-Invasion of Europe started 3:30 A.M. this morning

June 6-Everett Pixley and son Albert called today and stayed for supper-then went to Hospital to see Willie

June 18-Sunday-have been alone all day. Mabel's folks took dinner and went fishing-just started raining

June 22-Thursday-Mildred, Fred and Bob here for dinner-Bob home on Furlow

July 2-Sunday-Fred came and took me to church-stayed the rest of the day with Mildred

July 6-Archie came-went to West Hartford with him then to his house for a while-got home 9:40 P.M.

Aug.9-Wednesday-went to Unionville with Mary and Irving-lovely ride

Aug.22-Tuesday Mrs. Hadsell came this a.m.

Aug.28-Monday Mrs. Hadsell went home today

Aug.28-Monday Bob came for a while today.

Sept.1-Friday night-went with William when he went up to Madeleine's after Mattie who had been spending a few days up there

Sept.4-came home with Mildred and Fred who came up Saturday night-we all had a very nice time.

Sept.24-Sunday-our first frost last night. Mattie, Bill and the Boys called for a while-also Eleanor stopped in on her way home.

Oct.2-Monday-Julia and Billie came today

Oct. 13-Julia and Billie went home today

Oct.25-Wednesday-Bob, Archie and I planned for Bob to buy my land. Bob went back to his base Thursday.

Oct.27-Navy day-Rear Admiral Morrow.

Nov.6-Monday snow flurries all day first of the season - much colder

Nov.7-Tuesday-Election day for President

Nov.13-Monday-A.M.-7 o'clock-28 above zero. Archie, Dora, Mr. and Mrs. Root, her sister and I went to Westfield to look over my land- lovely day also

Nov.16-Thursday started snowing hard this afternoon at five o'clock-had been raining hard all day

Nov.19-Sunday went with Archie and Dora to see Willie. She does seem a lot better. Lovely weather we are having

Nov.26-Sunday-a lovely day-Madeleine and Harry brought Mabel home-she went up Friday to help Madeleine can meat. Mary, Irving and Mrs. Hadsell also called

Dec.3-Sunday-Archie and I went in to the Hospital to see Willie today-found her feeling quite like herself.

Dec.6-Red Cross met with Mrs. Johnson-8 present-had a very pleasant time.

Dec.20-Wednesday-Arthur and Greta came today-after dinner we went in to see Willie

Dec.24-Archie and family here for supper-went in to see Willie with Mattie and Bill-stopped to see Millie

Dec.25-Spent Christmas day with Irving--Mrs. Hadsell was there-had a nice time

Dec.29-2 above zero at 8 A.M.

Dec.30-2 below zero at 8 A.M.

JANUARY, 1945

Jan.1-This has been a rather lonely day as none of the children have been in and rather a cloudy day too but I am comfortable so won't complain

Jan.4-Mildred and I went to Hartford. Went in to see Willie. Al (St Pierre) came home-their third Wedding anniversary

Jan.29-Water pipes frozen this morning-been very cold for the past week-around zero

Jan.30-men came to thaw the pipes-how true we never miss the water till the well runs dry.

Jan.22-Harry and Madeleine brought Mrs. Seibert here to Board.

Mar.23-everything pure and white this morning-cloudy and looks as thought we might have more by night

Mar.21-Willie's Birthday-seven of us went in Irving's car to the Hospital and gave her a little surprise-Mary, Mrs. Hadsell, Mattie, Arthur who was home on Furlow, Mrs. Seibert, and I,-Ice cream and cookies were served - she enjoyed it very much.

Mar.25-Millie (French) came this afternoon - her Minister's wife brought her-she went to see her folks who live in Pleasant Valley

Mar.27-Tuesday- Mrs. Seibert went to Glastonbury with Arthur as he was home on furlow so he took her as far as East Hartford. Mary and Irving had gone to Detroit, Mich. the Sunday of March 25 to see Grace.

Apr .1-Mabel, Dim, Junior, Shirley and I went to the Easter Service, then in the afternoon Archie and Dora took Mildred and I in to see Willie, then up to see Alice and Earl for supper-had a very pleasant time.

Apr.2-Monday Irving and Mary's Anniversary Archie and Phillip and Buster, Arthur and Girlfriend, Mattie, Bill, Dim, Shirley, Mrs. Hadsell, and I. & Gladys

Apr.3-Thursday-Mrs. Hadsell came to visit me.

Apr.10-Mrs. Hadsell went over to spend a week with Mabel and help her with a Rug

Apr.12-President Roosevelt died at 3:35 this afternoon.

Apr.15-went to church with Mabel and family in the afternoon went to see Dr. Murphy on our way to the Hospital to see Willie-found her quite happy.

June 15-Strawberry supper and entertainment at Avon with Mabel and Family

June 16-Strawberry supper at Neighborhood House went-with Mabel and Family

June 17-went to children's concert at church with Mabel's Family

June 24-Sunday-Madeleine, Harry and Merton spent the weekend with Mabel. I went up to Archie's for dinner - he brought me home in the evening-had hot dog roast outside for supper-lots of folks there

June 26-Tuesday -went in to Hartford with Irving and Mary-went to see Willie-came out on the 5:27 bus - stayed overnight with Mildred-in the morning Mildred and I went in to Hartford with Mildred Louise-took the bus to Glastonbury and spent the day with Mrs. Seibert-had a lovely time-she has such a nice place to live. She got a letter saying she was to get her State Aid-we were thankful for her.

June 28-Thursday-did a little ironing but did not feel much like working after our trip.

July 1-Sunday Archie's folks took John & Dot Gisler to the train-they have spent two weeks with Archie's folks - so we went in to see Willie-found her comfortable.

July 22-Sunday Archie and family took me down to see Madeleine-stayed until Saturday 28th-had a very nice time. Came home with the man that works for Harry. Their folks live in Southwick. Merton also went with them to see Leonard.

Aug.14-Tuesday the war with Japan over today-praise the Lord for this victory.

Aug.19-Cousin Austin Stockwell and Lizzie were here today. Margrett and daughter over to Mabel's for a few days.

Aug.30-Thursday-Roy came to see his mother today.

Sept.2-Archie and Dora, children, Mrs. Hadsell and I went in to see Willie
Sept.4-Roy went home today

Sept.6-15 '45-Archie, Dora, Mrs. Hadsell and I took a wonderful trip south-saw so many places of interest-lovely weather all the time-will have so much to think of the long winter days ahead.

Sept.30-returned to standard time tonight

Oct.14-Sunday Archie, the boys and I went in to see Willie today-found her comfortable then went home with him to dinner and then up to Southwick to see Madeleine-got home about 8:30 and Mildred and Fred came in for a few minutes so I had a full day but a very

Oct.15-Monday washed today-not a very pleasant day-cold and chilly

Oct.16-Tuesday Irving and Mary went to the city. Mrs. Hadsell spent the afternoon with me-had a nice visit

Oct.17-Wednesday-I went up to Mattie's and Irving's for a while. Irving brought me home.

Oct.29-Tuesday Millie came to live with me today

Nov.14-Wednesday Millie and I went to Hartford with Archie-came out on the bus and had supper with Mildred-they brought us home.

Nov.16-Friday went with Mabel and Dim for groceries at Collinsville and then to the movies.

Nov.22-Thursday-Thanksgiving Day. Mabel and family and I spent the day with Madeleine and Harry-rained hard when we started but cleared later.

Nov.23-our first snow squall of the season

Nov.19-Tuesday-Millie went to Templeton to spend Thanksgiving

Dec.10-Mildred and Fred came up for dinner also Madeleine, Harry, Merton and Billie as he was home from the West Coast on furlow last Saturday

Dec.8-the family met at his house to welcome him home

Dec.17-Irving and I went to Westfield tonight to sign the deed for the sale of my building lot. Millie and Mary and Buster went with us. We stopped on the way home to see Madeleine

Dec.22-Saturday-went with Mr. & Mrs. Root after groceries.

Dec.23-Sunday-went to see Willie

Dec.24-Christmas Eve-Archie and Family came this evening-fire at Niles St. Hospital where Willie was. Willie O.K.

Dec.25-Christmas Day-sent telegram to Roy to let him know that his Mother was alright. Millie and I spent the day with Mildred. Fred Jr. came for us and brought us home. Had a quiet day. In the afternoon Archie took us in to see Willie-found her very much broken up which was no wonder after what she had been through.

JANUARY, 1946
Jan.1-No mail today-We are having more cold weather

Jan.2-Shirley's wedding day-reception at her home-31 present, Bertha Mae was Bride's Maid. They looked so sweet, but she seems like a little girl to me, but it is hard to realize that the children are growing up. I pray they may be happy.

Jan.5-writing to Roy tonight

Jan.10-Willie was taken from St. Francis Hospital, where they took her after the fire, to the Dawson Convalescent home on 5 Highland St.

Jan.13-Went to see Willie--Millie, Mary, Irving and I.
Jan.14-I went in to see Willie today. Millie stayed in the city to do some trading.

Jan.16 -10 above zero at 7:30 A.M.--still 10 above at 9 P.M.

Jan.20-Sunday - Archie and I went to see Willie. She is not so well today.

Feb.3-Sunday Millie and I went in to see Willie. Archie and Dora took us in. Willie did not look very well, but her mind was real clear. She was quite like herself

Feb.7-Monday-lovely winter-I did my washing

Feb.8-Tuesday Ironed, very cold 4 above zero at 7:30 A.M.

Feb.26-Tuesday Arthur, Greta and 5 year old Calvin, their youngest, came today.

March 6-Millie and I went to the city.

Mar.17-Sunday Mr. Milligan, his son Wilbur, his Daughter, Mrs. West and a Lady friend of Wilbur's - Millie's folks came today.

Mar.18 –Monday-Mildred's 30th Anniversary, also Mr. and Mrs. A.W. Vining's 50th Anniversary.

Mar.20-Wednesday-Millie left this a.m. will spend a couple weeks with her niece at Ballard Vale, Mass and then she and her brother will go to St. Andrews, N.B. for the summer. I went to see her off at Hartford.

April 2-Tuesday-quite a snow storm last night-went into Hartford with Mary and Irving-went to the Hospital to see Willie-came back early and went home with them as it was their 29th Anniversary -there were 19 present

April 5-Friday Mrs. Seibert came today

April 7-Archie and Dora took Mrs. Seibert and I in to see Willie

April 8-Monday-quite a snowstorm today

April 9-Mrs. Seibert went home today. She went in to city with Irving and   Mary

Apr.19-Good Friday Mildred and I went to city today. Bought Spring Hat and   Material for coat

Apr. 21-Easter Sunday Went to Church at Collinsville with Archie and Family-had dinner with them and in the afternoon went in to see Willie

Apr. 23-Tuesday Rev. Woodruff our minister called this afternoon-worked in my flowers and did my ironing.

Apr. 28-Sunday went to call on Mrs. Vining

May 2 –Thursday - Mrs. Charles Rowe and Mrs. Brown called the Nurseryman??

May 4-Saturday-Went to Mabel's for supper as the twins and their families were having their Birthday Party together as they usually do- only a day early as they were unable to have it on the 5th.

May 5-Sunday-went in to the Hospital to see Willie with Dora, Candy and Archie and then went to the Hospital to see Dorothy and her first baby a lovely little Boy, one day old.

May 12-Mothers Day-went to church with Mildred Louise and Myles and spent the rest of the day with Mildred

May 9th-Friday-Arthur Pixley came in for a while, expecting to take a new job up in Maine where he went the 12th of May

June 2-Sunday-Madeleine dropped in for just a minute to bring my Birthday present. Went up to Irving's for the afternoon and evening. Irving has been in bed for a week-wrenched his back

June 29-Saturday Willie passed away about 12:30 A.M.

July 2-Willie's Funeral at 9:30 A.M. Buried in Springfield. Roy got here Sunday night June 30th. Then went home Wednesday July 3.

July 4th-we had our Family reunion July 4th at Neighborhood House-40 present-lovely day.

July 3-Mildred, Fred and Bob moved their things in my hen house for storage until they could go into their new home which they are building and they came to live with me.
June (July?) 7-Friday-Mildred Louise was taken sick, Mildred stayed with me and cared for her - she was in bed 4 weeks.

July 25-Thursday-Had Doctor-went to bed

Sept.29,'46-Sunday-Grandma Paine day-children and grandchildren came to work for me. Shingled House and (did) many other jobs that needed doing very much-so lovely of them.
Present
26-had Picnic Lunch-a lovely day and all had a nice time.

Oct.30-Madeleine and family came as they were unable to come Sunday and mended and painted the woodshed.

Nov.20-Picked a Dandelion today

Nov.21-Millie went into the city with Bob and Mabel August

Nov.28-Thanksgiving Day-Charlie, Millie and I were planning on spending the day with Archie and Dora, but I was sick so Millie stayed home with me. Charlie went with Irving's folks, but the girls saw that we had a nice dinner with Millie's help.

Nov.30-Saturday-Flo Williamson called today.

Dec.2-very cold, around 20 above zero all day. Radio says 6 above tonight-some change when we have been having such lovely weather around 70.

Dec.10-Started surveying and making the new street post. Our place very warm-out our north kitchen window it was 64 above zero.

Dec.11-Built a new fire in the dining room today.

Dec.25-Christmas-we were invited to Mattie's. Charlie went. Millie stayed home with me as I was sick. Mildred came in and helped get the dinner, and stayed and had dinner with us. Received many presents and Christmas cards, and most of the children came in during the day.

JANUARY, 1947

Jan.18th-Signed the paper so Bob could borrow money at the Simsbury Bank on the first house he built on my land I sold him.

Jan.19-Buster started from Hartford for Fort Lauderdale, Florida to see Alfred. Buster drove down with a man going from Hartford

Jan.31-Friday-Lovely day-like spring-temperature in the 60's in the middle of the day.

Feb.15-Saturday Bob and others shingling the first house where the Barn used to be - lovely day.

Feb.16-Sunday-Raymond Cole and Patsy his oldest daughter called this morning on their way home from Pittsfield, Mass. Patsy is to be married in June. Archie, Dora, Candy, and Nancy also called in the evening.

Feb.21-Friday-snowing this morning hard and last night Radio said 2 inches of snow fell the first snow to amount to much this winter. 9 A.M. and still snowing hard.

Feb.23-Sunday-Millie, Charlie and I spent the afternoon with Archie and Dora and had supper and a very pleasant time.

Mar.3-Monday-Mabel came this afternoon and washed the floors in my dining room, bathroom and kitchen.

Mar.2-Sunday-Went with Archie, Dora, Nancy, Patty to the Hartford Hospital to see Shirley and her first Baby (Geo. A. Poirier, Jr.)

Feb.27-Thursday-Madeleine and family came home from Florida-arrived home 5:30 P.M.

Mar.10-Archie, Dora, Nancy and Patty came this evening. I was sick in bed with a cold.

Apr.19-Saturday-Irving and Mary took Millie and Charlie to B___ly, Canada. Started 12:30 Noon. They were here with me all winter.

Apr.20-Sunday-Archie, Dora and Nancy came in for a few moments. They had been to see Uncle Arthur who is sick at the Pettersen Convalescent home in West Avon.

Apr.21-Monday-rain this morning turning to snow this afternoon. The ground is quite white. Bleak and cold--regular March day.

Apr.24 -Mrs. Moody came to live with me.

May 30-Bill and Mattie invited all over to the Peoples Forest where they are living in their trailer to have a Picnic. Fred Jr. came and got Mrs. Moody and I. We stayed a while-quite a crowd.

July 16-Archie and Dora came this evening-did two jobs that needed doing for me.

Aug.10-Sunday-Archie and Dora came this afternoon returned from their trip after spending a week. Took Nancy, Pattie, and Phillip and spent a while with Aunt Millie in St.Andrews, Canada

Jun.17-Mildred moved into her New Home today.

June 23-Bill and Mattie and their 3 children started on their trip west. Bertha is to meet them at Buffalo, N.Y. and travel with them three weeks.

Aug.25-Dimock and Shirley arrived home this evening-had a lovely time.

Sept.21-Sunday-Buster called today--home on his first furlow.

Sept.26-our first heavy frost

Oct.6-Monday Millie came this afternoon.

Oct.17-82 degrees on the North side of our house 3 in the afternoon.

Nov.2-Sunday 7 A.M. nice morning a little colder than we have been having-have had a beautiful fall.

Nov.3-Monday-Archie and family came this evening

Nov.23-Sunday Archie and Dora came for a couple hours-rather cloudy today. Shirley came in with George Jr.

Nov.30-our first snow today.

Dec.1-15-above zero at 7:30 A.M.

Dec.8-Millie went to Boston with Dorothy and Al on their way to Maine. She went to see about her eyes.

Dec.11-everything pure and white this morning as it snowed last night

Dec.23-Tuesday--Our first big snowstorm.

Dec.25-Christmas Day-Millie and I spent the day with Irving and family-had-a nice time. Santa was wonderful to me as usual.

Dec. 30-Mr. Judd put in the gas heater.

Dec.31-Donnie Paine called today--home from the west coast for a few days-so glad to see him

Author's Note: The foregoing journal was obtained from the attic of the Dimock and Mabel Glazier home located on Bushy Hill Rd., in Simsbury, CT .The owner of the house, their Granddaughter, Rachel (Ferrante) Brown was kind enough to allow me to copy it and I have included it here verbatim. The house has since been sold.

COPY OF HANDWRITTEN WILL
By: Ella Gordon (French) Paine

Dec. 2, 1946
My dear Children,
These things I would like each of you to have:

Mildred
Electric Toaster (Sewing Machine/Motor crossed off added to Madeleine)
My best set of silver your children gave me.
The old gold Broach that was your Great Grandmother Stockwell's

Irving
The Safe
My Plain Gold band ring

Madeleine
My Best Set of green and white Dishes
The Gold Bracelet that Aunt Willie gave me
8 Silver Tea Spoons to match in small folder
Bar Pin that was Great Grandmother Stockwell's
Sewing Machine and Motor

Mabel
My wrist watch
The Broach that Alfred gave me
Electric Mix Master
6 knives and forks in red and white folder and
Organ

Mattie
My Engagement Ring
Parlor Clock
Sugar Shell & Butter Knife which was a wedding gift
The Silver soup ladle

Archie
My silver napkin ring which was my mother's - has her initials MHE on it
The old chest of drawers and the Handmade chair that was Aunt Willie's made by the
Shakers (Electric Toaster crossed off, added to Mildred)

Mary
The willow sandwich (?) tray
Tall standard cake dish not Plain
Silver cold meat fork

Dora
The necklace that she and Mattie bought for me--on trip at Old Orchard, Aug.1933
Tall standard cake dish plain
Silver Pie Knife

My dear Children,
The rest of the things in the home, divide as near equal as you can. It is my wish that each of you
will be pleased, and that they may be useful.

Lovingly, Mother

Author's Note: A copy of the foregoing list was found among the papers of Archie W. Paine, Sr. I do not know where the original is to be found, if still in existence. It would seem plausible that each child was given a copy of this for their own use, perhaps at the time their Mother went into the nursing home and the household was broken up

.

Descendants of: Merton K. Paine (Gen. IX, Paine Family) and
Ella G. (French) Paine

MILDRED LOUISE PAINE (GEN. X, Paine Family)
   b. Nov. 12, 1891 at Springfield, MA
   d. Oct. 30, 1984 at Avon, CT
   bur. Curtiss Cem., Simsbury, CT
   m. Mar. 17, 1916 at Simsbury, CT to
FERDINAND RUDOLPH AUGUST
   b. Sep. 21, 1892 at Burlington, CT
   d. Nov. 22, 1957 at Simsbury, CT
   bur. Curtiss Cem., Simsbury, CT

GENERATION XI
Children of Ferdinand R. & Mildred L. (Paine) August

Ferdinand Rudolph Jr.	b. Feb. 7, 1917 at Simsbury, CT
Albert Raymond	b. May 17, 1918 at Simsbury, CT
Dorothy	b. Dec. 23, 1919 at Simsbury, CT
Robert Burton	b. May 18, 1921 at Simsbury, CT
Mildred Louise	b. Jun. 19, 1923 at Simsbury, CT

ALBERT IRVING PAINE (GEN X, Paine Family)
   b. Apr. 1, 1896 at Springfield, MA
   d. Apr. 24, 1968 at Simsbury, CT
   bur. Curtiss Cem., Simsbury, CT
   m. Apr. 2, 1917 at Avon, CT to
MARY HADSELL
   b. Apr. 25, 1898 at Avon, CT
   d. Jan. 4, 1992 at Simsbury, CT
   bur. Curtiss Cem., Simsbury, CT

Albert Irving Paine World War I

GENERATION XI
Children of Albert I & Mary (Hadsell) Paine

Bernard Norman	b. Jan. 22, 1921 at Manchester, CT
	d. Oct. 20, 1922
Arthur Merrill	b. Jan. 29, 1923 at Manchester, CT
Donald Irving	b. Jun. 13, 1927 at Westfield, CT
Gladys Elizabeth	b. Nov. 29, 1928 at Westfield, MA

MADELEINE PAINE (GEN.X, Paine Family)
　b. Dec. 22, 1899 at Westfield, MA
　d. Apr 17, 1998 at Westfield, MA
　bur. New Cem., Southwick, MA
　m. Sept. 3, 1921 at Simsbury, CT to
HARRY KING SEIBERT
　b. Aug. 15, 1901 at Berlin, CT
　d. Sep. 22, 1983 at Westfield, MA
　bur. Southwick, MA

GENERATION XI
Children of Harry King & Madeleine (Paine) Seibert
Eleanor Grace	b. Sep. 19, 1922 at West Hartford, CT
Leonard Leroy	b. Mar. 15, 1925 at Avon, CT
William Howard	b. Feb. 4, 1927 at Avon, CT
Merton George	b. Feb. 16, 1929 at Cheshire, CT

MATTIE PAINE (GEN X, Paine Family)
　b. May 5, 1903 at Simsbury, CT
　d. Jan. 11, 1990 at Colorado Springs, CO
　bur. Arvada Cem., Arvada, CO
　m. Aug. 20, 1927 at Congregational Church, Avon, CT to

WILLIAM BOERUM WEED
　b. Apr. 18, 1904 at Bethel, CT
　d. Feb. 10, 1970 at Denver, CO
　bur. Arvada Cem., Arvada, CO

Mattie Paine　　　Age 21

GENERATION XI
Children of William B. & Mattie (Paine) Weed
Bertha Mae	b. Jun. 25, 1928 at Danbury, CT
Lois Mattie	b. Nov. 21, 1929 at Danbury, CT
William Boerum, Jr.	b. Jul. 27, 1932 at Simsbury, CT
Frederick Davis, II	b. Apr. 22, 1935 at Simsbury, CT

MABEL PAINE (GEN. X, Paine Family)
　b. May 5, 1903 at Simsbury, CT
　d. Oct. 10, 1980 at Simsbury, CT
　bur. Curtiss Cem., Simsbury, CT
　m. Feb. 18, 1925 at Simsbury, CT to

DIMOCK BURDETTE GLAZIER
　b. April 15, 1897 at Stafford, CT
　d. Mar. 8, 1979 Simsbury, CT
　bur. Curtiss Cem., Simsbury, CT

GENERATION XI
Children of Dimock B. & Mabel (Paine) Glazier

Shirley Mabel	b. Jul. 22, 1926 at Simsbury, CT
Dimock Burdette, Jr.	b. Dec. 18, 1927 at Simsbury, CT

ARCHIE WILLIAM PAINE (GEN. X, Paine Family)
b. Mar. 9, 1905 at Simsbury, CT
d. May 18, 1988 at Farmington, CT
bur. Curtiss Cem., Simsbury, CT
m. (1) Sep. 30, 1927 at Simsbury, CT to

ELDORA vanNESS STOUTENBURGH
b. Dec. 3, 1897 at Brooklyn, NY
d. Sep. 23, 1959 at Burlington, CT
bur. Curtiss Cem., Simsbury, CT

m. (2) Feb. 4, 1961 at Burlington, CT to

FLORENCE GLADYS BUTTLES
b. Nov. 16, 1904 at Collinsville, CT
d. Feb. 12, 1999 at Farmington, CT
bur. Curtiss Cem., Simsbury, CT

Archie W. Paine
Age 20

Authority: Births: Archie-Simsbury, CT, Eldora-Brooklyn, NY;
Marriage: Simsbury; Deaths: Archie-Farmington, CT, Eldora-Burlington, CT

GENERATION XI
Children of Archie W. & Eldora v. (Stoutenburgh) Paine

Beverly Marion	b. Dec. 27, 1928 at Hartford, CT
Archie William, Jr.	b. May 14, 1930 at Hartford, CT
Phillip Irving	b. Jan. 29, 1932 at Hartford, CT
David Alan	b. 1934 at Hartford, CT (stillborn)
	bur. Curtiss Cem., Simsbury, CT
Nancy Joan	b. Apr. 12, 1937 at Hartford, CT
Claudia Ann	b. Dec. 22, 1943 at Winsted, CT

Claudia (Candy) came to our family at the age of five months and was officially adopted in 1961.
Authority: Certified Copies of Births: Beverly & Archie

Memories of Archie W. and Florence B. Paine
In 1962, **Archie** and his wife, **Florence** began discussing retirement plans. Archie had been
living in Water Company (MDC) houses for the past twenty plus years and they needed to decide
where a permanent home would be located.

Dad (Archie) asked if she would like to go home to her hill. Mother (Florence) was overjoyed at the prospect. Thus it was decided that they would make Cemetery Rd. in Collinsville their permanent residence. Mother had lived in and around that vicinity for many years having been born on South St., which is just off the foot of Cemetery Rd. She had owned her own little home on Cemetery Rd. until she married Dad in 1961 and moved to the MDC house at Barnes Hill in Burlington, CT at that time she sold her house to her brother Everett Buttles and her sister Susie May Dyson. So moving back would locate them just a short walk down the hill from Everett and Susie May.

Dad then asked Mother to think about moving an old saltbox house from the bank of the Farmington River to their property on Cemetery Rd. Mother thought that would be a monumental task, *moving a whole house!* Dad explained that they would take it down piece by piece and rebuild on their own property. Mother thought the task was still a daunting one, but agreed.

The house, originally built in 1740 by E. J. Wilcox was under the ownership of the Baker's who had used it for a summer home until it was ravaged during the Aug. 19, 1955 flood that overflowed the banks of the Farmington River. It had stood unoccupied by the owners since that time. When the folks contacted them they were very interested in seeing it moved and safely restored in the village of Collinsville.

Dad and Mother carefully dismantled the house, saving the good lumber and numbering pieces as they went along. It was necessary to find replacement lumber for some which had been too damaged by the flood waters to be re-used. Dad located old chestnut from a barn, which fit in nicely with the wood in the original house. The original wide floors were put back down. In the den, which was added, they put down oak with cut nails to retain the ambience of the old building.
Mother was helping out one day in the dismantling, when a beam slipped and glanced along the back of her head, knocking her down. Fortunately she suffered no permanent injury, but did have a bad headache and very sore shoulders for a while.

The layout was changed a bit to make it more suitable to their needs, including indoor plumbing, which the old house did not have. The kitchen counters have marble tops and splashboards.

They were proud of the brick fireplace and brick wood box which enhance the great room. Mother was fond of mentioning that the panel above the mantel is a door turned sideways. It was painstakingly scraped down to its original wood. The staircase in the front hall was in sad shape too with many layers of peeling paint. There too it took many hours of scraping ending with a lovely staircase.

Dad and Mother both worked side by side with the dismantling and rebuilding, obtaining help when needed from family and contractors. Dad always said it would not have gotten done if not for her help. It was joint consultation and decision-making. And the end result was a beautiful home with a very happy contented couple residing there.

The retaining walls in the driveway were constructed by Dad, as were the stone steps leading to the side door, which enters into the kitchen and great room. He was aided on many weekends by, our brother, Dave Holloway. Dave helped with a lot of the heavy work that Mother was not strong enough to manage.

The house still retains the warm feeling of their tender loving care in the building of it and in their welcoming presence there. The door was always open to family, friends and new acquaintances. The "House in the Orchard" is a place they called home for many happy years. Dad died in 1988 and mother was able to live there an additional nine years. At the age of ninety-two she found it necessary to enter the Health Care Center there in Collinsville, and the house was sold.

Obituary
Farmington Valley Herald, May 26, 1988

REMEMBERING ARCHIE PAINE

There were some new tears in the Farmington River last week. Not everyone noticed them, but old-timers saw the crystalline droplets reflecting the sun, and knew that Archie Paine was now part of the ages. Archie was a river man, and there were none who knew her moods, her beauty and her fury better, and he was one of the few who could converse with her.

Archie Paine was many things to many people; family man, friend, naturalist, and most of all, a warm human being who held all of God's creatures in the same high esteem. Characteristically, he slipped off into the woods quietly, leaving behind a legacy that few of us ever amass. The Farmington River Valley is the richer for his having been at its center for the best part of this century.

MEMORIES OF ARCHIE W. PAINE
By: Dr. Keith C. Alderman

Author's note: On a recent visit to the home of Nancy and Jim Keane, Keith was reminiscing with us about our Dad. Upon his return home he wrote to Nancy. The following is an excerpt from that letter, dated April 20, 1999 and printed here with Keith's permission.

"You and your sister, Beverly, remarked that your father, Archie, and I had an unusual friendship. It is true. I don't think it happens very often that a man in his seventies and a young man in his twenties develop a strong and abiding friendship. But it happened.

And it happened almost by accident. I was working at Friendly's in Unionville at the time, and Archie, Florence and Mrs. Buttles used to come in sometimes. I knew Archie slightly from Village Lodge, and would always make sure that I would talk with him. He mentioned one day that he needed some help to do some work outside, and that the person who he had scheduled to help him didn't show up. I volunteered, figuring that whatever he had to do would only take an afternoon or so, and besides, how long and hard could a man in his seventies with a cane work anyway?

I met Archie at his house on Cemetery Lane one Saturday morning. I had been working two jobs, had been to a party the night before, and was not at my best the next morning. I was also dressed in a tee shirt and shorts and sneakers. I found it strange that your father was dressed in long pants, a shirt with long "short sleeves," suspenders, work shoes and a baseball cap.

All that day I worked with your father, taking apart the old foundation of the barn which was in back of the house. And all day long, too, I spent swatting mosquitoes, gnats, black flies, deer flies, and other biting insects. So on Monday, when I went next to work with your dad, I had long pants on. And the day after that, I wore a long sleeved shirt.

I soon found that I couldn't stand on a ladder, lift a rock, and hold my pants up at the same time. So I found and bought my first pair of suspenders. After dropping a few large stones on my toes, I went out and purchased a good pair of work shoes, too.

I had never known anyone to work outside in the rain before, but your dad was such a person. Before long, I too, had a cap with a brim to keep the rain off my glasses. It took, in all, just about a month, but at the end of that time, the transition was complete. I looked like he did.

And I had never worked so hard physically in my life. Your dad would just put his cane in his back pocket, and go to work.

I have never known anyone quite like your father. Even at this date, more than ten years after his passing, I have to say that he was my best friend. Unusual, I know. But so many meaningful things in life are slightly out of the ordinary, or unusual.

His friendship to me was priceless and the time I spent with your dad and Florence were some of the best days of my life. I know that perhaps people thought that my working with your dad was atypical. But I carry his presence with me in my thoughts and memories. His goodness and grace walk with me still."

EULOGY TO MY GRANDMOTHER
Florence Buttles Paine

By John J. Martinoli

The first time I remember meeting my new Grandmother, it was a snowy winter day in February, 1961, at a wedding in the house on Barnes Hill Road. I was twelve years old. Now that may sound strange to some of you—but let me assure you that I remember a lot from the first twelve years of my life, and I remember another Grandmother, who had died in 1959, a few months before my 10th birthday. I had always called her "Grammie". When I met my new Grandmother on that day in February I really didn't think much of it at the time-I guess I figured if she was OK with "Grampa", she was OK with me. Besides-it was pretty clear even to the Grandchildren that he liked her. I can't remember how or when I named her, (I'm almost 50 now) but for most of the next 38 years, I've called the only Grandmother I ever really got to know "Gram".

She was, to me and to most of the family that she inherited on that snowy day, a very special lady. She was certainly so to my Grandfather. It's only in the last several years that I have realized how special their relationship was. She was more vocal about their courtship and their dreams in the conversations we shared as she and I grew older. Looking back, I will treasure the times we shared, the small part I played in helping their dreams come true, and the lessons I learned from her, for the rest of my life. I'll also remember-fondly-the cherry pies. Oh, those pies. I never passed through the state without paying her a visit-and letting her know when I'd be visiting. And I always got pie. And she would always say it didn't come out very good. And I would always ask for another piece.

There was more to Gram than good pies, though. I remember spending a summer vacation when I was fourteen working-and working hard-at the house that now stands on Cemetery Road. Only it wasn't up on that hill. It was down by the river and we were taking it down. My cousin Bill and I had a great time knocking the plaster from the walls and a not so great time cleaning it up. We had a very frustrating time taking boards down without breaking them (because it was more fun to break things), and an absolutely boring time straightening and savings the nails we took out of the boards. But Gram had a very effective way of controlling our youthful exuberance-"Do it right, and you can have some pie when we get home," she'd say. We did it right. Gram always won. And she kept an eye on us too- she worked right along with us.

Yes, my Grandmother knew how to work. I think that's why she and Grampa made such a great team. They talked things over, made their plans, and worked together to get things done. One of my favorite stories, and one she told me often, concerned the house in the orchard. It wasn't always in the orchard, as most of you know. It seems that they were driving down by the river one day, and Grampa pointed out a house. "Girlie," he said, "Do you like that house?" "Yes", she said, "It's a beautiful house." To which he replied, "Do you want to buy it? We could fix it, and it could be our house." My Grandmother allowed as how it would be a great house, but she didn't want to live that close to the river. To which he replied "Well then, we'll buy it and move it up to Cemetery Road." She always insisted that she thought he was kidding. She always followed that comment up with the fact that she should have known better. Whenever I think of my Grandmother now, I think of her in the house in the orchard-a house that she vowed only to leave "When they carry me out feet first." As we all know, that was not to be. I still wish, with all my heart that we could have made it so. But there's one thing I cannot accept-I cannot accept the thought that my Grandmother's story does not have a happy ending. I bid her farewell now with two additional stories, one hers, one mine.
First, hers—I wasn't there when my Grandfather died. Gram was. This is how she described it. Grampa woke up early that morning, as usual. He got out of bed, smacked her on the bottom and said "C'mon Girlie, we've got a lot of work to do today." And went to the bathroom, just like always. There, as we all know, he died quite suddenly-not looking back on what used to be, but looking forward to what lay ahead.

My Grandmother lived on in that house for nine more years. Sadly, it was necessary for her to move to a full time care facility two years ago. She wasn't happy about it and neither was the family. She always talked about going home when she got better, always looking forward. She left us on a day in February, thirty eight years and 8 days after she officially joined our family, not looking back on what used to be, but looking forward to what lay ahead.

Here's my story—She's awake now. She awoke from her sleep in a familiar bedroom, amazed at how good she was feeling. She got up quickly, dressed without help and walked downstairs. She walked into a familiar kitchen and was greeted by a familiar voice, saying "Well, good morning, Girlie. What took you so long? Let's have some breakfast and get to work before the day is done."

CHAPTER TWO
GENERATIONS XI AND XII

Descendants of: Mildred L. (Paine) August & Ferdinand R. August

FERDINAND (FRED) RUDOLPH AUGUST, JR (GEN. XI, Paine Family)
b. Feb. 7, 1917 at Simsbury, CT
d. Oct. 10, 1983 at Hartford, CT
bur. Curtiss Cem., Simsbury, CT
m. June 26, 1940 at Avon, CT to
MABEL INEZ McLAUGHLIN
b. June 26, 1920 at Hartford, CT

GENERATION XII
Children of Fred R. Jr. & Mabel I. (McLaughlin) August
   Norman Frederick   b. Oct. 1, 1946 at New London, CT
   Roy Joseph   b. Apr. 10, 1948 at Preston, CT
    (Both boys adopted by Fred and Mabel)

ALBERT RAYMOND AUGUST (GEN. XI, Paine Family)
b. May 17, 1918 at Simsbury, CT
d. Mar. 9, 1989 at Simsbury, CT
bur. Curtiss Cem., Simsbury, CT
m. (1) May 30, 1941 at Avon to, CT
THEONA STRONG
b. May 20, 1919 at Avon, CT
d. May 30, 1976 at Simsbury, CT
bur. Curtiss Cem., Simsbury, CT

m. (2) Feb. 24, 1979 at Avon, CT to
ARDELLA WOOSTER MIRICK
b. Aug. 15, 1916 at Hartford, CT

GENERATION XII
Children of Albert R. & Theona (Strong) August
   James Albert   b. Jun. 19, 1942 at Hartford, CT
   Larry Strong   b. May 16, 1945 at Hartford, CT
   Michael Jay   b. Mar. 17, 1947 at Hartford, CT
   Sharyn Elizabeth   b. Sept. 8, 1948 at Hartford, CT

DOROTHY AUGUST (GEN. XI, Paine Family)
b. Dec. 23, 1919 at Simsbury, CT
m. Jan. 4, 1942 at Avon, CT to
ALBERT JOSEPH St. PIERRE
b. Sept. 26, 1918 at Berlin, NH

GENERATION XII
Children of Albert J. & Dorothy (August) St. Pierre

Barry Joseph	b. May 4, 1946 at Hartford, CT
Deborah Jean	b. May 14, 1950 at Gardiner, ME

ROBERT BURTON AUGUST (GEN. XI, Paine Family)
b. May 18, 1921 at Simsbury, CT
d. Jan. 22, 2010 at Simsbury, CT
bur. Curtiss Cem., Simsbury, CT
m. Jun. 26, 1948 at Avon, CT to
GLADYS ELEANOR THOMPSON
b. Oct. 31, 1921 at Avon, CT

GENERATION XII
Children of Robert B. & Gladys E. (Thompson) August

Betsy	b. Oct. 30, 1951 at Hartford, CT
Roberta	b. Jul. 1, 1953 at Hartford, CT
Lourie	b. Oct. 28, 1955 at Hartford, CT
Ann	b. Jun. 5, 1957 at Hartford, CT
Marnie Louise	b. Dec. 30, 1964 at Hartford, CT

Memories of Robert B. August

"GRAM and GRAMP"
Bits and pieces of the lives of ELLA G. and MERTON K. PAINE from about 1925 to 1950.

1. GRAM and DANCING at the AVON CONGREGATIONAL CHURCH
> Gram and Gramp were deeply committed to their Church (The Avon Congregational Church at Avon) and it was not unexpected that each of them in their own way would exercise their opinions as they thought appropriate. The story is that Gram "put her foot down" when the young people of the Church wanted to dance in the Fellowship Hall. (There was no more discussion on that issue).

2. COMMITTED CHURCH MEMBERS
> In those days each family customarily had its own pew in the Sanctuary where they would sit for Sunday service. I recall going there with my grandparents and sitting in the pew which would be on the west side toward the front. Incidentally, this is the same pew, which my wife Gladys and I occupied until the 1980's when we moved to the balcony. It wasn't that we were unhappy with our location or upset with anyone, but during recent years, the children came to the early part of the Sunday service, and it was our feeling that families with children could more readily sit in the main part of the Sanctuary, just prior to the children going to their Sunday school classes part way through the service.

3. THE "28 CHEVY
> Gramp had switched vehicles somewhere during his career and gave up his horse and buggy for an old 1928 Chevy. One time I was riding with him as he went to Avon Center from his home on Bushy Hill Road and he drove the full distance of 3 or 4 miles in second. He explained to me that he realized that other folks thought he was a little bit odd in doing this, but his comment was "you know, it is a lot faster than a horse and buggy, even this way."

4. <u>ALFRED AND HIS DRIVER'S LICENSE</u>

Alfred, who was a State Ward, lived with Gram and Gramp during his high school years in the early 30's, and when he was eighteen it was time for him to get his driver's license. He was not above telling an interesting story which most of the time, was approximately accurate. He and Gramp had driven in the old Chevy to Wethersfield, where in those days you would get your license. As Alfred got behind the wheel and the Police Officer who would be examining him, opened the door to get in the front seat beside Alfred, the officer shook the door a little bit, rattled the running board, and commented to Alfred, "you want me to approve your driving when you come in with a car like this? My Heavens, what have you been doing with this car?" Alfred's response was that it really wasn't his doing, but the "ole gent." (Alfred frequently called Gramp, the "ole gent.") used the car a great deal to go up into the back pasture to bring the cows down when it was time to milk them in the afternoon; and rather than getting out of the car to open the gate, he usually used one front fender or the other. Arthur got his license.

5. <u>THE ITINERANT "YANKEE PEDDLER"</u>

Gramp had moved his family in the late 1890's from Westfield, Mass. to Bushy Hill Rd., and there took up his livelihood partly in farming (which was, of course, a way of life for most rural people in those days) and as a typical Yankee Peddler delivering goods from door-to-door between Westfield and Simsbury. Gramp would make the round trip each week, leaving from Bushy Hill to Westfield by one northerly route; taking orders from the farm wives as he went, and then returning from Westfield another route. He would deliver the orders the next week as he went either to or from Westfield. I personally do not remember his having made the trip, but I do remember the stories about his being the last of the Yankee Peddlers along with another gentleman from Simsbury.

He also had a Country Store in a barn at his home at Bushy Hill from which he sold mostly kitchen packaged goods to local people. I remember particularly his having Shredded Wheat available on the shelves from which he measured out household products to his various customers. In this instance the can was marked "Mustard".

6. <u>GRAM and the MICE in the CHICKEN FEED BARREL</u>

When Gramp died in 1937, Gram decided that it wasn't necessary for her to hang up her shoes and become the "little old grandmother sitting in her rocking chair on the porch."

She continued raising chickens and selling a few eggs to those who would drive by on a weekly basis. On one occasion she was very much aware that mice were getting into her chicken feed and she developed a plan to rid herself of these marauders. On the occasion in question, she got herself a sturdy, lengthy stick and crept up on the barrel of chicken feed and "thump! thump! thump! beat the mice to a pulp. She then discarded the dead animals in the ever-present manure pile.

7. <u>ART and the OLD CAT</u>

Art Paine, a cousin and also a frequent guest of Gram's was fairly resourceful in many, many ways. He overheard his father, Irving, and Gramp talking about an old cat that was truly on its last legs. Art heard Gramp say that he would have to bury that feeble, old cat. Art took Gramp at his word and interpreted his statement to be exactly that. The old cat had to be buried. Art took the cat, dug a hole in the sawdust pile and buried the cat alive. It was only through happenstance that Art's father wanted to know what he had been up to when Art said he buried the cat as Gramp said needed to be done. Art was only trying to be helpful. They found the old cat coming up out of the sawdust pile wheezing and puffing and huffing.

31

8. <u>THE OLD HORSES' BURIAL GROUND</u>

Alfred was not above overly impressing a youngster several years his junior. One of those deep impressions on my mind is the explanation which Alfred gave to me that the depressions up through the cow pasture, which did not seem to be formed naturally, were the cave-ins where Gramp had shot old horses which were no longer of any value to him. The practice was (according to Alfred) to have someone hold the horse on the edge of the hole and then the other person would shoot the horse and they would then push the horse into the hole and cover it over. The explanation made good sense to me for a number of years until I realized that there were many more depressions than there possibly could have been old horses.

9. <u>ART, the OUTHOUSE and the HORNETS</u>

I have said that Art was resourceful. He frequently lived up to that characterization. On one occasion Gramp was in the out house out in back of the old store, probably reading his Sears & Roebuck catalogue and having his morning constitutional and a moment of uninterrupted seclusion. Well, almost uninterrupted. Art thought that it would be worthwhile to note the results it he were to take a long handled rake and stick it into the hole of a big hornet's nest that was under the eaves of the outhouse and on one occasion he proceeded to do so. He then lifted the trap door at the back of the outhouse and shoved the hornet's nest in under the seat of the outhouse when Gramp was above reading his catalogue. The results were immediate----

10. <u>VISITING GRAM AND GRAMP</u>

Like many grandchildren, a visit to Gram's was a special event. The remembrances are several, but I recall particularly a noonday meal in their dining room that was not simply a hurried affair, but one which started with Gramp offering a prayer and a full meal with napkins and tablecloth. Why I remember the little white porcelain elliptical shaped dishes with creamed peas, I will never know. In the kitchen was a long hand towel on a roller attached to the door at the foot of the stairs to Alfred's garret bedroom, where everyone (or at least we men folk) dried our hands after washing at the black cast iron sink.

Many the times I remember wriggling down between the cold, smooth sheets of the bed in the garret that was an extra room for grandchildren who came to visit.

11. <u>FOURTH OF JULY REUNIONS</u>

Since 1914, the family has always celebrated the 4th of July with a family gathering. These gatherings started at the homestead on Bushy Hill Road with a picnic in the orchard just south of the house. These were gatherings of all of the Paine relatives.

12. <u>GRAMP and the GLASS OF WINE</u>

Drinking in the Paine household was not forbidden, it just wasn't done. However, Gramp and Gram had some good neighbors across the street, the Krolikowski family, who were having a wedding. Again, this is a story related by Alfred and perhaps somewhat embellished. In any event, Gramp felt that they should accept the informal invitation for him to go up and wish the wedding party well and he proceeded to do so. On his return, he sang all sorts of interesting songs, walking down the middle of the road from the Krolikowski homestead to the Paine farm. The facts came out little by little, that Gramp had been offered a glass of wine and felt of course, that he sociably should accept the invitation.

13. <u>KICK THE CAN IN BUSHY HILL ROAD</u>

When I talk about Bushy Hill Road, I am talking about an old country dirt road that had few cars, and when there was a car, it was so unusual that anyone in the roadway would have ample warning to step aside. I remember playing "kick the can" in the street on one occasion.

14. <u>THE GANDER</u>

Gram kept one or two geese and a gander in a little fenced enclosure between the milk house and the street, which would have been a few feet north of their house. I recall vividly the fence, the milk house and the gander. I don't know how old I was, but I was tall enough so that my nose came up to the level of the beak of that gander when he proceeded to tell me that I was invading his territory. When I put my nose through the fence to get a better look at him, he proceeded to peck my nose. You tell me how old a little boy has to be to have his nose come up to the level of a gander's beak and I will tell you how old I was.

15. <u>GRAMPA FRENCH</u>

Grampa French was Gram's father, who lived with Paine's during the last few years of his life. He was a colorful character; had had an interesting career on the Constellation, the sister ship to the Constitution* and at the age of 90 as the only surviving member of the crew, was a guide in Boston Harbor to visitors who visited the ship**. Also in that year, he traveled along by ship to New Orleans, by train to visit his daughter, Alice Pixley in California, by train from California to visit his daughter Julie Waterman in Cleveland, Ohio and thence by train back to Hartford.

While there were times he was feeble, there were also times he was quite active indeed. At his age, he could play "the bones" and his music box with fingers which were still nimble.

16. <u>AUNT WILLIE, AUNT ALICE, AUNT JULIE and GRAM</u>

There were four siblings in Gram's family: Aunt Willie Taylor, who worked at Ethel Walker School; Aunt Alice Pixley who lived in California; and Aunt Julie Waterman who lived in Cleveland. The sisters occasionally returned to the homestead and visited with the family from time to time. "Billie" Waterman was Aunt Julie's daughter, and a sophisticated, mature young woman from the big City. When Billie visited, you can bet all the Paine males made certain to come visit at Gram and Gramp's.

Author's Notes:

*We have since discovered that the **Constellation**, which Grandpa French sailed aboard, was the **second Constellation**. The first Constellation had become so derelict that she could no longer perform her duties and was decommissioned and broken up in 1853. Pieces of her were incorporated into the new Constellation, which was launched in 1854. Grampa's sojourn aboard her was undertaken in 1859 when she sailed to patrol the African Coast to intercept slave ships which were no longer legally allowed to bring slaves to America. The story of the two Constellations can be found in Chapter Nine.

**The ship he visited in Boston Harbor was the USS Constitution, not the Constellation.

Grandpa's story is found in Chapter Five, **FRENCH**.

MILDRED LOUISE AUGUST (GEN. XI, Paine Family)
  b. Jun. 19, 1923 at Simsbury, CT
  d. Jul. 4, 1962 at Hartford, CT
  bur. Curtiss Cem., Simsbury, CT
  m. Apr. 1945 to
MYLES IRVING GANGELL
  b. Dec. 3, 1916

GENERATION XII
Child of Myles I. & Mildred L. (August) Gangell
  John Emerson   b. Nov. 26, 1948 at Waterville, ME
    (Adopted by Mildred and Myles)

Descendants of: Albert I. Paine (Gen. X, Paine Family) & Mary *(*Hadsell) Paine

ARTHUR MERRILL PAINE (GEN. XI, Paine Family)
  b. Jan. 29, 1923 at Manchester, CT
  d. May. 27, 1978 at Hartford, CT
  bur. Simsbury Center Cem., Simsbury, CT
  m. Sep. 2, 1950 at Simsbury, CT to

RUTH FRANCES ENGELKE
  b. May 11, 1931 at Hartford, CT
  d. Dec. 5, 2008 at Simsbury, CT
  bur. Simsbury Center Cem., Simsbury, CT

GENERATION XII
Children of Arthur M. & Ruth (Engelke) Paine
  Steven Arthur   b. Nov. 1, 1951 at Hartford, CT
  Linda Sue   b. Mar. 6, 1954 at Hartford, CT
  Amy Louise   b. Sep. 16, 1959 at Hartford, CT

DONALD IRVING PAINE (GEN. XI, Paine Family)
  b. Jun. 13, 1927 at
  m.(1) Feb. 15, 1952 At Pittsfield, MA to
JOYCE A. MAHLSTEDT
  b. May 8, 1931 at Watertown, CT
  d. Aug. 24, 1991 at Simsbury, CT
  bur. Curtiss Cem, Simsbury, CT

  m. (2) Oct. 5, 1996 at Avon, CT to
CONSTANCE P. DOUGLAS

GENERATION XII
Children of Donald I. & Joyce A. (Mahlstedt) Paine

Ellen Ann	b. Jan. 20, 1953 at Hartford, CT
Michael Robert	b. Jul. 23, 1954 at Hartford, CT
Susan Gail	b. Jul. 25, 1955 at Hartford, CT
Russell Alan	b. Nov. 25, 1956 at Hartford, CT
Timothy Gordon	b. May 1, 1958 at Hartford, CT
Donald Jeffrey	b. Nov. 13, 1961 at Hartford, CT
Donna Joy	b. Jan. 17, 1963 at Hartford, CT

GLADYS ELIZABETH PAINE (GEN. XI, Paine Family)
b. Nov. 29, 1928 at Westfield, MA
m. Sep. 19, 1953 at St. Bernard's Ch., Tariffville, CT to
EDWARD LAWRENCE KELLY, JR.
b. Aug. 13, 1929 at Tariffville, CT

GENERATION XII
Children of Edward L. & Gladys E. (Paine) Kelly

Thomas Michael	b. Oct. 24, 1954 at Hartford, CT
Rosemary	b. May 10, 1956 at Hartford, CT
Katherine Elizabeth	b. Dec. 20, 1960 at Hartford, CT
Barbara Ann	b. Nov. 9, 1962 at Hartford, CT

Descendants of: Madeleine (Paine) Seibert (Gen. X, Paine Family) & Harry K. Seibert

ELEANOR GRACE SEIBERT (GEN. XI, Paine Family)
b. Sep. 19, 1922 at West Hartford, CT
d. Apr. 27, 2010 at South Hadley, MA
m. Nov. 6, 1948 at St. Mary's Church, Westfield, MA to
CHARLES JOHN TOOLE
b. Dec. 3, 1923 at Holyoke, MA
d. Dec. 14, 2004 at Holyoke, MA

GENERATION XII
Children of Charles J. & Eleanor G. (Seibert) Toole

Anne Marie	b. Sep. 13, 1946 at Meriden, CT
Virginia Rose	b. Oct. 4, 1952, Holyoke, MA
Alice Madeleine	b. Apr. 17, 1954 at Holyoke, MA
John Charles	b. Apr. 11, 1956 at Holyoke, MA
Mary Patricia	b. Mar. 16, 1959 at Holyoke, MA
Debra Jean	b. Mar. 31, 1960 at Holyoke, MA
Michael Edward	b. Mar. 31, 1963 Holyoke, MA

LEONARD LEROY SEIBERT (GEN. XI, Paine Family)
b. Mar. 15, 1925 at Simsbury, CT
m. April 18, 1949 to
MAE ELIZABETH MacWILLIAMS
b. May 24, 1929 at Springfield, MA
d. Nov 15, 2000 at Westfield, MA

GENERATION XII
Children of Leonard & Mae Elizabeth (MacWilliams) Seibert
Cheryl Anne	b. Jul. 6, 1950 at Hartford, CT
Lynne Carol	b. Dec. 3, 1952 at Hartford, CT
Laurie Dee	b. Jun. 18, 1961 at Westfield, MA

WILLIAM HOWARD SEIBERT (GEN. XI, Paine Family)
b. Feb 4, 1927 at Avon, CT
m. May 17, 1952 at Granby, CT
CYNTHIA COLLEEN KARLSTROM
b. Aug. 13, 1932 at Springfield, MA

GENERATION XII
Children of William H. & Cynthia C. (Karlstrom) Seibert
Dale William	b. Sep. 10, 1953 at Westfield, MA
Patricia Ann	b. Dec. 13, 1955 at Westfield, MA
Terry Diane	b. Nov. 8, 1959 at Westfield, MA
Kim Amelia	b. May 22, 1962 at Westfield, MA
Christopher Howard	b. May 29, 1970 at Westfield, MA
Holly Cait	b. Dec. 20, 1971 at Westfield, MA

MERTON GEORGE SEIBERT (GEN. XI, Paine Family)
b. Feb. 16, 1929 at Cheshire, CT
m. (1) Mar. 21, 1952 at Suffield, MA to

ALICE THERESA MURPHY
b. Nov. 1, 1932 at Hartford, CT
d. Aug. 31, 1971 at Southwick, MA
bur. Southwick, MA

m. (2) Apr. 4, 1973 at Southwick, MA to
RUTH ELEANOR (EDWARDS) McNAMARA
b. July 13, 1936 at Braintree, MA

GENERATION XII
Children of Merton G. & Alice T.(Murphy) Seibert
Brenda Lee	b. May 18, 1954 at Springfield, MA
Douglas Holden	b. Oct. 23, 1956 at Springfield, MA

Child of Merton G. & Ruth E. (Edwards) Seibert
Bobbi Jo	b. Aug. 9, 1970 at Springfield, MA

(Ruth's child - adopted by Merton)

Descendants of Mattie (Paine) Weed (Gen. X, Paine Family) & William B. Weed

BERTHA MAE WEED (GEN. XI, Paine Family)
  b. Jun. 25, 1928 at Danbury, CT
  d. Feb. 1, 2003 at Colorado Springs, CO
  m. (1) Jan .6, 1949 at Seekonk, MA to
THOMAS FERLINGERE
  b. Aug. 28, 1922 at Rhode Island
  d. Jan. 8, 1989 at Providence, RI

  m. (2) Nov. 16, 1965 at Denver, CO to
WYLIE EDGAR DUKE, JR.
  b. Aug. 7, 1929 at Flora, IL
  d. Oct. 3, 1992 at Killeen, TX

GENERATION XII
Children of Thomas & Bertha Mae (Weed) Ferlingere
  Valerie Mae   b. Jan. 31. 1950 at Denver, CO
  Thomas Scott   b. Dec. 17, 1950 at Denver, CO
  Carol Anne   b. Nov. 26, 1952 at Denver, CO
  Ellen Grace   b. May 31, 1954 at Denver, CO
  Karen Louise   b. Jun. 26, 1957 at Denver, CO

Child of Wylie E. Jr. & Bertha Mae (Weed) Duke
  Wylie Christopher   b. Jun. 13, 1966 at Denver, CO

Memories of Bertha M. (Weed) Duke
Mother, (Mattie Paine Weed) was born in 1903, the year that the Wright brothers first flew their airplane at Kitty Hawk, North Carolina. Before she died in 1990, men had gone from the earth to the moon by rocket ship, and walked on the surface of the moon. She lived through two world wars (her brother Irving (Albert I. Paine) served in the first.) and the "great depression". She never forgot the flu epidemic of 1918, when many people died. Pneumonia and infections were serious and could be fatal because antibiotics were not discovered until the 1940's. Other diseases also were feared because, except for a smallpox vaccination, there were no immunization vaccines.

In mother's childhood, travel was largely by horse and buggy or wagon, and by train. Apparently the trains stopped at every community, and sometimes at different places in the same community. She grew up in Simsbury, CT on a farm. Then went to "Normal School" in New Britain, CT. She worked as a teacher in a one-room school before her marriage, boarding away from home during the week. One of the teacher's responsibilities was to light the stove in the schoolroom before the children arrived, in order to have the school warm for them. She told how she showed the "big" boys that poetry could be fun, by reading "Casey at the Bat" to them, while they sat heads down at their desks and eyes closed as they imagined what the poem was describing. "How they laughed", she said. Then she told them, "That's poetry!"
Mother and Dad, William Boerum Weed, were married in 1927. They first lived in Bethel, CT, and Dad helped his father on the farm. My sister, Lois, and I were born during this time. Then they lived for a short while in West Simsbury. I vaguely remember that Dad drove us there in an old Ford. There was an ice-house nearby our house. Ice was stored in large blocks packed in sawdust, then delivered from house to house in the summertime to keep food chilled in an ice-

box. Later there were electric refrigerators (for homes with electricity). We always had electricity since I can remember. However, an aunt did not for years. And not everyone had an indoor bathroom. For years at the Weed farm, the water at the kitchen sink was obtained by a hand pump. A bath was taken in a galvanized tub placed near the stove in the kitchen, where it was nice and warm.

Dad built our home on Stratton Brook Road in Simsbury, CT about 3 miles from the Paine farm. At that time, I don't know if anyone ever hired a contractor to build their home. The ones that I know about built their own, perhaps with the help of family members and/or friends. The cellar-hole was dug out with a big scoop shovel pulled by horses, usually. The first building was the "garage". My brothers were born here - at home with a doctor in attendance, and a woman friend, who came to take care of Mother, the home, and the rest of the children until Mother was able to carry on by herself. We lived in the garage for a few years until the house was built. I remember helping to nail down the sub-flooring. My brother Fred had his own hammer (full size) and "nail apron" that he carried around his neck by putting his head through the handle straps. He had his very own wood to pound nails into. It was a sawed-off section of tree trunk. He was about three years old at the time. And he managed to have just about every inch of the wood with a nail in it - all the way down, too. The house had 10 rooms. There was a cellar, 1st and 2nd floors, and an attic. There was a full bath upstairs, and a 1/4 bath on the first floor.

The furnace in the cellar was fueled with wood. Dad rigged up a power saw to cut the slab wood into stove lengths. Slab wood is the trimmings from logs, as they are squared off at the sawmill before being cut into boards. Dad would back a car up the driveway, block it securely, and take a wheel off. Then a pulley-belt was put around the wheel drum at one end and a wheel at the other end that was attached to an "axle" with a circular saw on it. That part was stationary. When the car was started and put in gear, the saw would activate. Part of the saw frame was a hinged shelf to support the length of wood. The operator then rocked the support back and forth, moving the wood up each time so that the saw cut the length desired. It made a very satisfying "z-z-zing". It was our children's job to toss the wood down the cellar door, and stack it neatly, ready to be used in the furnace. Sometimes we would stack it so as to make "rooms" and "walls" for a "fort" to play in.

The kitchen stove was a cast-iron range, with a warming oven and a hot-water tank. Later, Dad got mother an electric cook stove. It was more convenient, but it took some getting used to. And we missed the warmth of the old stove. The kitchen was large, and while Mother was ironing, she played word games on a big slate blackboard hanging on the wall near the table. We practiced writing our names backwards and upside down, wrote messages in Morse code, learned the states' capitols—for fun! For me school was an extension of the games. It was always assumed that we would finish school and we did. Later, when Dad became a forest ranger, this same blackboard became the place for phone messages and data about the current fire emergency. We were on a party line (phone number was - ring 3). The neighbors were very understanding of the situation, and as far as I know, never complained about the phone being tied up. At those times, Mother became secretary and dispatcher, too. Often when the fire wasn't put out until late at night , she became the "fast -food" cook as well, fixing and serving eggs and toast, and perhaps cocoa or coffee to the hungry, wet, dirty fire-crew before they went home. Dad never sent them away hungry late at night. There were no hamburger stands around. *No Macdonald's yet!*

After my sister and I graduated high school, Dad moved the family from the big house into a 33 foot trailer and moved us all "out West" to Colorado. There were no "throughways" except the Merritt Parkway, just finished in Connecticut. and no interstate highways at that time, so we took the "scenic route" over hill and dale, through town and country. And scenic it was, as we crossed the United States, the Great Plains, and great rivers, bringing our house behind us. We watched a wheat harvest under the Kansas sun in July. There were no trees for miles. The air was clear and the sky was big. We often camped overnight at a state park or state forest. One forest ranger in Ohio told us how their home had been a stop on the "Underground Railroad", and there was a secret room in the house. It all seemed like one grand adventure. I don't recall Mother complaining either. She *did* like to go places! And there were so many new sights, people and places. However, for two or three years, she was dreadfully homesick for her family. In Connecticut, Mother had severe arthritis. Dad thought the dry climate of Colorado would be a help to her. It was. She never again was bed-fast or lame from arthritis.

Every other year they went back east to visit the family, and that eased her homesickness greatly. In the between years, they traveled west to visit my brothers. Bill had married and moved to British Columbia where they lived for a number of years. Also, since Mother and Dad lived in Arvada, Colorado, more or less in the middle of the country, their home became the stopover for family and friends traveling through. They were always welcome and greeted with much pleasure.

Dad died in 1970. Mother continued her hospitality until she moved to Colorado Springs in 1984, often having family or friends visiting for days at a time. Dad's cousin remembers the time they were driving from the East Coast, and arrived around midnight. They found Mother waiting for them at the end of the lane, so they wouldn't miss the turn, which was difficult for a passer-by to find in the daylight - and even more difficult in the dark.

Mother lived with me from 1984 until her death in 1990. She enjoyed having her tea outdoors where she could watch the trees "dancing" in the wind. She was excited by every bird that came to the feeder. Mother liked to GO! She was ready and at the door waiting before you could find the car keys.

She was adventuresome, too. She was always ready to try something new. One time she was watching some men practice rappelling down a mountainside. If she had been dressed in slacks, I'm sure she would have tried it. Another time, she tried a recipe that included turkey, chocolate, and chili among the ingredients. (To say the least, it was unusual, but good.)

Mother enjoyed reading, and usually read something every day. Many times as a child, I remember that her light would be the last to go out. If it had writing, she read it! She liked to write, too. Mother was a "people person" and related to people from the heart. Her cheerful attitude and ready smile endeared her to everyone. She never forgot her manners, and was always gracious and thoughtful to others. She had a strong sense of what was decent, and what was not. To the end of her life she loved people and the Lord Jesus.

Before Mother passed away she had one great great grandchild. Her children and grandchildren live in Colorado, Washington, Nevada, Arizona, Oklahoma, California, Ohio, Georgia, and New York states.

The Depression and World War II occurred during my childhood. I didn't know there was a depression until after W.W.II and I went away to school. Some of my classmates were raised in the city. They remembered the bread lines and shortages. We always had a garden, and so did our neighbors. "We eat what we can, and what we can't, we can" So we canned the produce for the winter. Dad cobbled (repaired) our shoes when they needed soles, heels, or stitching. We had a cow and goats for milk and meat and sometimes butter. Route men drove their trucks house-to-house offering bread or milk and dairy or fresh fish. There were no supermarkets. Oranges were a wintertime treat (usually at Christmas). Bananas were rare.

For a teen-ager the war was a time of patriotism and excitement. The men of an age to be in the service were. Highschoolers were recruited for fire-fighting crews, my sister and I among them. So, as teen-agers, we were forest fire fighters! That was a "grown-up" job, and a necessary one.

We felt like we were doing an important service, and we worked hard to do it right. Neither did we want anyone to think that we were pampered because we were the Ranger's daughters.

During the war years, Mother and Dad took in a friend and her family - 2 adults and 4 children. The friend worked at Pratt and Whitney in Hartford, CT (as did Dad), in addition to his forestry work). Between everyone they kept track of ration books and there was always enough for everybody. Everyone helped. The work got done and there was time for play.

We made our own stilts and "clompers", (tin cans with string handles) to walk around on outdoors. We played games of ball, sliding, skating, skiing, hide & seek, climbing trees, swimming depending on the season. Indoors there were puzzles, Monopoly, word games, reading, Parcheesi, chess, checkers, etc. Visiting was done while our hands were busy shelling peas or snapping beans, or doing embroidery or other "hand-work", and around the dinner table. That was a merry time, as I remember. We had a radio. There was no TV yet.

We helped pitch hay. (No one had a baler.) For spending money we baby-sat, or worked for neighbors at .25 an hour. We worked picking strawberries for two cents a basket, and picked up potatoes in the field at five cents per 100-LB. gunnysack. My cousin had a paper route.

There was a difference between "helping" and "working". "Helping" was not for pay - but there was a great deal of satisfaction in knowing our efforts made a difference

LOIS MATTIE WEED (GEN. XI, Paine Family)
  b. Nov. 21, 1929 at Danbury, CT
  m. (1) Feb. 19, 1949 at Denver, CO to
MACK HORICE SUTHERLAND
  b. Jan. 2, 1919 at Oxford, MS
  d. Apr. 25, 1987 at Boulder, CO
  bur. Ft. Logan National Cem., Denver, CO

  m. (2) Aug. 2, 1975 at Colorado Springs, CO to
RONALD LEO TAYLOR
  b. May 14, 1937 at Denver, CO

GENERATION XII
Children of Mack Horice & Lois M. (Weed) Sutherland
  William Thomas   b. Feb. 17, 1951 at Denver, CO
  Dana Marie   b. Aug. 28, 1953 at Denver, CO
  Renee Michelle   b Sep. 15, 1957 at Denver, CO
  Dawn Terri   b. Nov. 13, 1961 at Denver, CO

Child of Ronald L. & Lois M. (Weed) Taylor
  Frederick Neal   b. Oct. 28, 1968 at Denver, CO

Memories of Lois (Weed) Taylor

I remember the old grocery store, there on the curved part of the driveway on the Merton K. Paine farm on Bushy Hill Rd., in Simsbury, CT. It was a picturesque, typical old store, with a long counter on the left as you came in with a cash register and scale on it with barrels of food stuffs in front of it and shelves all around the walls. It was also always kind of dark. I remember some of the boy cousins playing on the roof one fourth of July and getting in trouble for it.

The main family get together was on July 4th for a picnic in the orchard in back of the house. Aunt Willie Taylor lived upstairs for awhile but I can't remember if it was before or after Grandpa (Merton K. Paine) died.

Mom (Mattie P. Weed) went to school with Mr. Dodge, who became our generation's Simsbury High School principal - later Superintendent. Mom went to normal school, New Britain (CT) class of '25 by her pin.

Dad (William Boerum Weed) was raised on the Weed Homestead in Bethel (CT). He went to Storrs University studying animal husbandry, I believe. He and Mom lived on the homestead after their marriage. Bertha and I were born in Danbury; then went to the farm for our early years. From the homestead we all moved to Simsbury where we lived in the garage while Dad built the house. Dad was a Connecticut State Forest Ranger for years, taking on a wartime job at Pratt & Whitney during WW2. Bertha and I were on the fire crews for several years. We both went to school there in Simsbury for our 12 years. The boys, Bill (Jr.) and Fred, were both born there (in Simsbury). We always had a large garden and goats. I needed the goat milk for health reasons. Mom always canned and put up the produce for the next year's food supply. Dad was also a volunteer fireman on the town's force while we lived there.

Upon my graduation from high school in 1947, we moved to Colorado for Mom's arthritis. It, the move, seemed to help her quite a bit. Bert stayed there in the east as she was going to nursing school. The move to Colorado was somewhat like either pioneer times or the Beverly Hillbillies. We had an old station wagon, loaded and a 24' x 8' 1 bedroom trailer. Dad had built two sets of bunks in the bedroom for us kids. He and Mom had the sofa bed in the living room area. We moved from that big house in Connecticut with just what we could take in the trailer. Mom did say later that some things were stored with family members for them.

The Mississippi was in flood when we went through. I remember crossing the main river channel bridge and then driving ten miles through the flooded area with only stakes marking the sides of the road. It must have been quite a nervous time for Dad not knowing whether or not the road was in fact passable under all that muddy water, still there or washed away. To us kids it was just an exciting experience, seeing something new.

In Colorado, we settled in the Denver Metro area. Dad worked for the Forestry Dept. up in Gould for a while. The boys went to school and I found secretarial work and moved out on my own into an apartment.

Dad built their home in Arvada and they moved out of the trailer into it. They lived there, Dad until his death in 1970, and Mom until a couple years before she passed away in January, 1990.

I met Mack at the apartment house. He had an apartment there too, in the same building. We married in 1949.

Mack grew up on the north side of Chicago, during the Dillinger era. All his life he was an artist and photographer. He went to the Chicago Art Institute for several years. He served in the Army during WW2 in the Pacific Theater, ending up stationed at Lowry Air Base in Denver. After the service, he stayed there in the Denver area.

After our marriage we continued to live in several different homes there in Denver until finally buying our own place. All this time Mack worked as a photographer. For ten years we had our own studio, specializing in weddings, portraiture and babies. I learned to be a photographer during this time.

Our children were all born in Denver, the three eldest getting their education there. Dawn and Fred started school there with Dawn going one year in Meeker and finishing in Vernal, Utah as salutatorian. She then moved to Ogden and went to college there for a couple years.

After closing the studio, Mack worked as a Deputy Sheriff for Adams County, working his way up to Lieutenant in charge of communications. Soon after our divorce in 1969, he moved to Boulder and went to work at K-Mart, managing the Photo Dept. there until he retired.

After we closed the studio, I worked as Secretary/bookkeeper for several different companies. I went to work for MA Bell and was working there three years when I met and married Ron Taylor in 1975. We later renewed our vows on August 2, 1984 in Attica, Kansas.

Ron is five-eighths Apache Indian on his Mom's side of the family. His Dad was Cherokee and Dutch, born in Bangor, ME became orphaned and was raised in an orphanage in Maine, running away and living on the streets supporting himself from a young age in the Hell's Kitchen area of New York.

Our life together has been busy and diversified. We've had a towing business, where I learned to and did drive a tow truck and we've run a wrecking yard, both in the Denver area.

Ron tells me he is the original jack-of-all-trades. He's played semi-pro baseball and softball, been a roofer, a welder, a race car driver, both super stock and figure 8's, a mechanic and also had a large towing business, all prior to our marriage.

Shortly before our move to Meeker, we had a garage in conjunction with the towing business. We suffered a $100,000 loss during a burglary, closed the garage and moved to Meeker, where Fred finished grade school.

In Meeker we owned and operated a Motel, unique in that it was made of individual log cabins, many of which were a part of the original Fort Meeker settlement from pioneer days. Fort Meeker was a cavalry encampment. The original officer's quarters, hotel, cafe and parade ground (where City Hall now stands) are still all there. The hotel has a lot of stuffed and mounted animals hunted and killed by Teddy Roosevelt, really quite an interesting place. While we lived there we made the acquaintance of (Old) Doc Fredericks. He moved there with the cavalry as its dentist, He related incidents of Indian uprisings and all kinds of stories of that era.

While we had the motel, Ron undertook several sideline occupations to augment the motel income during slow winter months.

One winter it stayed 52 below for several weeks. Another winter the White River froze from the bottom up and the channel was completely solid with ice. The flowing part of the river was going by our door by mere yards and on through the city park where all you could see of the park was the top boards of the picnic tables. Everyone was all packed and ready to move out if need be. It got no worse though, thank goodness. Weeks later with sounds like cannon fire, the ice broke up, the river went back into its channel, all was well, and spring was on its way.

Roni opened a roto-rooter business, a locksmith/saw sharpening shop, and plowed drives and business parking lots. After the Oil Shale businesses were shut down by Uncle Sam, we sold the motel and moved to Attica, Kansas. Ron had had two massive strokes by then and per doctor's orders "to live—move lower and warmer." In Attica, Fred did his high school years and went on to Washburn University with honors, graduating in 1992.

In Attica, I worked as Bookkeeper/shipping clerk for Attica Engineering for four years, until they moved bookkeeping to Wichita where the main office is located. By this time the lowering, slowing economy was in the middle plains states, so employment was a little harder to find. Also by this time I was a little older. I found and kept an Asst. Manager's position at a convenience store in nearby Anthony for the four years, until we moved to Washington.

As Ron's health improved he reopened his saw sharpening shop and with it a small engine repair shop. Along with these two, he had 2 daily paper routes. We kept busy, paid the bills, and Ron got as well as he could, which is all we hoped for.

In Washington, I went back to work part-time in another convenience store. Ron found work as a Distribution Manager for a small weekly newspaper. I worked there, too, one day a week, as Distribution Center clerk. Along with this Ron has kept several other paper routes, until the paper expands, hopefully soon, and his workload will be enough that he'll be able to drop the routes.

Through all this moving and with diversified work schedules, I have managed to raise my own five children as well as Ron's five, (five girls and five boys between us) At this writing we have 24 grandchildren.

WILLIAM BOERUM WEED, JR. (GEN. XI, Paine Family)
   b. Jul. 27, 1932 at Simsbury, CT
   m. Jun. 16, 1956 at Escondido, CA to
ALBERTA RUTH BERRY
   b. Jan. 6, 1939 at Walnut, CA

GENERATION XII
Children of William B. Jr. & Alberta R. (Berry) Weed
Rosemarie Nina	b. Mar. 27, 1957 at Escondido, CA
Daniel Patrick	b. May 27, 1961 at Ranch-Big Creek, B.C., Canada

FREDERICK DAVIS WEED, II (GEN. XI, Paine Family)
   b. Apr. 22, 1935 at Simsbury, CT
   m. (1) Apr. 22, 1956 at Yuma, AZ to
JO DONNA BERRY
   b. Dec. 5, 1935 at Riverside, CA
   d. Dec. 17, 1993 at Cottonwood, AZ
   bur. Cottonwood, AZ

   m. (2) Sep. 2, 1995 to
RUTH (RUTHIE) ELAINE LONG
   b. Dec. 13, 1941 at Jacksonville, IL

GENERATION XII
Child of Frederick D. & Jo Donna (Berry) Weed
Michael Davis	b. Oct. 12, 1956 at CA
	d. Jan.30, 1987 at CA
	bur. Ashes strewn along California coast

EXCERPTS FROM BIOGRAPHICAL SKETCH
JO DONNA BERRY WEED

Written by her husband, Fred D. Weed, II

Jo Donna grew up in the rural area around Pomona, Walnut and what is now Rowland Heights, a commuter city east of Los Angeles, CA.

Her mother called her "Kitten" and she was a cat lover all of her life. She felt confident in bean fields, citrus and walnut groves and on horseback. Being Daddy's "Little Girl" she helped him build and repair harvesting equipment. After her Mom and Dad separated, she moved to Escondido, CA with her mother and attended junior college for a couple of years.

In the course of time, a handsome young "Mountain Man" from Colorado (Fred) moved in next door and promptly dated her younger sister, Ruth---once!! Jo Donna was advised by her loving younger sister, "Don't go out with that guy - he's a dud!!" When Fred's brother, Bill, asked Ruth for a date, Jo Donna felt compelled to chaperone her little sister and agreed to double date with Fred. That was the beginning of the end.

Jo Donna and Fred were married the next spring, April 22, 1956. Shortly afterward they moved to a few miles from Fred's parents in Denver, CO, where Fred had a job in construction. Jo Donna took the opportunity to get to know the family and develop a close relationship with her mother-in-law and learn the finer arts of homemaking and hospitality. However, it did take her a long time to get used to the Weed's weird sense of humor.

In 1959, Fred took a job with the U.S. Geological Survey as a surveyor to establish the field survey data for the photogrametric compilation of topographic maps. This required moving every three to six months with the seasons from South Texas to Northern Montana and everywhere in between.

This lasted until 1967. By that time their son, Michael, was in the third grade and had attended 12 schools. It was advised that they settle down to give Michael a chance to develop socially and put down some roots.

Jo Donna and Fred finally settled in the Salt Lake City area for about 14 years. They moved from there to Verde Valley, AZ in 1981. Fred has been involved in the construction business while Jo Donna's primary interests were in art, where she produced several lovely pastels, in gardening and in history.

In the 37 years Jo Donna and Fred were married, their life was indeed a moving experience. Due to his work, they lived in over 45 different places where she visited the local historic sites, museums
and libraries. Jo Donna was a compulsive gardener, starting a garden nearly everywhere they lived and giving most of the produce to friends. She was physically strong from all the garden and yard work. She found it rewarding and emotionally satisfying and she had a zest for life even with the cancer hanging over her like the Sword of Damocles for 22 years.

Jo Donna had strong beliefs and opinions, yet was tolerant of others' viewpoints even when she disagreed. Filled with faith, courage and conviction, she never considered divorce, and would often say "murder, yes—divorce, no!!"

She was somewhat "country", yet with a flair of feminine elegance and dignity, and was comfortable at a formal occasion. A quiet type by nature, she felt uncomfortable in the limelight, yet held Fred's hand encouraging him and helping him succeed in speech club, church and business.

Jo Donna was never one to complain. She loved to the end and entered her rest on December 17, 1993.
What else can I say? Joey was my best friend and companion for most of my life. The song "The Wind Beneath My Wings" makes me think of Joey when I hear it—and cry a little—a final tribute to "the wife of my youth."

44

Descendants of: Mabel (Paine) Glazier (Gen. X, Paine Family) & Dimock B. Glazier

SHIRLEY MABEL GLAZIER (GEN. XI, Paine Family)
  b. Jul. 22, 1926 at Simsbury, CT
  d. Jul. 20, 1968 at Hartford, CT
  bur. Curtiss Cem., Simsbury, CT
  m. (1) Jan. 2, 1946 at Simsbury, CT to
GEORGE A. POIRIER
  b. Plymouth, CT

  m. (2) May 16, 1951 at Maryland to
LEONARD FERRANTE
  b. at New York

GENERATION XII
Child of George A. & Shirley (Glazier) Poirier
  George Aloysius, Jr.   b. Feb. 27, 1947 at Hartford, CT

Children of Leonard & Shirley (Glazier) Ferrante
  Rachel Ella   b. Feb. 5, 1952 at Hartford, CT
  Bonnie Lee   b. Aug. 16, 1961 at Hartford, CT

DIMOCK BURDETTE GLAZIER, JR. (GEN. XI, Paine Family)
  b. Dec. 18, 1927 at Simsbury, CT
  d. Jul. 17, 1986 at Hartford, CT
  bur. Center Cem., Granby, CT
  m. Jun. 23, 1956 at Warehouse Point, CT to
CATHERIN JANE SCHAUB
  b. Nov. 15, 1937 at Harrisburg, PA
  d. June 15, 1987 at Hartford, CT
  bur. Center Cem., Granby, CT

GENERATION XII
Children of Dimock B. & Catherin J. (Shaub) Glazier, Jr.
  Dale Ella   b. July 17, 1959 at Hartford, CT
  Dimock Burdette III   b. Oct. 19, 1965 at Hartford, CT

Descendants of: Archie W. Paine (Gen. X, Paine Family) &
            Eldora van N. (Stoutenburgh) Paine

BEVERLY MARION PAINE (GEN. XI, Paine Family)
  b. Dec. 27, 1928 at Hartford, CT
  m. Apr. 30, 1949 at St. Bernard's R.C. Church, Tariffville, CT to
JOHN JOSEPH MARTINOLI
  b. Aug. 19, 1929 at Hartford, CT
  d. Dec. 20, 1990 at New Haven, CT
  bur. Ashes strewn at Naugatuck State Forest, Beacon Falls, CT

Authority: Birth Certs. - John & Beverly, Hartford, CT
  Marriage Lic. – Simsbury, CT
  Death Cert. – John, New Haven, CT

GENERATION XII

Children of Beverly M. (Paine) Martinoli & John J. Martinoli

John Joseph, Jr.	b. Dec. 16, 1949 at Hartford, CT
Jill Elizabeth	b. Sep. 12, 1951 at Hartford, CT
Edward William	b. Dec. 10, 1952 at Waterbury, CT

Memories of Beverly M. (Paine) Martinoli

My earliest memory of the farm on Bushy Hill Rd., in Simsbury, CT is following Grandpa, Merton K. Paine, on his chores around the farm. Whenever he could take the time to have me tag along, I was there. I apparently used to like to ride on the back of one of the draft horses when he was plowing. The hames made great handles. I do not remember the incident of my being knocked off the horse into a freshly plowed furrow, because I forgot to duck when Grampa drove the team under an apple tree. However, *I seem to remember it,* as it was an oft told story. This according to my mother happened when I was age two or three and the incident gave Mom all kinds of worry, as to possible other dangers of being out on the farm. However, it did not stop me from skipping along after Grampa whenever I had the opportunity. Accordingly he nicknamed me "Skipper".

Our adventures were many, growing up on the farm. We lived next to the old farmstead in a house Dad built us on property Grandpa deeded to him. Dad originally built us four rooms and then added another four over a period of the next ten years. The milk house and old General Store stood between the two houses.

We roamed the farm at will as we grew older, helping when ordered to do so, but mostly I remember, the wonderful fun filled days and the freedom of fields, woods and pasture.

We had adventures with bee's nests, birds, horses, bringing down the cows from pasture for milking, and one mean old yellow rooster in particular who chased us, *especially me*, every time I ventured into the chicken yard! Collecting the eggs was not much fun, when I had to be on close lookout for that mean old thing!

I named one of a litter of pigs "Pinky" and then cried inconsolably when he was taken with the rest of the litter to the slaughterhouse. Dad made a rule then and there "No more naming the animals which were to be sold for food!" Grandpa Paine caught Junior Glazier and me switching the cows in the barn one day. Junior, being fleet of foot, managed to elude Grandpa and run home. Grandpa was so angry he took a swipe at me as I tried to get past him and gave me a black eye. He was sorry and so was I. Needless to say, we did not switch the cows again.

Spring was a tough time of year for Mama, as we were constantly coming in wet and dirty from running through wet barnyards and streams which were always full during the spring thaw. (There were no automatic washers and dryers in those days).

I remember my brother, Archie, coming in wet so many times one day that Mama had run out of dry clothes for him and in despair, finally put him in one of my dresses thinking to shame him into staying home and dry. No such luck! He thought it was great and went proudly next door to show Grandma and Grampa Paine and then to Aunt Mabel and Uncle Dim's on the other side of us to show them, and our cousins! They all found it very amusing. Fat chance anyone would mistake him for a girl. He was all boy!

1900 — 1910
With Best Wishes

Merton Paine + tea cart + mules

Taken in Sunsbury
Conn. In front of grist

46a

I remember the smell of ground coffee each time I walked into Grandpa's General Store. I don't remember that the store was in operation in the years that we lived there. But that coffee smell lingered.

Dad, who had gone to Conn. Agricultural College (now UCONN) and qualified for a State Forestry position, worked for the State of Connecticut for a few years and then took a job with the Metropolitan Water District, which supplies the cities of Hartford and West Hartford with water. He worked for them until his retirement in 1967.

My first five years of school were spent at Simsbury Elementary School. In June of 1940, before I was twelve, Dad moved us from our home in Simsbury, CT to Barkhamsted, CT. to Metropolitan Water District property, where we lived for a year and a half.

The change in schools was rather drastic, since Simsbury had individual classrooms for each grade and Barkhamsted had two rooms for eight grades. It was quite a change for me, since I, being very social or one could say, nosy, had a hard time concentrating on my own business when the teacher was running three other grades! My grades slipped a bit and mother mentioned that she would perhaps need to look into boarding me out with Simsbury cousins if I was not going to be able to make the adjustment. Not wanting to leave the family for such a lengthy time, I put my nose to the grindstone and brought my grades back up.

It was in Barkhamsted that brother Phil had a bad accident at the age of eight. We had just arrived home from a week's vacation at Lake Champlain. Dad was mowing the lawn, and we three children were about 35 feet up a maple tree in the back yard playing tree tag. Phil reached for a limb above him to climb higher, stepped on a rotten limb and not having a solid hold on the limb above, fell the 35 feet to the ground, missing Dad who had just passed under the tree with the mower.

He broke his leg, both wrists and smashed his elbow. Orthopedics being what they were in those days, the folks were given two choices, operate and take a chance that the arm would be out straight and unbendable, or operate and set the bones to allow healing in the bent position. They opted for the bent position, reasoning that he would have more use of his arm that way. From what I discerned over the years it was the right decision, since he was able to do just about anything he set his mind to accomplish.

Our home in Simsbury was rented for a number of years and eventually sold. It is still there, though changed somewhat in looks. What used to be a driveway leading to our house, and on to the barn, is now a street.

The farm acreage was sold and developed and there are now homes where the barn once stood and where the animals pastured and where the hay and cornfields once grew.
The old farmstead still stands too, also changed in appearance over the years, but still recognizable.

We moved to Burlington, CT, from Barkhamsted, again to water company property, in January 1942, where I finished seventh grade, went on to eighth and then on to Canton High School.

In Burlington, Dad was put in charge of the patrols, which guarded the water company property. This was right after Pearl Harbor, and fear of espionage was rampant. Guardhouses were set up at all the dams and other crucial points where explosions could endanger the water supply to the city. They had to be manned twenty-four hours a day. It was a time when we used blackout curtains on the windows and learned some of the art of self-defense when it was being taught to the men who would make up the patrol groups.

Candy came to live with us there in May of 1944 at the age of five months, and stayed until she finished nursing school, moved to a nursing position in Boston, met Greg Bishop and married and began raising her own lovely family. She was officially adopted into the family in 1961, but became our baby sister immediately upon her arrival in '44. At the age of three she became my rival for Johnny's affections. It was rather trying to have to sit and wait to go out on my dates with him while he read her a story. Of course he started the whole procedure by bringing her books! She announced to anyone who would listen that if I didn't marry him she would when she grew up.

Pat came to live with us in mid 1944 and stayed through the rest of her school years, until her marriage. She and Nancy were fairly close in age, so got to be close friends. Living as far out from town as we did, it was great for them to have each other.

Phyllis (Dee-Dee) Stoutenburgh, our cousin, came to live with us in late 1944 or early 1945 after her mother passed away. Uncle Gill, her Dad lived in Boston and was unable to care for their three daughters. Phyllis lived with us until she grew up and married Michael Vernesoni.

I remember boarding one of Uncle Harry Seibert's tough little ponies in our barn one winter. He had several at the farm in Southwick, MA. They gave pony rides in the summer, and looked for boarding out in the winter months. My job was to care for him and ride him when weather permitted. It was a task I loved. His name was Chubby and he was a barrel shaped brown and white, tough little guy, with a mind of his own. I was sad to have Uncle Harry take him back.

Mama passed away there at Burlington in Sept. of 1959. She had been ill since 1951 with angina, and had her good days and her bad days. Archie and I were married and had families by then. Johnny and I had moved to Oxford in Feb. of 1952, so I wasn't much help during her illness. Phil and Jackie married soon after. Nancy, Pat, Candy and Dee-Dee were still at home and helped out tremendously. Pat married in January of 1955 and Nancy and Jim, that September.

As the years passed and mother began to have more down days, Aunt Mabel came to help. Uncle Dim worked for MDC at that time and he would bring her when he came to work and then take her home when his day's work was done. I remember that Aunt Mildred would come too sometimes so that mother wouldn't be alone, while Dad was working. It was such a comfort to Dad to know that his sisters were there. Candy and Dee-Dee were in school of course and Dad was relieved to know that the two young girls didn't have to bear the full burden of house chores. Aunt Mabel continued to help out after Mother passed away and until Dad and Florence married in 1961.

Many of us were briefly housed back at Barnes Hill with our own families, while awaiting moves to new homes or relocating to new jobs. Great family get-togethers were held there, with our own immediate family and the gathering of the clan as well. The grounds were spacious and well suited to picnics, ballgames and horseshoes which were among the favorite pastimes at the gatherings.

The family lived in the ten-room Barnes Hill farmhouse until Dad and Mother (Florence) built their own home in Collinsville. Two other families, who worked for MDC, occupied the house for a time but then retired or moved on to other jobs.

The house, empty for many years, was torn down in 1997, since the MDC had come to feel it a liability to maintain. I greeted this event with great nostalgia as did my siblings since it was a house so intertwined with our growing up years. It seemed like a true ending to our childhood.

THE GATHERING OF THE CLAN

Our clan gatherings to celebrate Independence Day were held yearly at the Merton K. Paine homestead on Bushy Hill Rd. in Simsbury, CT, in the orchard when weather permitted. I can't remember rainy 4ths of July. Perhaps we had them but I just recall the camaraderie of being with all of our cousins, the wonderful picnic, especially the homemade root beer and the watermelon and topping off the day with wonderful fireworks, which the older boys were allowed to set off. We younger children were allowed to hold the sparklers and cautioned not to drop the wires on the ground when the sparkle was gone. Of course, someone always managed to drop at least one, which was impossible to find in the dark. The rule was no bare feet at fireworks time! Woebetide the child who had not put on his or her shoes and stepped on a hot wire!

Those reunions began as the French Family Reunion in 1914 and were held annually apparently at the Paine Homestead. They were still referred to as the French Reunion in 1920 as snapshots of that year have revealed. It is unclear when the annual get together of Independence Day became the Paine Reunion but it had that reference in 1929 when pictures were taken in front of the house Dad was building on our property beside Grandpa & Grandma Paine's. Since that date it has been called the Paine Reunion.

The get-togethers, were held in the orchard into the late thirties, and then changed to the Bushy Hill Neighborhood House. The earliest minutes of the gathering reflect that it was held in July 1942 at our home in Burlington, Conn. There were **no reunions** held during the war years of 1943, 1944, 1945, due to the fact that many of the men in our family were away serving their country as well as due to food rationing and the gasoline shortage. The reunion in 1946 was again held at Bushy Hill Neighborhood House. From then until 1959 the picnics were held either there or at our home in Burlington, Conn.

From 1959 through 1968 they were held at Camp Gertrude Bryant, in West Avon, Conn. In 1969 we began holding our gatherings at the Coon Club in West Simsbury, CT and they have been held there ever since.

Attendance over the years has fluctuated greatly. As the families grew, attendance numbered in the eighties and nineties. The largest attendance was in 1975 when 102 were present. As the parents passed away, children of my generation began having their own picnics with their children and grandchildren. Many also live too far away to attend, thus attendance has gradually dropped until 1998 when there were only 35 present. However, the tradition continues, and the entire clan is always welcome.

ARCHIE WILLIAM PAINE, JR. (GEN. XI, Paine Family)
  b. May 14, 1930 at Hartford, CT
  m. (1) Apr. 7, 1949 at Torrington, CT to
ELIZABETH ANN FULOP
  b. Oct. 13, 1929 at Torrington, CT

  m. (2) May 9, 1954 at Winsted, CT to
DOROTHY MARGARET HUFTEN
  b. Jul. 10, 1932 at Hartford, CT

GENERATION XII
Children of Archie W. & Elizabeth A. (Fulop) Paine, Jr.
  Archie William, III   b. Nov. 15, 1949 at Torrington, CT
  David Alan   b. Jan. 11, 1952 at Torrington, CT

Early photos of the French Reunion, July 4th

Children of Archie W. & Dorothy M. (Huften) Paine, Jr.

Holly Beth	b. Sep. 14, 1961 at Hartford, CT
Samanthe Lee	b. May 14, 1965 at Hartford, CT

PHILLIP IRVING PAINE (GEN. XI, Paine Family)
   b. Jan. 29, 1932 at Hartford, CT
   d. Dec. 24, 1996 at New Britain, CT
   bur. Curtiss Cem., Simsbury, CT
   m. (1) Nov. 26, 1951 to
JACQUELINE FRECHETTE
   m. (2) Jan. 29, 1963 at Hartford, CT to
BARBARA ANN (LAITE) BARNUM
   b. Mar. 3, 1935 at Bristol, CT

GENERATION XII
Children of Phillip I. & Jacqueline (Frechette) Paine

Deborah Ann	b. Dec. 4, 1952 at Hartford, CT
Phillip Timothy	b. Dec. 30, 1953 at Hartford, CT

Children of Phillip I & Barbara (Laite) Paine

Phillip Irving, Jr.	b. Sep. 8, 1962 at Winsted, CT
Lynn Scott	b. Dec. 3, 1963 at Putnam, CT
Linda Starr	b. May 13, 1965 at Hartford, CT
Darren Allen	b. Feb. 21, 1970 at Hartford, CT

NANCY JOAN PAINE (GEN. XI, Paine Family)
   b. Apr. 12, 1937 at Hartford, CT
   d.Dec.7, 1999 at Hartford, CT
   bur. Village Cem., Collinsville, CT
   m. Sep. 10, 1955 at Newington, CT to
JAMES MICHAEL KEANE
   b. Jul. 27, 1932 at Hartford, CT

GENERATION XII
Children of James M. & Nancy J. (Paine) Keane

Michael	b. Jun. 16, 1956 at Hartford, CT
Gregory	b. Feb. 6, 1958 at Hartford, CT
Theresa Marie	b. May 16, 1959 at Hartford, CT
Cynthia Margaret	b. May 18, 1962 at Hartford, CT
Mary Elizabeth	b. May 23, 1967 at Hartford, CT

CLAUDIA (CANDY) ANN PAINE (GEN. XI, Paine Family)
   b. Dec. 22, 1943 at Winsted, CT
   m. Jun. 3, 1967 at Collinsville, CT to
GREGORY JAMES BISHOP
   b. Oct. 14, 1941 at Chelsea, MA

GENERATION XII

Children of Gregory J. & Claudia A. (Paine) Bishop

Amy Beth	b. Apr. 22, 1972 at Boston, MA
Seth Joel	b. Jan. 21, 1977 at Concord, MA
John Michael	b. Jan. 2, 1981 at Concord, MA

A Tribute to Nancy (Paine) Keane
By Candy (Paine) Bishop

MEMORIES OF A SISTER

How long ago was it? I must have been about five or six when Nancy took Phyllis and me on one of those walks. The sun glistened on snowy-crusted fields. Golden grasses blew in the wind from snowy beds. It wasn't the usual reservoir trek, but down to where Barnes Hill ended and beyond. To me this was a big adventure. We finally came to a culvert big enough for us to crawl through. You had to be careful not to fall into the water that gushed through to the other end. I discovered that there were advantages to being the smallest. I could go through almost without bending over. Maybe it was a slippery rock or hurrying to catch up with the others that caused my fall, but down I went. As I slid, one of my boots quickly filled with icy water. My foot was numb with cold and soon I was shivering. My big sister seated me on a rock, pulled off my boot and one very wet sock. And taking a woolen mitten from her hand she placed it on my foot. To this day I can still remember the instant warmth and comfort that resulted from this one selfless act. To her it was no big deal; just an every day thing; something anyone else would do. But I knew better. "My sister is a genius," I thought. "Who else would have thought of a mitten?" I was yet to learn that it was a way of life for her, and that her creative and resourceful thoughtfulness would later influence my own life. "But now your hand will get cold." I said, as she helped me on with my boot. "I'll just keep it in my pocket." She said smiling. Then putting her other hand in mine she added, "C'mon, Honey, let's go home."

CHAPTER THREE
GENERATIONS XII AND XIII

**Descendants of: Ferdinand R. August, Jr. (Gen. XI, Paine Family) &
Mabel I. (McLaughlin) August**

NORMAN FREDERICK AUGUST (GEN. XII, Paine Family)
 b. Oct. l, 1946 at New London, CT
 m. Mar. 21, 1970 at Wilkes Barre, PA to
VIRGINIA LLEWELLYN
 b. Sep. 25, 1945 at Wilkes Barre, PA

GENERATION XIII
Children of Norman F. & Virginia (Llewellyn) August
Lisa Paige	b. Sep. 10, 1971 at Vandenberg AFB, CA
Megan Elizabeth	b. Nov. 15, 1975 at Hartford, CT
Shelley Lynne	b. June 21, 1977 at Hartford, CT

ROY JOSEPH AUGUST (GEN. XII, Paine Family)
 b. Apr. 10, 1948 at Preston, CT
 m. Apr. 2, 1977 at Bristol, CT to
VERGENE CONOPASK
 b. Nov. 10, 1948

GENERATION XIII
Children of Roy J. & Vergene (Conopask) August
Travis Seth	b. Sep. 20, 1977
Forrest Wesley	b. June 20, 1984
Justin Orion	b. July 28, 1981

Descendants of: Albert R. August (Gen. XI, Paine Family) & Theona (Strong) August

JAMES ALBERT AUGUST (GEN. XII, Paine Family)
 b. Jun. 19, 1942 at Hartford, CT
 m. Nov. 26, 1966 at Havelock, NC to
JANICE FAYE PAGE
 b. Jul. 3, 1945 at Portsmouth, VA

GENERATION XIII
Child of James A. & Janice F. (Page) August
Todd	b. Aug. 19, 1972 at New Britain, CT

(adopted at 6 1/2 weeks of age)

LARRY STRONG AUGUST (GEN. XII, Paine Family)
 b. May 16, 1945 at Hartford, CT
 m. Jan. 31, 1969 at Simsbury, CT to
JACQUELINE YVETTE TELLIER
 b. Nov. 18, 1945 at Simsbury, CT

GENERATION XIII
Children of Larry S. & Jacqueline Y. (Tellier) August

Kari Lynn	b. Aug. 5, 1969 at Hartford, CT
Keith	b. Feb. 20, 1973 at Hartford, CT
Kirstin	b. Oct. 17, 1978 at Hartford, CT

MICHAEL JAY AUGUST (GEN. XII, Paine Family)
b. Mar. 17, 1947 at Hartford, CT
m. Dec. 20, 1969 at Lafayette, CO to
JANE ELLEN BALL
b. Jun. 22, 1948 at Denver, CO

GENERATION XIII
Children of Michael J. & Jane (Ball) August

Shawn Michael	b. Jul. 1, 1973 at Longmont, CO
Steven Matthew	b. Apr. 11, 1976 at Longmont, CO
Shannon Mitchell	b. Jul. 27, 1979 at Fort Collins, CO

SHARYN ELIZABETH AUGUST (GEN. XII, Paine Family)
b. Sep.18, 1948 at Hartford, CT
m. Jul. 31, 1971 at Avon, CT to
SAMUEL W. BIRINGER
b. Jul. 25, 1943 at New Britain, CT

GENERATION XIII
Children of Samuel W. & Sharyn E. (August) Biringer

Laura	b. Nov. 14, 1976 at Bristol, CT
Heidi	b. Mar. 16, 1980 at Bristol, CT

Descendants of: Dorothy (August) St. Pierre (Gen. XI, Paine Family) & Albert J. St. Pierre

BARRY JOSEPH St. PIERRE (GEN. XII, Paine Family)
b. May 4, 1946 at Hartford, CT
m. June 9, 1972 at Avon, CT to
ROBERTA KONE
b. May 13, 1943 at Hartford, CT

DEBORAH JEAN St. PIERRE (GEN. XII, Paine Family)
b. May 14, 1950 at Gardiner, ME
m. Feb. 6, 1971 at Collinsville, CT to
ANTHONY ASARO
b. Aug. 16, 1949 at Torrington

GENERATION XIII
Children of Anthony & Deborah J. (St. Pierre) Asaro
Amanda Lisbeth	b. Mar. 3, 1973 at Hartford, CT
Jason Matthew	b. Oct. 11, 1977 at Hartford, CT

Descendants of: Robert B. August (Gen. XI, Paine Family) &
Gladys E. (Thompson) August

BETSY AUGUST (GEN. XII, Paine Family)
b. Oct. 30, 1951 at Hartford, CT
m. Apr. 24, 1976 at Avon, CT to
JAMES PATRICK McCLURE
b. Aug. 1, 1953 at Post, TX

GENERATION XIII
Children of James P. & Betsy (August) McClure
Scott Nathanael	b. Aug. 16, 1983 at Alexandria, VA
Kate Joanna	b. Dec. 3, 1986 at Pomona, CA

ROBERTA AUGUST (GEN. XII, Paine Family)   (retained surname August)
b. Jul. 1, 1953 at Hartford, CT
m. (1) Sep. 20, 1975 at Avon, CT to
NORMAN ROBERT SHIELDS
b. Aug. 30, 1953 at Lead, SD

m. (2) Aug. 1, 1987 at W. Lynn, OR to
GREGORY GORDON PARSONS
b. Oct. 30, 1947 at Birmingham, AL

GENERATION XIII
Children of Gregory G. Parsons & Roberta August
Andrea August Parsons	b. Mar. 24, 1990 at Portland, OR
Emily Greer August	b. May 24, 1993 at Portland, OR

LOURIE AUGUST (GEN. XII, Paine Family)   (retained surname August)
b. Oct. 28, 1955 at Hartford, CT
m. Jul. 25, 1988 at Medford, MA to
LOREN EDWARD BERNARDI
b. Jun. 7, 1954 at Chicago, IL

GENERATION XIII
Children of Loren E. Bernardi & Lourie August
Galen Hanson August	b. Jun. 7, 1990 at Beverly, MA
Larkin Thompson Bernardi	b. Apr. 11, 1992 at Beverly, MA

ANN AUGUST (GEN. XII, Paine Family)
  b. Jun. 5, 1957 at Hartford, CT
  m. (1) Jun. 28, 1980 at Avon, CT to   (retained maiden name August)
DANIEL LOUIS SCHMIDT
  b. Jan. 3, 1954 at Portville, NY

  m. (2) Jul. 27, 1991 at Avon, CT to
PHILIP CHARLES BAIERWICK
  b. Feb. 15, 1955 at Hartford, CT

GENERATION XIII
Children of Philip C. & Ann (August) Baierwick
  Rebecca Ann   b. Dec. 20, 1994 at Hartford, CT
  Sarah Abigail   b. Mar. 10, 1998 at Hartford, CT

  NOTE: see page 161 for Family of Marnie Louise August

Descendants of: Mildred L. (August) Gangell (GEN. XI, Paine family) & Myles I. Gangell

JOHN EMERSON GANGELL (GEN. XII, Paine Family)
  b. Nov. 26, 1948 at Waterville, ME
  m. Sep. 13, 1975 at Collinsville, CT to
JANICE BRISTOL
  b. Mar. 20, 1950 at Hartford, CT

GENERATION XIII
Children of John E. & Janice A. (Bristol) Gangell
  Elizabeth Anne   b. Jan. 8, 1978 at Winsted, CT
  Paul Emerson   b. Aug. 17, 1981 at Torrington, CT

Descendants of: Arthur M. Paine (Gen. XI, Paine Family) & Ruth F. (Engelke) Paine

STEVEN ARTHUR PAINE (GEN. XII, Paine Family)
  b. Nov. 1, 1951 at Hartford, CT
  m. Nov. 12, 1978 at Tariffville, CT to
JANE BARRITT
  b. May 31, 1955 at New Orleans, LA

GENERATION XIII
Children of Steven Arthur & Jane (Barritt) Paine
  Christy Ann   b. Nov. 16, 1978 at Denver, CO
  Cathryn Ruth   b. Jul. 21, 1982 at Hartford, CT

LINDA SUE PAINE (GEN. XII, Paine Family)
  b. Mar. 6, 1954 at Hartford, CT
  m. Oct. 20, 1979 at Simsbury, CT to
MARK L. LANDRIGAN

GENERATION XIII
Children of Mark L. & Linda Sue (Paine) Landrigan

Lauren Elizabeth	b. Jan. 22, 1982 at Hartford, CT
Ryan Merrill	b. Feb. 2, 1986 at Hartford, CT

AMY LOUISE PAINE (GEN. XII, Paine Family)
b. Sep. 16, 1959 at Hartford, CT
m. Jun. 7, 1986 at Simsbury, CT to
WILLIAM CARL WOLF
b. Feb. 2, 1957 at Hartford, CT

GENERATION XIII
Children of William C. & Amy L.(Paine) Wolf

Jeffrey Allen	b. Nov. 9, 1990 at Franklin, NH
Margaret Elizabeth	b. Apr. 7, 1994 at Franklin, NH

Descendants of: Donald I. Paine (Gen. XI, Paine Family) & Joyce A. (Mahlstedt) Paine

MICHAEL ROBERT PAINE (GEN. XII, Paine Family)
b. May 20, 1954 at
m. Nov. l, 1980 at Simsbury, CT to
JEAN (JEANNIE) VERONICA KNIFFIN

GENERATION XIII
Children of Michael R. & Jeannie (Kniffin) Paine

Michael Robert, Jr.	b. Oct. 24, 1984 at Hartford, CT
Sarah Jean	b. Nov. 7, 1986 at Hartford, CT

SUSAN GAIL PAINE (GEN. XII, Paine Family)
b. Jul. 25, 1955 at Hartford, CT
m. Jun. 24, 1989 at Simsbury, CT to
DUANE STAGG
b. Mar. 26, 1955 at Eunice, LA

RUSSELL ALAN PAINE (GEN. XII, Paine Family)
b. Nov. 25, 1956 at Hartford, CT
m. Sep. 20, 1980 at Simsbury, CT to
MARY (MOLLY) MARGARET WILLIAMS

GENERATION XIII
Children of Russell A. & Molly (Williams) Paine

Julie Lynn	b. Aug. 22, 1981 at Hartford, CT
Jeffrey Alan	b. May 2, 1983 at Hartford, CT

TIMOTHY GORDON PAINE (GEN. XII, Paine Family)
b. May 1, 1958 at Hartford, CT
m. Mar. 29, 1986 at Baltimore, MD to
LYNNE COLLINS

GENERATION XIII
Children of Timothy G. & Lynne (Collins) Paine
Christopher Nicholas	b. Sep. 18, 1986 at Baltimore, MD
Kali Nicole	b. Mar. 6, 1990 at Seattle, WA

DONALD JEFFREY (DJ) PAINE (GEN. XII, Paine Family)
b. Nov. 13, 1961 at Hartford, CT
m. Oct. 12, 1985 at Falls Church, VA to
CYNTHIA (CINDY) LANGILIER

GENERATION XIII
Children of Donald J. (DJ) & Cindy (Langilier) Paine
Joshua Robert	b. June 19, 1990 at Hartford, CT
Sheana Joy	b. Sep. 14, 1991 at Hartford, CT
Remi Maxwell	b. Jun. 1, 1994
Grady Gerard	b. Jul. 2, 1996, Falls Church, VA

DONNA JOY PAINE (GEN. XII, Paine Family)
b. Jan. 17, 1963, at Hartford, CT
m. (1) June 9, 1987 at Simsbury, CT to
ROBERT MacKENZIE

m. (2) Nov. 25, 1995 at Simsbury, CT to
SEAN DAVID CROMBEZ
b. Dec. 13, 1968 at Tecumseh, MI

GENERATION XIII
Children of Sean D. & Donna J. (Paine) Crombez
Nicole Joyce	b. Dec. 27, 1996 at Grand Rapids, MI
Jan Alexander	b. Feb. 17, 1999 at Hartford, CT

Descendants of Gladys E. (Paine) Kelly (Paine Family) & Edward L. Kelly, Jr.

THOMAS MICHAEL KELLY (GEN. XII, Paine Family)
b. Oct. 24, 1954 at Hartford, CT
m. Apr. 4, 1982 at Tariffville, CT to
SUE CHISOLM
b. Oct. 1, 1955 at Augusta, GA

GENERATION XIII
Child of Thomas M. & Sue (Chisolm) Kelly
Jeffrey Michael	b. Oct. 25, 1983 at Jacksonville, FL

ROSEMARY KELLY (GEN. XII, Paine Family)
b. May 10, 1956 at Hartford, CT
m. May 7, 1988 at Simsbury, CT to
HAROLD QUAGLIAROLI
b. Nov. 19, 1957 at Hartford, CT

KATHERINE ELIZABETH KELLY (GEN. XII, Paine Family)
   b. Dec. 20, 1960 at Hartford, CT
   m. Nov. 1, 1986 at Simsbury, CT to
ROBERT MARINO
   b. Aug. 6, 1960 at New Britain, CT

GENERATION XIII
Children of Robert & Katherine E. (Kelly) Marino
   Rachel Elizabeth   b. Mar. 24, 1991 at Hartford, CT
   Amanda Lynn   b. Aug. 18, 1994 at Hartford, CT

BARBARA ANN KELLY (GEN. XII, Paine Family)
   b. Nov. 9, 1962 at Hartford, CT
   m. Sep. 3, 1988 at Simsbury, CT to
TIMOTHY ANDREW PINTO
   b. Mar. 11, 1964 at Hartford, CT

GENERATION XIII
Child of Timothy & Barbara A. (Kelly) Pinto
   Jennifer Rose   b. Jul. 10, 1991 at Hartford, CT
   Timothy Andrew, Jr.   b. Jun. 20, 1994 at Hartford, CT

Descendants of Eleanor G. (Seibert) (Gen. XI, Paine Family) & Charles J. Toole

ANNE MARIE TOOLE (GEN. XII, Paine Family)
   b. Sep. 13, 1946 at Meriden, CT
   m. to
ROGER DENIS OUIMET
   b. Feb. 23, 1944 at Montreal, CAN

GENERATION XIII
Children of Roger D. & Anne Marie (Toole) Ouimet
   Lisa Marie   b. Feb. 25, 1968 at Holyoke, MA
   James Joseph   b. Aug. 5, 1970 at Holyoke, MA
   David John   b. Jun. 12, 1976 at Holyoke, MA

VIRGINIA ROSE TOOLE (GEN. XII, Paine Family)
   b. Oct. 4, 1952 at Holyoke, MA
   m. (1) to
WILLIAM JOSEPH DOYLE, III
   b. Sep. 5, 1952 at Holyoke, MA

   m. (2) Aug. 15, 1987 at Amherst, MA to
CHARLES HENRY SHAW
b. Sep. 18, 1950 at Brookline, MA

GENERATION XIII
Children of William J. Doyle, III & Virginia R. (Toole) Doyle
(now known as Virginia Rose Toole-Shaw)

William Joseph IV	b. Apr. 14, 1971 at Holyoke, MA
Katie Marie	b. Feb. 12, 1975 at Holyoke, MA
Brandon David	b. Apr. 3, 1978 at Greenfield, MA
Christopher Michael	b. Mar. 21, 1980 at Greenfield, MA

ALICE MADELEINE TOOLE (GEN. XII, Paine Family)
b. Apr. 17, 1954 at Holyoke, MA
m. (1) to
THOMAS BUTLER

m. (2) Aug. 24, 2985 at Granby, MA to
RICHARD COPLEY SCOTT
b. Oct. 10, 1945

GENERATION XIII
Child of Thomas & Alice M. (Toole) Butler

Thomas Michael	b. Jul. 13, 1971 at Holyoke, MA

JOHN CHARLES TOOLE (GEN. XII, Paine Family)
b. Apr. 1, 1956 at Holyoke, MA
m. Dec. 29, 1990 at Cambridge, MA to
MARIE ADELAIDE MENDONCA
b. at Portugal

DEBRA JEANNE TOOLE (GEN. XII, Paine Family)
b. Mar. 31, 1960 at Holyoke, MA
m. Nov. 1977 at So. Hadley, MA to
DAVID CLEGG
b. Apr. 1960 at Holyoke, MA

GENERATION XIII
Children of David & Debra J. (Toole) Clegg

Shannon	b. Mar. 31, 1978 at Holyoke, MA
David Charles	b. Sep. 18, 1979 at Holyoke, MA
Theresa Grace	b. Mar. 18, 1982 at Holyoke, MA

MICHAEL EDWARD TOOLE (GEN. XII, Paine Family)
b. Mar. 31, 1963 at Holyoke, MA
TRUDY NAZAR
b. Dec. 23, 1951

GENERATION XIII
Child of Michael E. Toole & Trudy Nazar

Daniel Nazar-Toole	b. Sept. 29, 1993 at Greenfield, MA

Descendants of: Leonard L. Seibert (Gen. XI, Paine Family) &
Mae E. (MacWilliams)Seibert
CHERYL ANNE SEIBERT (GEN. XII, Paine Family)
   b. Jul. 6, 1950 at Hartford, CT
   m. Feb. 18, 1989 at Huntington, MA to
RICHARD EDGAR BENOIT
   b. Nov. 14, 1944 at Springfield, MA

GENERATION XIII
Child of Richard E. & Cheryl A. (Seibert) Benoit
   Lucille (Lucy) Seibert   b. Sep. 3, 1993 at Springfield, MA

LYNNE CAROL SEIBERT (GEN. XII, Paine Family)
   b. Dec. 3, 1952 at Hartford, CT
   m. May 20, 1972 at Southwick, MA to
RICHARD HAROLD COWLES
   b. Jan. 31, 1946 at Westfield, MA

GENERATION XIII
Children of Richard H. & Lynne C. (Seibert) Cowles
   Erin Seibert   b. Mar. 6, 1985 at Springfield, MA
   Ryan Seibert   b. Aug. 13, 1987 at Holyoke, MA

LAURIE DEE SEIBERT (GEN. XII, Paine Family)
   b. Jun. 18, 1961 at Westfield, MA
   m. Oct. 27, 1990 at Southwick, MA to
DANIEL PAUL BERESFORD
   b. Sep. 4, 1959 at Hartford, CT

Descendants of: William H. Seibert (Gen. XI, Paine Family) &
Cynthia C. (Karlstrom) Seibert

DALE WILLIAM SEIBERT (GEN. XII, Paine Family)
   b. Sep. 10, 1953 at Westfield, MA
   m. Nov. 17, 1973 at Granby, CT to
KATHLEEN MARY ALLEN
   b. Jul. 9, 1954 at Westfield, MA

GENERATION XIII
Children of Dale W. & Kathleen M. (Allen) Seibert
   Daniel Joseph   b. Mar. 30, 1976 at Westfield, MA
   Sarah Ann   b. Jan. 11, 1978 at Westfield, MA
   Brian Howard   b. Jul. 3, 1981 at Westfield, MA

PATRICIA ANN SEIBERT (GEN. XII, Paine Family)
 b. Dec. 13, 1955 at Westfield, MA
 m. Sep. 11, 1976 at Granby, CT to
GREGORY ARTHUR BLAIR
 b. Apr. 13, 1956 at Granby, CT

GENERATION XIII
Children of Gregory A. & Patricia A. (Seibert) Blair
Jacob Uriah	b. Aug. 15, 1978 at Springfield, MA
Jonathan Adam	b. Nov. 12, 1980 at Springfield, MA
Amanda Jean	b. Mar. 6, 1984 at Springfield, MA

TERRY DIANE SEIBERT (GEN. XII, Paine Family)
 b. Nov. 8, 1959 at Westfield, MA
 m. Oct. 29, 1983 at Suffield, CT
WILLIAM ALLEN TROY
 b. Aug. 8, 1965 at Westfield, MA

KIM AMELIA SEIBERT (GEN. XII, Paine Family)
 b. May 22, 1962 at Westfield, MA
 m. Oct. 20, 1984 at Chicopee, MA to
GLEN DAVID RICHARDS
 b. Nov. 11, 1961 at Chicopee, MA

GENERATION XIII
Children of Glen D. & Kim A. (Seibert) Richards
Bryce Andrew	b. Jun. 19, 1988 at Manchester, CT
Kelsey Leigh	b. Aug. 4, 1990 at Manchester, CT
Jared David	b. Mar. 27, 1993 at Manchester, CT
Hayley Catherine	b. Aug. 5, 1995 at Manchester, CT

Descendants of: Merton G. Seibert (Gen. XI, Paine Family) & Alice T. (Murphy) Seibert

DOUGLAS HOLDEN SEIBERT (GEN. XII, Paine Family)
 b. Oct. 23, 1956 at Springfield, MA
 m. Feb. 23,1980 at Southwick, MA to
DENISE AUFIERO
 b. Apr. 23, 1958 at Passaic, NJ

GENERATION XIII
Children of Douglas H. & Denise (Aufiero) Seibert
Kristofer Douglas	b. Jun. 22, 1983 at Springfield, MA
Corey Michael	b. Sep. 21, 1985 at Springfield, MA

Descendants of: Merton G. Seibert (Gen. XI, Paine Family) & Ruth (McNamara) Seibert

BOBBI JO SEIBERT (GEN. XII, Paine Family)
   b. Aug. 9, 1970 at Springfield, MA
   m. Oct. 20, 1990 at Southwick, MA to
STEVEN DALE HILL
   b. Feb. 10, 1970 at Macs Creek, MO

GENERATION XIII
Child of Steven D. & Bobbi Jo (Seibert) Hill
   Steven Dillon   b. Aug. 28, 1992 at Bremerton, WA

Descendants of: Bertha M. (Weed) Ferlingere (Gen. XI, Paine Family) &
                Thomas Ferlingere

VALERIE MAE FERLINGERE (GEN. XII, Paine Family)
   b. Jan. 31, 1950 at Denver, CO
   m. (1) Jan. 31, 1970 at Denver, CO to
LOYD THOMAS BAKEWELL
   b. Feb. 22, 1942 at Salt Lake City, UT

   m. (2) Jun. 3, 1989 at Waynoka, OK to
DANNY VEARL BECK
   b. July 5, 1950. Lindsay, OK

GENERATION XIII
Children of Loyd T. & Valerie M.(Ferlingere) Bakewell
   Jonathan David   b. May 1, 1971 at Denver, CO
   Caroline Joy   b. Apr. 13, 1973 at Denver, CO
   Daniel Joseph   b. Apr. 24, 1979 at Denver, CO

Child of Danny V. & Valerie M.(Ferlingere) Beck
   Whitney Hope   b. Feb. 14, 1992 at Chickasha, OK

THOMAS SCOTT FERLINGERE (GEN. XII, Paine Family)
   b. Dec. 17, 1950 at Denver, CO
   m. Jan. 15, 1971 at Green Bay, WI to
SHARON ANN RICE
   b. Nov. 8, 1951 at Green Bay, WI

GENERATION XIII
Children of Thomas S. & Sharon A.(Rice) Ferlingere
   Cellina Louise   b. Apr. 9, 1972 at Denver, CO
   Jason Thomas   b. Apr. 27, 1973 at Green Bay, WI

KAREN LOUISE FERLINGERE (GEN. XII, Paine Family)
    b. Jun. 26, 1957 at Denver, CO
    m. (1) Nov. 13, 1975 at Colorado Springs, CO to
KENNETH HOLT McILHENNY
    b. Nov. 13, 1952 at Torrington, WY

    m. (2) Jan .6, 1989 at Buffalo, NY to
FRANK RUCKINGER
    b. Dec. 24, 1946 at Altoona, PA

GENERATION XIII
Children of Kenneth H. & Karen L. (Ferlingere) McIlhenny
    Seth Holt   b. Jul. 23, 1976 at Colorado Springs, CO
    Sarah Louise   b. Jul. 23, 1976 at Colorado Springs, CO
    Sage Hudson   b. Mar. 26, 1980 at Cheyenne, WY

Descendant of: Bertha M. (Weed) Duke (Gen. XI, Paine Family) & Wylie E. Duke, Jr.

WYLIE CHRISTOPHER DUKE (GEN. XII, Paine Family)
    b. Jun. l3, 1966 at Denver, CO
    m. Aug. 13, 1988 at Aspen, CO to
ELIZABETH ANN CIPRIANO
    b. Dec. 5, 1967 at El Paso, TX

GENERATION XIII
Children of Wylie C. & Elizabeth A. (Cipriano) Duke
    Jonathan Christopher   b. Oct. 17, 1991 at Denver, CO
    Ashley Elizabeth   b. Jan. 10, 1993 at Denver, CO
    Victoria Rose   b May 8, 1995 at Denver, CO

Descendants of: Lois M. (Weed) Sutherland (Gen. XI, Paine Family) &
               Mack H. Sutherland

WILLIAM T. SUTHERLAND (GEN. XII, Paine Family)
    b. Feb. 17, 1951 at Denver, CO
    m. (1) Aug. 15, 1970 at Denver ,CO to
KAREN LEE FISHER
    b. Aug. 14, 1951 at Denver, CO

    m. (2) Nov. 4, 1978 to
JAIME LEE SUMMERS
    b. Nov. 5, 1967

    m. (3) to
JACKIE LEE RIDELL

GENERATION XIII
Children of William T. & Karen Lee (Fisher) Sutherland
Sean Michael	b. Sep. 25, 1971 at Denver, CO
Spencer Matthew	b. Aug. 30, 1975 at Denver, CO

Children of William T. & Jaimie L.(Summers) Sutherland
William Bradley	b Jun. 10, 1979 at Denver, CO
Richard Thomas	b. Apr. 27, 1981 at Denver, CO

Child of William T. & Jackie L. (Ridell) Sutherland
Thomas Lee	b. Aug. 13, 1984 at Phoenix, AZ

DANA MARIE SUTHERLAND (GEN. XII, Paine Family)
b. Aug. 28, 1953 at Denver, CO
m. Mar. 17, 1983 at Meeker, CO to
DUANE MARSH
b. Mar. 16, 1943 at Rio Blanco County, CO

GENERATION XIII
Child of Duane and Dana M. (Sutherland) Marsh
Frederick Lee	b. Nov. 24, 1982 at Meeker, CO

RENEE MICHELLE SUTHERLAND (GEN. XII, Paine Family)
b. Sep. 15, 1957 at Denver, CO
m. (1) Dec. 22, 1973 at Denver, CO. to
MICHAEL JAY WAGNER
b. Jul. 21, 1953 at IN

m. (2) Jun. 7, 1980 at Denver, CO to
SCOTT LICINI
b. Sep. l5, 1951 at Allentown, PA

m. (3) Jun. 22, 1991 at Marino, CA to
RICK HENTGES
b. Mar. 19, 1957 at CA

GENERATION XIII
Children of Michael J. & Renee M. (Sutherland) Wagner
Eric Michael Wagner-Hentges	b. Jan. 27, 1975 at Denver, CO
Joshua James	b. Jul. 22, 1976 at Denver, CO

Child of Scott & Renee M. (Sutherland) Licini
Anthony Scott	b. Feb. 1983 at Wurzberg, West Germany

DAWN TERRI SUTHERLAND (GEN. XII, Paine Family)
  b. Nov. 13, 1961 at Denver, CO
  m. (1) Jun. 22, 1980 at Ogden, UT to
DAVID MICHAEL LEONARDI
  b. May 7, 1958 at Ogden, UT

  m. (2) Mar, 31, 1986 at Longview, WA to
STEVE GREGG
  b. Jan. 19, 1951 at Longview, WA

GENERATION XIII
Child of David M. & Dawn T. (Sutherland) Leonardi
  Gabriel James   b. Aug. 5, 1982 at San Francisco, CA

Descendants of: Lois M. (Weed) Taylor (Gen. XI, Paine Family) & Ronald L. Taylor

FREDERICK NEAL TAYLOR (GEN. XII, Paine Family)
  b. Oct. 28, 1968 at Denver, CO
  m. Jun. 30, 1993 at Athol, KA to
TINA MARIE HUDSON
  b. Nov. 10, 1967 at Phillipsburg, KA

Descendants of: William B. Weed, Jr. (Gen. XI, Paine Family) & Alberta R. (Berry) Weed

ROSEMARIE NINA WEED (GEN. XII, Paine Family)
  b. Mar. 27, 1957 at Escondido, CA
  m. (1) Mar. 18, 1978 at Pasadena, CA to
McCONNELL EARL KNIGHT, JR.
  b. Sep. 10, 1951 at Indiana
  d. Nov. 2, 1983 at Pasadena, CA

  m. (2) Feb. 10, 1985 at Pasadena, CA to
COLIN ALEXANDER CATO
  b. Nov. 1, 1946 at London, England

GENERATION XIII
Children of McConnell E. Jr. & Rosemarie N. (Weed) Knight
  Angela Michelle   b. Mar. 2, 1979 at Pasadena, CA
  Geoffrey Michael   b. Jun. 11, 1980 at Pasadena, CA

Child of Colin A. & Rosemarie N. (Weed) Cato
  David Alexander   b. Aug. 16, 1986 at Glendale, CA

DANIEL PATRICK WEED (GEN. XII, Paine Family)
b. May 17, 1961 at Ranch-Big Creek, B.C., Canada
m. Oct. 14, 1986 at Big Sandy, TX to
CARA LYNNE EDWARDS
  b. Jan. 1, 1963 at Dayton, OH

GENERATION XIII
Children of Daniel P. & Cara L. (Edwards) Weed
   Lacy Danielle   b. Nov. 5, 1987 at Glendale, CA
   Tiffany Lynne   b. Dec. 6, 1989 at Cottonwood, AZ
   Ashley Cherie   b. Dec. 6, 1989 at Cottonwood, AZ

Descendants of: Shirley (Glazier) Poirier (Gen. XI, Paine Family) & George A. Poirier

GEORGE ALOYSIUS POIRIER, JR. (GEN. XII, Paine Family)
   b. Feb. 27, 1947 at Hartford, CT
   m. Dec. 31, 1988 at Bradford, VT to
JANICE EILEEN MURPHY
   b. Nov. 12, 1952 at Manchester, CT

Descendants of: Shirley (Glazier) Ferrante (Gen. XI, Paine Family) & Leonard Ferrante

RACHEL ELLA FERRANTE (GEN. XII, Paine Family)
   b. Feb. 5, 1952 at Hartford, CT
   m. Aug. 12, 1995 at Collinsville, CT to
HERMAN BROWN
   b. Apr. l, 1945 at Hartford, CT

BONNIE LEE FERRANTE-GLAZIER (GEN. XII, Paine Family)
   b. Aug. 16, 1961 at Hartford, CT
   m. Sep. 24, 1988 at Avon, CT to
VICTOR PHILIP DELBON
   b. Sep. 15, 1959 at Hartford, CT

Children of Victor P. & Bonnie L. (Ferrante-Glazier) Delbon
   Christopher James   b. Jul. 11, 1986 at Hartford, CT
   Victoria Lynn   b. Jan. 5, 1989 at Hartford, CT

Descendants of: Dimock B. Glazier, Jr. (Gen. XI, Paine Family) & Catherin J. Schaub

DALE ELLA GLAZIER (GEN. XII, Paine Family)
   b. Jul. 17, 1959 at Hartford, CT
   m. Jun. 3, 1978 at Granby, CT to
JOHN RAYMOND HELLER, JR.
   b. Apr. 12, 1958 at Hartford, CT

GENERATION XIII
Children of John R. & Dale E. (Glazier) Heller, Jr.
   Kristin Ann   b. May 24, 1982 at Hartford, CT
   Chelsea Lynn   b. Jun. 10, 1986 at Hartford, CT
   Catherin Sue   b. Oct. 2, 1990 at Hartford, CT

DIMOCK BURDETTE GLAZIER, III (GEN. XII, Paine Family)
b. Oct. 19, l965 at Hartford, CT
m. Oct. 15, 1995 at Granby, CT to
BRENDA JEAN HART
b. Dec. 17, 1971 at Hartford, CT

Descendants of: Beverly M. (Paine) Martinoli (Gen. XI, Paine Family) & John J. Martinoli

JOHN JOSEPH MARTINOLI, JR. (GEN. XII, Paine Family)
b. Dec. 16, 1949 at Hartford, CT
m. May 6, 1972 at Philadelphia, PA to
KATHRYN LABOURE MARGARET LOFTUS
b. Jul. 10, 1950 at Philadelphia, PA

GENERATION XIII
Children of John J. & Kathryn L. M. (Loftus) Martinoli, Jr.
  John Daniel   b. Apr. 5, 1977 at Pensacola, FL
  Susan Elizabeth   b. Aug. 3, l979 at Fredericksburg, VA

JILL ELIZABETH MARTINOLI (GEN. XII, Paine Family)
b. Sept. 12, 1951 at Hartford, CT
m. (1) Nov. 27, 1971 at Seymour, CT to
PAUL JOSEPH MARINO
b. Dec. 5, 1952 at Derby, CT

m (2) at Oxford, CT to
MICHAEL GERRY

m. (3) Jun. 6, 1986 at Oxford, CT to
JOSEPH A. DeFELICE
b. Dec. 14, 1952 at Derby, CT

GENERATION XIII
Child of Paul J. & Jill E. (Martinoli) Marino
  Meegan Angela   b. Dec. 5, 1972 at Derby, CT

EDWARD W. MARTINOLI (GEN. XII, Paine Family)
b. Dec. 10, 1952 at Waterbury, CT
m. (1) Apr. 11, 1981 at Oxford, CT to
LISA ANN (NARDI) WARD

m. (2) Apr. 8, 1995 at Oxford, CT to
CAROL ANN DEAN
b. Apr. 15, 1971 at New London, CT

GENERATION XIII
Child of Edward W. & Lisa A. (Nardi) Martinoli
  David Edward   b. Oct. 15, 1982 at Derby, CT

Descendants of: Archie W. Paine, Jr. (Gen. XI, Paine Family) & Elizabeth A. (Fulop) Paine

ARCHIE WILLIAM (PAINE, III) HOLLOWAY (GEN. XII, Paine Family)
  b. Nov. 15, 1949 at Torrington, CT
  m. (1) Jan. 2, 1971 at Oxford, CT to
SHARON ANN GREEN
  b. Jan .9, 1953 at Fort Dix, NJ

  m. (2) Jun. 10, 1995 at Warwick, RI to
KAREN LINDA TENNETT
  b. Mar, 22, 1963 at Providence, RI

GENERATION XIII
Child of Archie W. P., III & Sharon (Green) Holloway
  Kristy Beth Holloway   b. Apr. 7, 1971 at Millington, TN

Children of Archie W. P. III & Karen L.(Tennett) Holloway
  Heather Nicole   b. July 26, 1996 at Warwick, RI
  William Archie   b. Sep. 9, 1997 at Warwick, RI

DAVID ALAN PAINE HOLLOWAY (GEN. XII, Paine Family)
  b. Jan. 11, 1952 at Torrington, CT
  m. (1) Nov. 12, 1971 at Warwick, RI to
MARIAN ELLEN ROONEY
  b. Jul. 7, 1954 at Boston, MA

  m. (2) Sep. 18, 1993 at Fitchburg, MA to
MELANIE RAE REID
  b. Jan. 22, 1971 at Fitchburg, MA

GENERATION XIII
Children of David A. P. & Marion E. (Rooney) Holloway
  Michelle Marie   b. Mar. 8, 1972 at Warwick, RI
  Sarah Nicole   b. Jan. 12, 1977 at Fitchburg, MA

Children of David A. P. & Melanie R. (Reid) Holloway
  Christopher Alan   b. Apr. 15, 1995 at Leominster, MA
  Matthew David   b. Aug. 25, 1997 at Leominster, MA

Descendants of: Archie W. Paine, Jr. (Gen. XI, Paine Family & Dorothy M. (Huften) Paine

SAMANTHE LEE PAINE (GEN. XII, Paine Family)
  b. May 14, 1965 at Hartford, CT
TODD UNDERWOOD
  b. Aug. 21, 1961 at Minneapolis, MN

m. April 2001 to
MATHER CARSWELL

GENERATION XIII
Child of Samanthe Lee Paine
Lucas M. Paine   b. Nov. 13, 1981 at Torrington, CT

Children of Todd & Samanthe L. (Paine) Underwood
Allen Matthew   b. Dec. 16, 1989 at Pensacola, FL
Victoria Blair (Tory)   b. Feb. 16, 1994 at Fairhope, AL

Child of Mather and Samanthe Lee (Paine) Carswell

Daniel Robert Ono   b. May 19, 2001 at Pensacola, FL

Descendants of: Phillip I. Paine (Gen. XI, Paine Family) & Barbara A. (Barnum) Paine

PHILLIP IRVING PAINE, JR. (GEN. XII, Paine Family)
b. Sep. 8, 1962 at Winsted, CT
m. (1) to
KAREN STICKLES

m. (2) Jul. 20, 1991 at Collinsville, CT to
DAWN OSTHEIMER
b. Nov. 10, 1960 at Springfield, MA

GENERATION XIII
Child of Phillip I. Jr. & Karen (Stickles) Paine
Jeffrey Allen   b. Jun. 30, 1986 at New Britain, CT

Child of Phillip I. Jr. & Dawn (Ostheimer) Paine
Joshua Thomas   b. Dec.3. 1997 at Hartford, CT

LYNN SCOTT PAINE (GEN. XII, Paine Family)
b. Dec. 3, 1963 at Hartford, CT
m. (1) to Sandra

GENERATION XIII
Children of Lynn S. & Sandra Paine
Beth Marie   b. 1984 at New Britain, CT
Laurie   b. 1986 at New Britain, CT

Descendants of Nancy J. (Paine) Keane (Gen. XI, Paine Family) & James M. Keane

GREGORY KEANE (GEN. XII, Paine Family)
b. Feb. 6, 1958, at Hartford, CT
m. Mar. 4, 1989 at Farmington, CT to
PATRICIA SYMONDS
b. Aug. 1, 1949 at New Britain, CT

GENERATION XIII
Children of Gregory & Patricia (Symonds) Keane
Julia Kelleher   b. Oct. 2, 1990 at Hartford, CT
Margaret O'Connell   b. Jul. 2, 1992 at Hartford, CT

THERESA MARIE KEANE (GEN. XII, Paine Family)
   b. May 16, 1959 at Hartford, CT
   m. Oct. 21, 1995 at Burlington, CT to
JAMES UDO SCHRIJN
   b. Oct. 23, 1960 at Hartford, CT

CYNTHIA MARGARET KEANE (GEN. XII, Paine Family)
   b. May 18, 1962 at Hartford, CT
   m. Dec. 17, 1994 at Southbridge, MA to
MARK CARRON
   b. Jul. 8, 1962 at Springfield, MA

GENERATION XIII
Children of Mark & Cynthia M. (Keane) Carron
Cole Alysia	b. Feb. 22, 1993 at Worcester, MA
Mackenzie Hope	b. Feb. 12, 1995 at Worcester, MA

Descendants of Claudia A. (Paine) Bishop (Gen. XI, Paine Family) & Gregory J. Bishop

AMY BETH BISHOP (GEN. XII, Paine Family)
   b. Apr. 22, 1972 at Boston, MA
   m. Jun. 3, 2000 at Concord, MA to
PETER JULIO ANASTACIO
   b. May 26, 1967 at Gafanha da Encarnacao, Ilhavo 3830 Portugal

GENERATION XIII
Child of Peter J. and Amy Beth (Bishop) Anastacio
Charlotte Rose	Feb. 13, 2007 at Beverly, MA

SETH JOEL BISHOP (GEN. XII, Paine Family)
   b. Jan.21, 1977 at Concord, MA
   m. Sep 1, 2007 at Weston, MA to
KELLY MARIE LADD

JOHN MICHAEL BISHOP (GEN. XII, Paine Family)
   b. Jan 2, 1981 at Concord, MA
   m. Sep. 30, 2006 at Wayland, MA to
HEATHER JEAN DURNFORD
   b. Sep. 2, 1984 at Newton, MA

CHAPTER FOUR
GENERATION XIII & XIV

Descendant of: James A. August (Gen. XII, Paine Family) & Janice F. (Page) August

TODD JAMES AUGUST (GEN. XIII, Paine Family)
b. Aug. 19, 1972 at New Britain, CT
m. Mar. 5, 1995 at Midway, GA to
APRIL NICOLE MULKEY
b. 1974.

GENERATION XIV
Child of Todd J. & April N. (Mulkey) August
  Ricki Samantha Icelene   b. Nov. 15, 1995 at Anniston, AL

Descendant of: Larry S. August (Gen. XII, Paine Family) & Jacqueline Y. (Tellier) August

KARI LYNN AUGUST (GEN. XIII, Paine Family)
b. Aug. 5, 1969 at Hartford, CT
m. May 15, 1993 at Wethersfield, CT to
STEVEN JAMES PAYETTE
b. May 13, 1969 at Hartford, CT

GENERATION XIV
Child of Steven J. & Kari L. (August) Payette
  Alyssa Marie   b. Oct. 8,1994 at Hartford, CT

Descendant of: Debra J. (Toole) Clegg (Gen. XII, Paine Family) & David Clegg

SHANNON CLEGG (GEN. XIII, Paine Family)
b. Mar. 31, 1978 at Holyoke, MA

GENERATION XIV
Child of Shannon Clegg
  Sara Jean   b. Nov. 4, 1993 at Northampton, MA

Descendants of: Valerie M. (Ferlingere) Bakewell (Gen. XII, Paine Family) &
        Loyd T. Bakewell

JONATHAN DAVID BAKEWELL (Gen. XIII, Paine Family)
b. May 1, 1971 at Denver, CO
m. Jul. 29, 1995 at Lindsay, OK to
JENNIFER DAWN JOHNSTON
b. Mar. 13, 1973 at Weatherford, OK

CAROLINE JOY BAKEWELL (GEN. XIII, Paine Family)
   b. Apr. 13, 1973 at Denver, CO
   m. Dec. 14, 1995 at Rota, Spain to
CHARLES JOHN MARTENS
   b. Feb. 6, 1975 at Las Vegas, NV

Descendant of: Thomas S. Ferlingere (Gen. XII, Paine Family) &
                  Sharon Ann (Rice) Ferlingere

CELLINA LOUISE FERLINGERE (GEN. XIII, Paine Family)
   b. Apr. 9, 1972 at Denver, CO
   m. Dec. 9, 1955 at Siesta Key, FL to
MICHAEL SCOTT DAVIS
   b. Nov. l, l966 at Ashtabula, OH

GENERATION XIV
Child of Cellina L. Ferlingere
   Haley Marie   b. Mar. 7, 1989 at Warren, Ohio

Descendant of: Renee M. (Sutherland) Wagner-Hentges (Gen. XII, Paine Family) &
                  Michael J. Wagner

ERIC MICHAEL WAGNER-HENTGES (GEN, XIII, Paine Family)
   b. Jan .27, 1975 at Denver, CO
   m. Sept. 18, 1993 at Carmel Valley, CA to
NINA MARIE WILCOX MULVEY
   b. New York City, NY

Descendants of: John J. Martinoli , Jr. (Gen. XII, Paine Family) &
                  Kathryn Laboure Margaret Loftus

JOHN DANIEL MARTINOLI (GEN. XIII, Paine Family)
   b. Apr. 5, 1977 at Pensacola, FL
   m. Sep. 24, 2004 at Wyncote, PA to
JOANNE LATHAM BRISTOW
   b. Nov. 9, 1974 at Bryn Mawr, PA

GENERATION XIV
Children of John D. & Joanne L. (Bristow) Martinoli
   Zachary John   b. Sep. 22, 2006 at Paoli, PA
   Tyler Evan   b. Aug. 4, 2008 at Paoli, PA

SUSAN ELIZABETH MARTINOLI (GEN. XIII, Paine Family)
   b. Aug. 3, 1979 at Fredericksburg, VA
   m. May 1, 1009 at Media, PA to
JOSEPH PATRICK KENNEY
   b. Mar. 30, 1978 at Philadelphia, PA

Descendants of: Jill E. (Martinoli Marino) DeFelice (Gen. XII, Paine Family) &
Joseph A. DeFelice & Paul J. Marino

MEEGAN ANGELA MARINO (GEN. XIII, Paine Family)
  b. Dec. 5, 1972 at Derby, CT
  m. Apr. 29, 2000 at Oxford, CT to
TIMOTHY FANNING DUNN
  b. Aug. 4, l971 at Washington, DC

GENERATION X1V
Child of Meagan A. & Timothy F. Dunn
  Calie Elizabeth   b. Jan. 24, 2003 at Rockville, MD

PAUL JOSEPH DEFELICE
  b. Dec. 17, 1978 at Derby, CT
  m. Mar. 12, 2005 at North Haven, CT to
MEGAN ANN GLENNON
  b. Oct. 1, 1978

GENERATION XIV
Child of Paul J. DeFelice and Megan A. (Glennon) DeFelice
  Gianna Grace   b. Feb. 15, 2010 at New Haven, CT

Descendant of Edward W. Martinoli (Gen., XII Paine Family) & Lisa (Nardi) Martinoli

DAVID EDWARD MARTINOLI (GEN. XIII, Paine Family)
  b. Oct. 15, 1982 at Derby, CT
  m. Dec. 16, 2007 at Naugatuck, CT to
SAVHANNA PERKINS
  b. Nov. 15, 1987 at Bridgeport, CT

GENERATION XIV
Child of David E. & Savhanna (Perkins) Martinoli
  Wyatt John   b. Jan. 25, 2007 at Waterbury, CT

Descendant of: Archie W. (Paine, III) Holloway (Gen. XII, Paine Family) &
Sharon (Green) Holloway

KRISTY BETH HOLLOWAY (GEN. XIII, Paine Family)
  b. Apr. 7, 1971
  m. to
VIRGILIO PAUL MARINELLI, JR.

GENERATION XIV
Children of Kristy B. (Holloway) & Virgilio P. Marinelli, Jr.
  Kelsey Montana   b. June 18, 1996 at Virginia Beach, VA
  Virgilio Paul, III   b. Nov. 4, 1997 at Ohio

**Descendants of David A. (Paine) Holloway (GEN. XII, Paine Family) &
Marian E. (Rooney) Holloway**

MICHELLE MARIE HOLLOWAY (GEN. XIII, Paine Family)
   b. Mar. 8, 1972 at Warwick, RI
   m. Jul. 10, 1999 at Warwick, RI to
GLENN MANUEL CREAVEN
   b. Jan. 29, 1972 at Waterbury, CT

GENERATION XIV
Children of Michelle M. (Holloway) & Glenn M. Creaven
   Kaylah Ellen   b. Jul. 15, 2008 at Worcester, MA
   Sydney Antonia b. Jul. 15, 2008 at Worcester, MA

SARAH NICOLE HOLLOWAY (Gen. XIII, Paine Family)
   b. Jan. 12, 1977 at Fitchburg, MA
   m. Sep. 21, 2003 at Eisenhower House, Newport, RI to
JEREMY CARR
   b. Sep 18, 1975 at Toledo, Ohio

GENERATION X1V
Children of Sarah N. (Holloway) & Jeremy Carr
   Caleb Dale   b. Jun. 8, 2004 at Worcester, MA
   Sawyer Michael   b. Mar. 8, 2006 at Leominster, MA
   Audry Lillian   b. Aug. 23, 2007 at Leominster, MA

Descendant of: Samanthe L. Paine (Gen. XII, Paine Family)

LUCAS M. PAINE (GEN. XIII, Paine Family)

GENERATION XIV
Child of Lucas M. Paine & Crystal Ann Webb
   Abigail Marie Davidson   b. Sept. 27, 1999 at Foley, AL

Child of Lucas M. Paine & Lisa Blair
   Christopher Berkley Paine   b. Jan. 10, 2002 at Foley, AL

CHAPTER FIVE
FRENCH

We begin this section of the genealogy with the arrival in this country of **John French** who came to America with his wife **Sarah** and their first six children aboard the **Caledonia**, which arrived in the Port of New York on July 24th, 1832. **(see immigration page 92)**

GENERATIONS I & II
JOHN FRENCH (GEN. I French Family)
  b. Sep. 13, 1800 at Taunton, Eng.
  d. Sep. 20, 1879 at Norristown, PA
  m. Nov. 2, 1819 in England to
SARAH WEBBER
  b. Mar. 1, 1800 in England
  d. Apr. 23, 1869

Children of John & Sarah (Webber) French

Frederick W.	b. Jul 20, 1820 at Taunton, Eng.
	d. Apr. 18, 1893 at Boston, MA
Ethelinda W.	b. Apr. 10, 1822 at Taunton, Eng.
	d. 1877 at Philadelphia
Alfred W.	b. Feb. 11, 1824 at Bath, Eng.
	d. Apr. 16, 1834 at Lansingburgh, NY
Mary Ann	b. Feb. 23, 1826 at Bath Eng.
	d. May 12, 1899 at Philadelphia, PA
Lavinia W.	b. Dec. 21, 1828 at Bath Eng.
	d. Mar. 27, 1934
Clarissa	b. Mar. 1, 1832 at Bath, Eng.
	d. Nov. 23, 1915 at Cardington, PA
Thomas	b. Jun. 21, 1834 at Lansingburgh, NY
	d. Apr. 1, 1911, at New York City, NY
William Henry	b. Oct. 16, 1836 at Newark, NJ
	d. Jan. 7, 1932 at Simsbury, CT
Joseph	b. Dec. 23, 1838 at Rahway, NJ
	d. Aug. 23, 1842 at Philadelphia, PA
Sarah E.	b. Aug. 21, 1842 at Philadelphia, PA
John E.	b. May 31, 1845 at Philadelphia, PA

The foregoing record of the FRENCH FAMILY, was given to Alice Landon (French) Wheeler, whose first husband was George Elbert Cole.

Elbert C. Cole, of Williamstown, Mass signed the following on Feb. 18, 1927. "This is a copy of the data sent me by my mother, Alice L. Wheeler, received Feb. 18, 1972. Mother was given the information by her father, Wm. H. French."

William R. Cole attests to the following "The above is a true copy of data sent me by my brother, Elbert C. Cole, March 29, 1975." then goes on to say "Our grandfather William H. told me of living next door to John Wilbank on Callowhill St., Phila., (ca. 1851-2) where a new bell for

Independence Hall was being made: that the cracked bell was to be melted down as scrap as a part of the deal; that his sister (Clarissa?) married a Wilbank boy and later owned the bell.* (In an interview in the Springfield, Mass. Sunday Republican, May 27, 1928, grandfather, William H. French, is reported to have called his sister Caroline Wilbank. It appears that there was an error in reporting.) I am now seeking clarification of this matter with Mrs. John Fred Wilbank, 426 Madison Ave., Prospect Park, PA 19076.

WILLIAM HENRY FRENCH (GEN. II, French Family)
  b. Oct. 16, 1836 at Newark, NJ
  d. Jan. 7, 1932 at Simsbury, CT
  bur. Jan. 9. 1932 at Oak Grove Cem. in Springfield, MA
  m. Nov. 2, 1865 at Richmond, VA to
MARY H. DUGAN (widow of Frier, Fryer)
  b. Sep. 9, 1838 at Harpers Ferry, Jefferson City., West VA
  d. Jun. 9, 1907, at Chester, MA
  bur. Oak Grove Cem. Springfield, MA
  m. (1) May 26, 1860 Harpers Ferry? Jefferson City. VA? to
WILLIAM N. FRYER
  She was widowed before she had their child. It seems probable that Wm. N. Fryer died in the Civil War.
  m. (2) Nov. 2, 1865 at Richmond, VA to
WILLIAM H. FRENCH
Authority: Certified Copies of Death Records: Wm. H. French-Simsbury, CT Vital Records: Mary H. (Dugan) French-Chester, MA Vital Records, Vol. 4, P.19; Certified Copy of Marriage, Commonwealth of Virginia, Page 57 Line 1 records of Commonwealth Vital Records.

William H. French & Mary (Dugan, Fryer) French

Author's Note: *See Addendum Re: Letter of Employment recommendation from
<u>U.S. Grant, General</u> -Discovered 2006, Recorded on Page 159

<u>**GENERATION III**</u>
Child of Widow Mary H. (Dugan) Fryer
   Wilberta Fryer   b. Mar. 21, 1862 at Winchester City, VA**

Children of William H. & Mary H. (Dugan) French
   Thomas J.   b. 1866 at Washington, DC;
                                   d. Nov.15, 1888,
                                   bur. at Springfield, MA (<u>place</u> of death questioned)
   Ella Gordon   b. Jun 14, 1868 at Washington, DC
   Alice Landon   b. Dec. 13, 1869 at Omaha, NB
   George W.   b. 1871 at Washington, DC
   Clara   b. Oct. 13, 1873 at Washington, DC
   Julia R.   b. 1876 at Harpers Ferry, W.VA

Author's Note:
**All of the foregoing (wife and children) were listed as members of the household of William
H. French in the 1880 Census- Index for Jefferson County, West Virginia. F562 V. 5 E.D.2-Sheet
18 Line 25. Copy of Official Census obtained from Morman Vital Record Files.
***Have found no proof in Liberty Bell Histories pertaining to Wilbank ever owning bell.
****1880 Census refers to Wilberta as being born in Harpers Ferry. (Believe this in error)

WILBERTA FRYER
  b. Mar. 21, 1862 at Winchester, VA
  d. Jun. 29, 1946 at Hartford, CT
  bur., Jun. 30, 1946 at Oak Grove Cem., Springfield, MA
  m. to
CLARENCE H. TAYLOR
  d. Sep. 13, 1924
  bur., Oak Grove Cem.., Springfield, MA

Child of Wilberta (Fryer) & Clarence H. Taylor
  Roy   b. 1891?
                           d. Jan. 9,1961
                           bur. Oak Grove Cem. at Springfield, MA
Authority: Wilberta (Fryer) Taylor-Certified Copy of Death, Hartford, CT Vital: Have been unable to locate a record of birth in VA. A visit to Oak Grove Cemetery in Springfield MA showed a written record of burial there, but a visit to the lot area showed no placement of a monument.

COPY OF ARTICLE IN SPRINGFIELD, MASS. NEWSPAPER
SUNDAY, SEPTEMBER 16, 1924

Chasing Slavers with old Wooden Navy
William H. French, 87 Years Young, Served on "Constellation" Engaged in Suppressing Slave Trade off African Coast and later Enlisted as Private in Civil War

Springfield enjoys the distinction of being the home city of an unusual number of veterans of various military campaigns whose personal experience would rival the most stirring book of adventure. Of this colorful group none has a more varied and fascinating story of personal experience to tell than William H. French, a vigorous, wholesouled "youngster" of 87 years, whose early life's journal closely rivals that of Sinbad the Sailor.

Mr. French ranks as the oldest member of John J. Leonard Post, Veterans of Foreign Wars, and except for one of the few living members of the Mexican War, now more than 100 years old, he would enjoy the distinction of being the oldest member of the national organization. He served in the old "wooden navy" during the years immediately preceding the Civil War, fought through that conflict as a member of one of the most colorful regiments to be recruited in Massachusetts, put in an adventurous apprenticeship aboard a Provincetown "whaler" during the early '50s, and narrowly escaped a two years' cruise aboard a big East Indies "windjammer," which afterward foundered with her entire crew while rounding Cape Horn.

With all these interesting experiences to his credit it would be unusual if Mr. French did not possess material for an exceptional story of adventure. Happily, he is blessed with an agile memory and more than ordinary ability to recount his varied experiences in a manner that makes him a prime favorite among the members of the local post of the Veterans of Foreign Wars, even though that organization claims a number of "soldiers of fortune" who could spin exceptional yarns of their own.
Mr. French was born in Newark, N.J., spent his early boyhood in Philadelphia, but most of his adventures had their beginning along the Commercial Street waterfront of Boston in the days when a walk along that old thoroughfare was equivalent to a ticket of adventure.

At Work at Age of Eight

"We didn't have compulsory schooling in those days," Mr. French explained in recounting some of his many experiences, "and I was compelled to go to work when I was no more than eight years old. My father wanted to make a shoemaker out of me, but I had other plans, and I ran away from home three times before I reached maturity. I remember the Old Bowery in New York in its prime, as well as Old Five Points before the Mission House was built there. I worked as a gas fitter's apprentice, while they were building the Crystal Palace for the first World's Fair ever held, when I was no older than the average grammar school boy of these days."

Moreover, he was born with the spirit of the typical adventurer in his blood. The sea called him, as it called hundreds of boys in those days of clipper ships and long whaling voyages, and like his kind, he responded.

His first adventure came in 1853, when he was scarcely 17 years old, the result of a casual visit to the old Commercial Street waterfront in Boston. The shipping firm of Capen & Bangs was one of the most famous of its kind in those days, and young French strolled down to their wharf one day to look over the "Wild Wave", an East India "windjammer" of 2000 tons which was about to sail for Calcutta and other ports in the Far East.

Obeying an irresistible impulse Mr. French agreed to sign aboard as an apprentice seaman, and his brother, with whom he lived in Chelsea, gave his consent. The ship was to be gone two and a half years and Capt. Knowles, the skipper, proved to be a typical sailing master of those days. He had been married but a short time before and his orders to set out on the two and a half years' cruise probably had much to do with his ill nature, which he visited upon the seamen and apprentices with anything but a light hand.

To make the young apprentice's life more miserable a temporary crew of typical "wharf rats" was shipped to sail the ship from Boston to Nova Scotia where a crew of "bluenose" seamen was to be shipped for the major portion of the cruise.

Runs away from ship

"The beat across the bay was enough to cure me of any desire to make that two years' cruise," Mr. French declared with a laugh in recounting the experience, "and I took the first opportunity to skip out."

"This came while we were outfitting in Nova Scotia. We had taken aboard a cargo of shipbuilding timber for Liverpool, where we were to unload before going to London for our cargo for the East Indies, and the new crew had been shipped, when I asked Capt. Knowles if I could go ashore with four boys to get a few things. He consented and we went ashore. I found an excuse to leave my friends soon after we were out of sight of the docks, and that's the last I saw of them.

"An old side-wheeler ran between that port and Boston in those days, stopping at some of the Maine ports. I went down to the dock where this boat was tied up and pretended to be a terrible greenhorn who never had seen a steamer. The crew laughed at my red hair - it was flaming red in those days - and readily agreed to let me go aboard. Then, when nobody was looking, I slid under a lifeboat turned bottom upward on the upper deck, and crawled up into it as far as I could.

"Just as I expected, an hour or so later I heard the captain of the steamer with Capt. Knowles coming along the deck, hunting for me. The crew declared I had not left the boat. That red head of mine made me stand out among a million and they swore they would have seen me if I had gone ashore. Anyway, they didn't find me, and after a time I heard the paddle wheels going, which told me I was safe. I crawled out and looked around. We were well down the harbor, while a quarter of a mile away I could see the "Wild Wave" beating her way out of the harbor. Then I went up on the bridge to see the captain, who took the affair with a hearty laugh, and I paid my fare back to Boston.

"The 'Wild Wave' finished that trip all right, but on the next trip with most of the old crew aboard, she foundered rounding Cape Horn. If I had gone on her it is quite probable I would have gone down with her, for the way I was then there is little doubt but that I would have signed on at the end of the first voyage."

He then put in 14 months aboard a Provincetown whaler, which made a profitable cruise - for the owners - to the Bay of the Arabian Desert, where whales had been seen a short time before.

They were not as large as the Arctic whales, but rich in whale oil, nevertheless. The largest taken by his ship was a humpback whale which produced 130 barrels of oil. His most interesting adventure was when they captured an 80-barrel sperm whale, the first and only "spouter" he ever saw.

"I was pulling a tub oar," he explained, "when I saw this whale coming right toward my side of the boat. Not knowing anything about the habits of whales I was frightened nearly out of my wits. I called the attention of the man in charge of the boat to the whale and he turned the huge thing very easily. A whale has a tender nose and all you need to do is to touch that nose to turn him. One of the men reached out when the whale had almost reached the boat and hit him smartly on the nose with a boathook. The whale turned without touching us and sank. But it came up again a minute later right under the mate's boat, lifting it high in the air, then smashing it into bits. Fortunately not a man was lost and it really was funny to see them slide down that whale's back into the water. We picked them up and got several harpoons in the whale and eventually landed it.

"My experiences on that voyage illustrate how the owners of whalers took advantage of seamen who shipped with them. I was to get a proportionate amount of the entire catch during the voyage, which would have amounted to the value of about 10 barrels of oil. But the joker in that agreement was the fact that you had to buy everything you used out of Capt. Ryder's 'slop chest.' When they paid me off in Provincetown at the end of the voyage I found that I had exactly $5 coming to me. I was no longer a member of the crew then, so I could speak my mind, and I did. But it didn't do any good. They had me and they knew it. And they had the nerve to ask me to ship for another voyage. That $5 barely paid my fare back to Boston and I had to borrow money from my brother to fit myself out with clothes."

Mr. French's most interesting experience came as a member of the crew of the old sloop of war, "Constellation,"* sister ship of the famous "Constitution," better known as "Old Ironsides," both of which were built in 1795. He shipped aboard the "Constellation" in April, 1857, as a landsman after a brief time aboard the old receiving ship, "Ohio", in the Charlestown Navy Yard.
*Mistaken for original Constellation declared derelict in 1853. 2nd Constellation built 1854.

Adventures in Slave Trade
The "Constellation" was the flagship of a fleet of six vessels, which were to join a British fleet of equal armament to suppress the slave trade off the West Coast of Africa. Aboard the "Constellation" was Commodore Jack Inman, commander of the fleet, and a famous figure in United States naval history, while the ranking officer aside from the commodore was Capt. Nickerson, a typical New England sailor of the days of the old wooden navy.

"I count the three and a half years I spent with that old fleet as the most interesting experience of my life," Mr. French declared. "We went to Liberia first to ship 25 natives under the leadership of John Tobey to do the heavy work in the hot climate, such as manning the supply boats pulling between the supply base on shore and the ship. No white man could have stood that killing work and Com. Inman knew it. Similar crews were put aboard the other ships in the fleet, and then we set out for the 'Slave Colony' farther down from Liberia. We made our headquarters at Loango, and with the English vessels we plied up and down the coast in search of slave runners.

"To give an idea of the kind of life we led, we were allowed 48 hours' shore liberty every six months, all of which had to be spent on the British island of St. Helena, where Napoleon spent his last days. It was a barren island, some distance off the coast of Africa, and no soil covered the rocks until you had reached a point several hundred feet above the shore. The island was covered with a sparse growth fit only for sheep, and the shanties, like the one in which Napoleon lived, were built for the shepherds.

"I was ashore there several times, for on one visit Com. Inman was ill and we had to stay there six weeks. On this trip I got two souvenirs of the island, a dogwood, or ironwood cane, which I cut not 20 feet from the spot where Napoleon's hut stood, and a geranium which I took from his grave. At that time the body had been removed and taken to France, but the French maintained its guard of honor just the same, even though the island was British. We had plenty of liquor along in those days because we needed it. So while one of the men was giving the French guard a drink I grabbed one of the geranium plants from the grave and hid it under my arm.

"I was lucky enough to get some of the roots, and it grew nicely aboard ship. Later I took it to the home of my brother in Chelsea, where it thrived for many years. I was proud of that plant, perhaps because I had stolen it from under the eyes of that Frenchman. I've got the old cane yet. The wood is one of the hardest kind in the world to carve, but I worked the figure of a man and a woman on it and I'm quite proud of it.

"We spent some time on St. Helena and I climbed all over it. Before we left I knew every rock on the island. I was a member of the crew of the captain's gig, and as Capt. Nickerson often visited Col. Ross, commander of the Scotch regiment on the island, and Lady Ross, I had plenty of opportunity to explore the island while we were waiting for him to go aboard ship after his visits.

Chasing a Slave Runner
"The cruises up and down the coast in search of slave runners were fascinating. As an inducement to the sailors, the Government offered a bounty of $25 a head for every slave aboard any slave runner we might take. This was divided proportionately to rank, from the commodore down. I received quite a little nest egg in addition to my navy pay when I quit the service.

"The slave dealers had their game quite well organized. They had agents ashore who kept them posted on our whereabouts by code signals. We could see their signals flashing at night many times from their shore lookouts. They established big buildings in the interior, something like barracks, and these usually were full of natives in charge of drivers armed with long black snake whips. They traded for them and made enormous profits. They got them for something like $25 a head delivered, while the slave runners averaged about $800 a head for them in the Southern slave market.

"The first slave runner we caught was a fast little bark, 'Cora'. We were sailing in the wind one-day when the lookout called out, 'Sail Ho!' and we made out this little bark going in the same direction at a smart clip. Commodore Inman climbed into the rigging to have a look at her and I heard him declare, 'She's a slaver, all right; she's loaded with slaves.'

"Commodore Inman called on the entire crew to trim the vessel for the chase. He got up the carpenter to spruce up the rigging, several of the crew manned pumps to wet the sails so they would push the sloop along. Once in awhile we'd fire a shot, but that didn't scare them any, because we didn't try to hit them. Then I heard Commodore Inman telling Capt. Nickerson what would happen after darkness fell.

"'I know just what he'll probably do,' he said. 'He'll square his yards and think he's leaving us on this course. But we'll just fool him by squaring our own yards the minute it gets dark, and keep right up with him.'

Capturing Cora

"It was uncanny the way it worked out. The minute it became dark Commodore Inman ordered the course changed, and we nearly ran the 'Cora' down. Our jib was almost in her rigging when the lookout shouted a warning. Commodore Inman put a lieutenant in charge of the slaver, and then the lieutenant called us up from the gig. He sent us to pull up the hatches, and 705 natives came tumbling up out of the hold, yelling and cringing. They ran forward and crouched in the bow like so many animals.

"The funny part of it was that nobody aboard that ship would admit he was the captain. All of them shrugged their shoulders when the lieutenant asked for the skipper, but there was one man all covered with diamonds and he afterwards turned out to be one of the owners of the 'Cora,' as well as the famous 'Wanderer,' a speedy yacht which ran between the West Coast and the Southern States for years and never was caught.

"It was a fearful job, cleaning and doctoring those natives. They were nearly starved, but they responded to treatment and after keeping them awhile we landed them in Monrovia, Liberia, where according to custom, they were colonized. This was somewhat different from the way the British treated them, and shows how expensive this slave business was to the United States. Our government realized nothing out of the slaves and paid $25 a head above the cost of maintaining the fleet.

"On the other hand, the British always took the slaves they caught to the West Indies, where they were compelled to put in a certain term of years on plantations before they were liberated. The British made a profit from it, which, while it was questionable, more than paid for the cost of maintaining a fleet on the 'Slave Coast.'"

"It was a joke to the slave runners, too, for we had to release the crews of the ships and merely put the captain under bond. But where they made hundreds of thousands of dollars on a single cargo of slaves they could well afford the loss of an occasional vessel and the forfeiture of the captain's bond. They were taken to New York, where the captured vessel was sold at auction, as the prisoners landed; after that they could do whatever they pleased. Usually they bought another vessel and went right back slaving again.

The Slaver's Wager

"In our squadron was the little sloop 'St. Mary,' under Capt. Taylor. This vessel made one of the smartest catches ever made on the 'Slave Coast.'' The slaver was the 'Nightingale,'' a 2000-ton ship which came out from the United States with her skipper boasting that he would take back 1000 slaves with him. He made friends with all of the officers of the 'Constellation,' from

Commodore Inman down. Many a night I had heard him talking with them down in the cabin. Finally he admitted, and even boasted, that he was a slaver and that they never would catch him. The officers declared just as positively that he never would do it and I heard them making bets that he would or wouldn't.

"We didn't hear anything of the 'Nightingale' for weeks, although the fleet knew where she was. One evening the 'St. Mary' was cruising up the coast and came to the Bight of Benin shortly after dark. They were sailing across the opening when somebody spotted light clear at the end of the bight. Capt. Taylor sailed the 'St. Mary' out of sight, then hove her to and manned several boats with all oars muffled. They crept up to the 'Nightingale' in the darkness and were over her sides before the crew knew anything about it. The 'Nightingale' was bringing slaves aboard as fast as they could be packed below decks and several hundred were aboard when the crew of the 'St. Mary' surprised them. That captain was the maddest man in Africa, for he had planned to sail that night with 1000 slaves.

"The 'Wanderer' was the ship everybody hoped to catch, but they never did. Soon after the 'Nightingale' was taken the captain of the 'San Jacinta,' one of the ships of our fleet, came into port. 'I hear you've taken a slaver,' he said to one of officers of the 'St. Mary's.' 'Who is her captain?'. They pointed to the bejeweled man who had commanded the 'Nightingale.' 'Why, that's the captain of the '"Wanderer."' the officer declared. The man denied it for a time, then admitted that he was, but that is all the good it did us. No charge could be brought against him. The 'Wanderer' never was caught, and the best we could do was to put him under bonds after the 'Nightingale' was taken. Without a doubt he went back to the 'Wanderer' and made several more voyages with her. But we had the satisfaction of capturing two of his ships at least."

Enlists for Civil War

The Civil War broke out while Mr. French was on the West Coast of Africa, and while his enlistment ran out shortly after war was declared, it was several months before he returned to the United States and received his "big discharge" - quite an honor to a Navy man in those days - at the Kittery Navy Yard in New Hampshire. The fact that he was in the Naval Service when the war broke out qualified him for "foreign war" service, although he did not see actual fighting until several months later when he enlisted with the 24th Mass. Vols. soon after President Lincoln's call for 300,000 volunteers.

Previous to his enlistment, however, something remained to be done. This consisted of a vacation with his "matie," Ike Nodine, ship's barber aboard the "Constellation," to have a good time on the $1330 they brought home between them from their three and a half years' African cruise. It took them exactly 13 weeks to go through with the program, then Mr. French returned to Boston, spent a few weeks at his old trade as a shoemaker. He could not resist the call of duty and adventure, so he enlisted in February 1862, in the 24th Regt., under Col. Stevenson and in a short time they were in New Bern, N.C

William H. French   Age 90

Drove Band to Woods

While in the service Mr. French won further distinction as a member of the famous 24th Regt. Band, one of those interesting musical organizations recruited hurriedly during the war that gained high distinction before the close of the struggle. Gilmore's Band, a famous Boston organization, accompanied the regiment to North Carolina, but returned to Boston within a short time. The return of the band left the outfit hungry for a good musical organization, so Col. Stevenson's father, a wealthy resident of Boston, offered to outfit a band if one could be recruited from within the regiment. "Johnny" Armstrong, one of Mr. French's "pals" in the service, was the first to sign the agreement and Mr. French quickly followed. The nucleus of the band was eight men with previous musical experience, but so vehement were their efforts that the other members of the regiment drove them into the woods to practice with instruments loaned by a New York regiment. At the close of the war the band consisted of 20 men, equipped with the beautiful instruments Col. Stevenson's father had furnished as he had promised, and was one of the finest bands in the Union Army.

Wherever the regiment went the band made a name for itself: on an island in the harbor of Charleston, S.C.; in St. Augustine, Fla.; and later in Richmond, where the regiment was quartered when the war ended. Following the close of the war the band was engaged to play twice a week at Jefferson Davis' old headquarters, being one of the few bands connected with Federal forces to enjoy this distinction.

Mr. French was in Richmond for several months following the war, during which time he courted and married his wife. He was the first man to be married in Richmond following the close of the war, his wedding taking place a few days before the 24th Regiment was ordered back to Boston.

Mr. French tells of walking with a group of Confederate officers on the night the news of Lincoln's assassination was received. He heard the boys crying the news and ran down hill to get a copy of the paper. When he returned, his Confederate friends asked him if they had understood rightly that Lincoln had been shot. On being told that such was the case they sobered immediately. "This is one of the worst things that could happen," one of them declared. "It will make things hard for us."

Comes to Springfield
Following his marriage and discharge from the service Mr. French went to Harpers Ferry, VA., his wife's native town, where he conducted a canal store for several years. Later he lived in Millbury and came to Springfield more than 45 years ago. At the close of the war a number of Harpers Ferry families came to Springfield, where the men took positions in the United States Armory. Mr. French and his wife came here to visit some of their Harpers Ferry friends on one occasion and were induced to remain here. For more than 30 years he conducted a restaurant, most of the time on State Street near Walnut Street. He retired from that business 17 years ago following the death of his wife.

.

Although his days of adventure ended years ago, Mr. French delights in recounting his many and varied experiences. He is an exceptional entertainer and despite his 87 years, he can dance an old-fashioned "breakdown" or a cakewalk with as much spirit as a youngster of 20. At the Maj. John J. Leonard Post socials he invariably is one of the principal entertainers, either with a banjo or other musical instrument, as a singer of oldtime songs or as a dancer. He can dance the old or the new ones with equal skill and agility, and as tirelessly as his younger comrades.
One of his favorite songs is "The Bowery Sleigh Ride," which he learned 80 years ago when as a small boy he attended the performances of Welch & Mann's circus in Philadelphia and heard Dan Rice, the most famous white-faced clown of his day, sing his old favorites.

"Dan wrote his own songs," Mr. French explained, "but never published them. 'The Bowery Sleigh Ride' was one of them, so I imagine I'm the only man living today who knows it, or at least who can sing it."

Mr. French is a member of E.K. Wilcox Post, G.A.R., in the affairs of which he takes an active interest. He cannot resist the lure of entertaining, as is shown by his activities as a member of the Veterans of Foreign Wars. He also has served with "Jim" Anderson in the latter's holiday entertainments for the inmates of York Street Jail.

AUTHORS NOTE: The foregoing is an exact copy of the article without corrections. (See addendum page 156 re: **end of war employment recommendation** signed U S Grant, Gen.)

The following is an exact copy of an article, as it appeared, probably in mid 1930, in a (Springfield?) MA, newspaper. Though not dated the article does state that Grandfather, W. H. French was 93 years old at the time.

CIVIL WAR VETS HOLD REUNION IN THIS CITY
Gathered at Memorial Hall for Meeting and Reminiscences:
Four Regiments in Individual Reunions

The fast thinning ranks of Western Massachusetts veterans of the Civil War assembled at Memorial Hall this morning for the second annual reunion of all the "boys in blue" resident in the vicinity. Grizzled veterans, many of them wearing the blue coats and slouch hats that they wore so proudly over three score years ago, congregated in groups to fight again bloodlessly the battles in which they valiantly followed the Stars and Stripes, But their numbers are diminishing rapidly and of the thousands that once formed their ranks only a scant hundred remain in this vicinity.

The morning was devoted to registration and individual reunions of four of the Western Massachusetts regiments of the G.A.R. Those regiments which held reunions this morning were the 10th, 17th, 31st and 46th. The 37th regiment, which is also from the vicinity, postponed its individual reunion until Sept. 12, but many of the members of the 37th were present to meet old comrades from their own and other regiments.

The first veteran to arrive was George W. Frost, 85 years old, of the 46th Regiment, but he was soon followed by others. Mrs. Mary M. Marell, secretary of the reunion, was kept busy registering the veterans. Besides the veterans from the five Western Massachusetts regiments, representatives from a number of other regiments who are now resident in this vicinity were present. The registration list showed members from the 28th (?) New York Infantry, the 16th New York Heavy Artillery, the 2d, --, 8th, 24th and 52d Massachusetts Infantry, and the 29th Ohio Infantry. By noon there were 96 veterans registered, with a few more expected to bring the registration up to about 100.

W. H. French Is Oldest

W. H. French, 93 years old, of the 22d Massachusetts Infantry, was the oldest veteran attending the reunion who had registered up until noon today. Mr. French was in the navy from 1857 to 1861 on the United States man-of-war "Constellation", when they heard that war had broken out between the States. It was six months after the war had broken out before they heard of it and received orders to come home immediately. There being no Suez Canal at that time they had to sail around the Cape of Good Hope and it took them six months more to get home. Mr. French said that the entire crew nearly worried themselves sick for fear they would not get home in time to get into the fight. The "Constellation" joined Admiral Farragut's fleet in the Mississippi River. Later Mr. French joined the 22d Massachusetts Infantry and saw 42 months more of service. Mr. French was the first man married in Richmond, VA, after the evacuation of that city. During the

Sesquicentennial exhibition at Philadelphia, Mr. French was stationed on the "Constellation" to show visitors around, he being the only living veteran having served on that vessel.
At 12:30 a dinner was served to all the veterans in Memorial Hall. Mayor Fordis C. Parker was the guest of honor and welcomed the veterans to the reunion. After the dinner the afternoon was turned over to a smoke talk, at which the veterans got together to talk over old times and renew old friendships. A program of music was provided by the committee, including the Philharmonic Quartet of Springfield and banjo selections by Anthony Loprat, but the major part of the afternoon was spent in going over old times.

A touch of the old days was given to the veterans by Maj. A. Frank Hutchins, 82 years old, 26th N.Y. Staff, of Deerfield. Maj. Hutchins who was a member of that great Civil War band headed by Patrick Sarafield Gilmore, entertained his comrades by playing old-time war airs on his cornet. Maj. Hutchins was surrounded by a large group of veterans, who had their memories of the old days sharply revived as he played the tunes so familiar to them.

The following is from the Springfield Daily Republic Friday, January 8, 1932:

<u>WILLIAM H. FRENCH</u>
<u>WHO SAILED IN OLD WOODEN NAVY, DIES</u>

William H. French, 95, the oldest member of the E. K. Wilcox post, Grand Army of the Republic, and the last survivor of the old wooden-bottom fleet of the United States navy, died yesterday at the home of his daughter, Mrs. M. K. Paine, at Simsbury, Ct. His death came a few minutes after that of Lucius W. Bigelow, 90, the last of Simsbury's Civil war veterans. The two men became cronies late in life. Mr. Bigelow served with Co. F, 12th Connecticut volunteers, and Mr. French with the 24[th] Massachusetts infantry during the Civil war.

The death of Mr. French brings to a close a life filled with unusual adventures and a life the span of which saw this country grow from an isolated nation, more than half of whose eventual territory was either under foreign flags or control[l]ed by Indians, into a world power. When Mr. French was born at Newark N.J. October 16, 1836, the "wild west" began soon after one had passed the Ohio River and California and Texas, and most of the territory between these states were part of Mexico.

When he was a little boy, Mr. French's parents moved their home to Philadelphia, where his father maintained a shoemaker's shop. At odd moments he worked in his father's shop. (1)
Next door was the workroom of a German-American bell maker. He was at work on a bell for Independence Hall. It was to replace the Liberty bell, which had cracked. The cracked original lay in the bell maker's shop a derelict, (2) given in part payment for the new model. Mr. French's sister owned that bell when she married into the bell maker's family. And it was this sister, Mrs. Caroline Wilbank, (3) who prevented the use of the relic as material for new bells and later presented it to the City of Philadelphia.

But the old bell didn't endear the shoemaker's trade to a venturesome boy of 16, and William French ran away to sea. He fished on the Grand Banks. He sailed on a clipper ship, swapping cargoes from Newfoundland to Liverpool and from Liverpool to Calcutta.
When he was 17, he wandered down to Provincetown and set sail on the Ehermaphrodite brig Lewis Bruce under Capt. Ryder (4) for a whaling voyage in tropical seas. For three years he followed the spume and blow of the whaling ways. In the spring of '56 he was back on Cape Cod again, and going up to Boston saw a chance to ship with the crew of the Constellation, sister ship of the Constitution ("old Ironsides") for African coast-guard duty. Some of that crew were

brought aboard unconscious, knocked over the head with a blackjack or given an overdose of Jamaica rum and shanghaied for the difficult duty of chasing slave runners. But Mr. French went aboard under his own power, a volunteer.

At that time the Constitution had finished her famous fighting days and was tied up at her dock at Boston, not seaworthy. But the Constellation had been cut down to a 22-gun sloop to continue the longest fighting career in the history of the United States navy.

She stopped in Liberia to pick up 20 black Krumen for the heavy work of loading supplies under a tropical sun. Commodore Jack Inman, one of the keenest and best captains in the United States navy sailed up and down Africa from Fernando Po to the Gold coast and back again, with 48 hours off every six months at St. Helena. During that time there were many exciting chases of slave runners and years later Mr. French delighted in telling stories of those adventurous months.

In 1928 when Mr. French visited the Boston navy yard, where work had started on the reconstruction of the Constitution, he told with relish of the capture of the barque Cora, one of the most notorious slave runners of that day and one of the fastest. Her commander, Capt. Lathrop, was also captured. In telling of the capture of the Cora, Mr. French said "We got aboard of her and before we could get the hatches open, we could smell niggers--705 aboard. Naked and half starved, they came swarming up through the hatches and rushed for the forecastle. Some were scabbed with scurvy and others filth. Oh, awful. I hope I shall never live to see such another sight."

Discharge came in October, 1861, and he returned to a shoemaker's shop with his brother in the city of Boston. The Civil War had already begun.

Following President Lincoln's call for 300,000 volunteers for the war of rebellion in 1861, Col. Thomas G. Stevenson recruited the 24th Massachusetts infantry. (5) Mr. French closed his shoemaker's shop and enlisted. The regiment was organized at Camp Meigs, Reidville, and it left the state December 9, 1861. On January 6, of the following year the 24th embarked at Annapolis on board a transport and sailed for Hatteras Inlet as a part of Burnside expedition. For the greater part of the four years during which this regiment was in active service in the Civil war it was in North Carolina around Newberne.

The regiment saw considerable active fighting, and on September 28, 1864, it participated as part of Gen. Terry's division in the advance of the army of (up) the James toward Richmond. A daring reconnaissance along the Central railroad brought the troops within 2 1/2 miles of the rebel capitol. The 24th was the last regiment to leave Richmond the following year after Lee's surrender. From April 8, 1865 to January 20, 1866, the regiment was stationed at Richmond to guard the city and military prisoners. During this time, Mr. French fell in love with a southern girl and just before the regiment was mustered out of service on January 20, 1866 and sent back to Boston, he married her. (6)

On being mustered out of the service, Mr. French went with his bride to live for a short time at Harpers Ferry. They then went to Washington, where Mr. French entered business. He was wiped out in the postwar panic that in that city brought with it the downfall of the only governor the District of Columbia ever had.

Looking for new enterprise the wanderer went west on a Missouri river sidewheeler and took up residence in the boom city of Omaha, Neb. Times were hard until '69 when two railroads, the Central Pacific, crawling over the Rockies, and the Union Pacific, creeping out over the plains met at Omaha and he saw the final golden spike driven in the first transcontinental railroad. There was a frenzy of prosperity. But wanderlust seized him again and Mr. French was off with the tide that settled the ranges following the establishment of transcontinental connections. He took a quarter section 85 miles north of Omaha and moved out among the Indians to till the soil, until inexperience forced the abandonment of the project. (7)

There were other travels, and finally Mr. and Mrs. French came to Millbury.(MA) where for more than 20 years Mr. French conducted a restaurant at State and Walnut streets. He retired 24 years ago to settle down at Simsbury (CT) in a little brown farmhouse with his daughter, Mrs. Paine. (Ella G. French)

He always said that the Civil war never frightened him. Whales had frightened him, especially the bull that came up under the first mate's boat, splitting it like an eggshell and spilling all of them into the sea like toothpicks. That was another of the old stories he loved to tell. What a panic there was! The old bull thrashing after the floundering sailors, with his mouth wide open and bos'n saving the day by hitting him over the nose with a boat hook. But the Civil war? "Never turned a hair." Private French used to say.

Besides his daughter at whose home he died, Mr. French leaves four other daughters, Mrs. W. S. Taylor of Simsbury, Mrs. Clarence A. Wheeler and Mrs. A C. Perley (Pixley), both of Los Angeles, Cal., and Mrs. W. H. Waterman of Cleveland; one brother, James E. French of Staten Island, N.Y.; 19 grandchildren and 33 great-grandchildren. (8) He was a member of E.K. Wilcox post, G.A.R. and Maj. John J. Leonard post, Veterans of Foreign Wars, in this city. (9)

The funeral will be held at the home of Mrs. Paine tomorrow afternoon at 1, Rev. John Pail Clark of the Avon Congregational church officiating. Burial will be in Oak Grove cemetery in this city. (Springfield, MA)

FOOTNOTES TO THE OBITUARY OF WILLIAM H. FRENCH
Written March 31, 1978 **by William R. Cole, Grandson of William H. French** (Mr. Cole's address at the time was Lincoln University, PA, 19352).

1. John French's home (and shoemaker shop) was on Callowhill Street (in Philadelphia). John Wilbank, the bell maker, had a finishing shop next door but his foundry was a few miles north in Germantown.

2. I think Granddad was in error about the old bell being in the shop. The city of Philadelphia sued Wilbank for $400 because he refused to take the bell down and haul it up to Germantown. John W. figured that the $400 was not enough to cover the value of the scrap metal and the cost of the operation.

3. "Mrs. Caroline "Willbank" was wrong on two counts; there is only one **L** in **WILBANK** and "**CAROLINE**" was probably **CLARISSA** (something that I have to pin down)
Author's Note: Cert. Copy Death Record from PA. State Registrar spells name as **CLARISSA W. WILBANK.** Copy obtained Feb. 5, 1996

4. The Lewis Bruce was once careened somewhere along the Gulf of Arabia for hull cleaning. The sailors were busy at scraping barnacles when a bunch of Arabs made an attack, shooting the captain in the belly. I do not remember being told whether Captain Ryder survived or not but I do know that (just as he later became a damn yankee) I never heard him (granddad) speak of Arabs as other than damn treacherous Ayrabs.

5. The battle flag of the 24th Mass. Volunteers hangs in the State house in Boston. Granddad gave me a full story of how he came to volunteer. One day a man came into his shop with a handful of greenbacks, saying that, "A man was giving them away in a saloon." Together the two went to the saloon where a recruiting agent was offering $200 and one-month furlough (in which to spend it) so Granddad joined up pronto.

6. The marriage took some doing. Mary Dugan Fryer was a young widow with one child (Wilamena; or Aunt Willie") she had come from Harpers Ferry when her husband died. Four months pregnant with her first child, she went to live with an aunt in Richmond. Finally the Dugans were convinced of honorable intentions and a military wedding, the first such after occupation, followed with the regimental band playing the wedding march.

7. My mother, **Alice Landon French**, was born on Dec. 13, 1869, in a small shack that they called "The Dry Goods Box". Three weeks later "The Blizzard of 1870" (as it was long remembered) struck and for three days the little house shuddered with the family staying in and under the bed. Granddad would chop off a chunk of bread for a meal. A snowball served as a drink. On the following summer Granddad built a dugout and turned the dry goods box into a chicken house. Throughout the next winter they all stayed cosy (cozy) but in the first blizzard the chicken house was blown a half a mile down the prairie.

7a. Aunt Willie told me this story: As a six-year-old she went to stay with her aunt while Granddad and his brother-in-law drove to Omaha to be gone three days. There was great danger from grass fires and this aunt had been told how to start a backfire. Well, the worst happened, smoke appeared in the distance, the backfire was started but it set fire to the house which burned to the ground. Despite this, the in-laws stayed in Nebraska and prospered but the French family had had enough and came east to Washington. Granddad worked on the Capitol when the House and Senate wings were being added. He later went to Harpers Ferry (where Aunt Julie was born) and eventually to Millbury, MA arriving on July 1, 1881. The next day President Garfield was shot.

8. "Mrs. A C. "Perley" should read "Mrs. A C. "Pixley". She was Clara French and he was Albert Pixley. My mother married Clarence Wheeler about sixteen years after Dad's death. Mrs. W. H. Waterman was Aunt Julie. The Watermans lived many years in Springfield where Uncle Bill was a foreman in the Bemis and Call plant where small tools were made. Later, he moved to Cleveland. On July 25, 1914, Uncle Bill took me with the Bemis and Call baseball team (he was the manager) to nearby North End Playground where Bemis and Call handily defeated Goatesville 4-2. For details see my 1914 diary and my Spaulding Baseball Score Book for 1914 and 1915.

9. Granddad once took me to visit the G.A.R. Post quarters in Springfield. His death in 1932 left two survivors.

P.S. One little note more on the Omaha days. About four years ago Avis Waterman told me that Grandmother French was greatly admired by a prairie Indian. He would stop by the house almost daily for a look at this beautiful brunette who he called, a "fine squaw".

READ MORE ABOUT WILLIAM H. FRENCH AND HIS LIFE ABOARD CONSTELLATION IN THE CHAPTER ON CONSTELLATION.

GENERATION III
ELLA GORDON FRENCH (GEN. III, French Family)
  b. Jun. 14, 1868 at Washington, DC
  d. Mar. 28, 1957 at Avon, CT
  bur. Curtiss Cem., Simsbury, CT
  m. Jan. 7, 1891 at Springfield, MA to
MERTON KINGSLEY PAINE (GEN. IX, Paine Family)
  b. Jul. 6, 1870 at Belchertown, MA
  d. Aug. 14, 1937 at Hartford, CT

Children of Merton K. & Ella G. (French) Paine are (GEN. X, Paine-Shepard Genealogy, compiled by Clara Paine Ohler) and may also be found in Chapter One of this book.

ALICE LANDON FRENCH (GEN. III, French Family)
  b Dec. 13, 1869 at Omaha, NB
  d. Jan 26, 1943*
  m. (1) to
GEORGE E. COLE
  b. 1866
  d. Feb. 12, 1907
  m. (2) about 1923 to
CLARENCE WHEELER

Alice's address Los Angeles, CA (listed in W.H. French obit.) *(Information of Alice's death obtained from Journal of Ella G. (French) Paine. Journal beginning on page 8.)

GENERATION IV
Children of George E. & Alice L. (French) Cole
  Clarence
  Elbert d. 1976
  William R.

CLARA FRENCH
  b. Oct. 13, 1873 at Washington, DC
  d. Jan. 26, 1961 at Gardena, CA
  bur. Inglewood Park Cem.
  m. to
ALBERT C. PIXLEY

Clara's address Los Angeles, CA (listed in W.H. French obit.) Info. Clara's death given in remembrance card Mispagel Mortuary, Los Angeles

JULIA R. FRENCH
  b. 1876 Harpers Ferry, W.VA
  m. to
WILLIAM H. WATERMAN

The Waterman's lived for many years in Springfield, MA. Later moved to Cleveland, (OH)
Julia's address Cleveland (listed in W.H. French Obit)
The following is correspondence sent to my father, Archie W. Paine, Sr. from William R. Cole,
Lincoln University, PA. (RD 1, Box 87) Zip 19352

11 Feb. 1978

Dear Archie,
What a splendid letter. I'm sorry for all the illness among the Paines and hope better news is on
the way. Mary is ready for a shopping trip and this will be brief.

The enclosure will interest you, I feel sure.

Did Grandpa French ever tell you the story of the Liberty Bell? How his sister married John
Willbank, a Philadelphia bell-maker who had a contract with the city to make a new bell for
Independence Hall (which he did and it still hangs there), getting the old bell for scrap? How his
sister prevented its destruction? If you are interested I'll send you some material about it.
Again, thanks and best wishes to you both. Bill

Enc! Copy of Mother's Thanksgiving Letter, Nov. 29, 1894
(Written while my parents were living in Northhampton, Mass.)

Nov. 29, 1894 10 P.M.
We have had such a pleasant time today. Father and Mother French, Clara, Julia, George, Ella,
Merton, and Mildred have been here and went home on the 9 P.M. train. Everything went off
pleasant and all said they had a fine time. They danced, sang and did everything else. Henry
Macy was here also and played the Banjo so we had music and a general good time. Pa sang:
The Lazy Club and When I Went Out A Sleighing. Elbert went to bed at six o'clock and went
right to sleep, Clarence has been sick but is nearly well now and has been just as good as a little
kitten. He is sitting on the floor now playing. Clara is engaged to Mr. Albert Pixley and I
shouldn't be surprised if there was another wedding before another Thanksgiving. We have all
been quite well this past year and feel very Thankful for being spared. Papa got me a new
Rocking chair and Turkish rug for a Thanksgiving present.   Alice L. Cole

(From Bill Cole) For several years during the 90's my parents, George E. Cole and Alice
Landon (French) Cole, while living in Northampton, MA and then in West Charleston, VT, had
friends and relatives in for Thanksgiving. Each would write about the past year and all writings
were sealed (to be opened and read the next year.) My brother Elbert (died in '76) had the
originals that are now held by his widow, Margaret G. Cole of Middlebury, VT
(signed)
William R. Cole
Lincoln Univ. PA
11 Feb. 1978
P.S. My father died 12 Feb.1907, age 41

1 April 1978
Dear Archie,
This will be a hurried note, as the mailman will be coming here soon. But I do want to get these
enclosures to you soon. I am sorry to read of all the health troubles that have piled up on the
clan. I surely hope that your recent checkups were not countdowns as you suggested as possible!

From your response about our family history I suspect that I have some records that may fill gaps in yours.

The obituary of W.H. French is from the Springfield Republican of Friday, Jan.8,1932. Fit the three sheets together you will find interesting reading. The red numbers refer to my Footnotes on the Obit and two extra copies are enclosed (the kids may want them).
Now for the "sister" of Granddad, there were FIVE. The roster is enclosed with a few extra copies, also.
I have two more newspapers relating to our hero; the Spring. Union of July 27, 1926 (which has his picture in a sailor uniform and his attempts to get a job as a guide on the Constellation at the Philadelphia Sesquicentennial that summer. He came here and I took him to Philly where he spent much of the summer telling yarns on the old ship and collecting money for refitting the Constitution, rotting away in the Boston Navy Yard.), and the Sunday Republican of May 27, 1928 which contains a fuller account of his adventures. Before making more copies from these I have to do something about preservation for the paper is starting to crumble.

> *The letter to Mrs. Wilbank (whose husband was the grandson of the bellmaker) followed a telephone conversation with her. She lives in Philly and I hope to get in and spend a day with her very soon. I stop here with best wishes to you all,*
>
> *Bill*

enc. Letter to Mrs. Wilbank
obituary from Repub., Jan.8,1932 (three sheets)
footnotes to obit (three sets of two sheets each)
record of the French family (four copies)

Obituary, footnotes and record of French family have been recorded previously.
I will include the letter to Mrs. Wilbank here.

19 May, 1975
Mrs. John F. Willbank
426 Madison Avenue
Prospect Park, PA 19076

Dears Mrs. Willbank:
Since talking with you recently, I have hunted up some records and am enclosing a copy of data on the French family as a bit of background.

My grandfather, William H. French, was almost ninety-six when he died in Simsbury, CT, at my Aunt Ella Paine's home. He used to visit us in Vermont frequently and I had many happy hours listening to his yarns of an adventurous life. He often told me the liberty bell story and of his escapades in Philadelphia as a young boy sided and abetted by his older brother William H. (??Perhaps he meant Thomas?) Here is a thumbnail sketch of his life.

At the age of about sixteen he ran off to sea on a whaler for two years; joined the navy and sailed on the USS Constellation chasing slave ships off the Gold Coast for three and a half years; discharged in 1860, he joined the 24th Massachusetts Volunteers and was in the civil war for four years, ending in the occupation of Richmond where he met a young widow, my grandmother; homesteaded near Omaha; built the first cottonwood plank sidewalks in Omaha; mother (Alice L. French) was born 13 Dec., '69; big blizzard three weeks later nearly killed the family; gave up *farming in '72 and came east to Harpers Ferry for a few years; moved to Massachusetts; ran a small store and restaurant in Springfield; married my mother off to George E. Cole in '90; retired several years later and moved to a small farm west of Springfield; made frequent visits to his five living children; spent the summer of 1927 here, off and on; stayed occasionally with a nephew, Charles French, on Baltimore Ave, Phila.; declined the mayor's invitation to ride in the parade for the opening of the Sesquicentennial in a "handsomely decorated car as the Sole Surviving Crewman of the USS Constellation while it was till on active duty" because of ill health at the time; later spent most of the summer on the old ship telling yarns to visitors and collecting money (over $1400) for Constitution rebuilding fund; lived with my Aunt Ella for a few years; worn-out, took to his bed in Dec.,1931; two weeks later quietly looked at his daughters, Ella, Willy (Wilhamina*) and Alice, said "Goodbye, girls" and died. He is buried in Laurel Hill Cemetery** in Springfield beside his wife.*

James Cole, the first of my family in America, came to New England from England in the 1620's, was a member of the party that settled Hartford, CT, in 1635. The tribe finally reached northern Vermont.

I hope to see you before long and swap information about our mutual forbears and the fascinating story of the bell.

Sincerely,
Bill Cole

*name was Wilberta
**Name of Cemetery is Oak Grove-

IMMIGRATION

Thanks to Elizabeth P. Bentley who transcribed Customs Passenger List and put them in a book "Passenger Arrivals at the Port of New York 1830-1832" I have been able to obtain the following immigration information. Our great-great grandfather, John French, brought his wife Sarah and their six children to this country in 1832.

They embarked from Liverpool on the ship Caledonia, captained by Hugh Graham, and arrived in the Port of New York on July 24th, 1832. According to the record the Caledonia was the 509th ship to arrive in the Port of New York that year.

Found in the passenger lists:

John French	Age 32
Sarah French	Age 32
Fredk French	Age 11
Adeline French	Age 10 (believe this to be Ethelinda)
Alfred French	Age 8
Mary Ann French	Age 6
Lavinia French	Age 3
Clarissa French	Age 4 months

CHAPTER SIX

THE PAINE-WHITE CONNECTION

The following letter has been in the family as long as I can remember, and was among my father's important papers at the time of his death:

PEREGRINE WHITE'S POSTERITY
A LETTER FROM ONE OF THE EIGHTH GENERATION

"They have been having quite a pother in the Boston papers over the posterity and relics of Peregrine White, the first white child born in New England.

It was all raised in connection with the alleged carelessness of the White family concerning the preservation of the old house he used to occupy in Marshfield. The house proved to be, after all, of a date considerably later than Peregrine's death; though the farm was his, and has remained in the family ever since, until now that it has passed out of the hands of Sybil White, a lineal descendant.

Criticisms on this instance of growing irreverence for ancestry awakened a great many responses from descendants of Peregrine, which, if they serve no other purpose, form all together extremely interesting evidence that the old New England families are not decaying into extinction, despite the forebodings of medical pessimists.

Among the most noteworthy contributions to this evidence is a letter received from Annie Preston of Northfield, whose interesting poem of "Susanna White," printed in these columns, last summer, will not have been forgotten. She writes as follows:

William and Susanna White arrived on board the Mayflower at Plymouth Rock, December 22, l620. Peregrine White, the first English child born in New England, was son of the above, born in November 1620, while the ship was anchored in Cape Cod bay, between Cap Cod and Plymouth.

Daniel White was son of Peregrine; John White, who married a Miss Skinner, was son of Daniel; John White, son of John White, married Mary Grover, lived for many years in Mansfield, and was a merchant there.

This couple had nine children, names respectively John, Abial, Otis, Calvin, Mary, Rachel, Lovina, Azubah and Susanna, all born and christened at Mansfield.

Susanna, the heroine of the poem published, some time ago in the Republican, was engaged to be married to William French, but he being killed at the battle of Bunker Hill, at the intercession of his mother, she married his brother, John French, at Providence, R.I. They afterward moved to Dublin, N.H., where they lived a few years, and then removed to West Northfield, Mass., where they ended their days.

This couple had 11 children. "Grandmother French" was very wise in Bible lore, and was remarkable for her mental powers and the strength of beauty of her Christian character. She died in the autumn of 1836, but is still remembered with pleasure by many people in the community.

Four of her daughters married, brought up families, died and are buried in West Northfield. All were useful Christian women, Susanna married Aaron Beals and at his death married Mr. Lovejoy—both of New Hampshire; Polly married John Caldwell; Lovina married James Caldwell and Achsah married Aaron Preston.

Their descendants, as may be said of most large New England families, are widely scattered. Some of them are: Dr. John E. Preston of Salem, N.J., Otis Preston of Elkland, Pa., Mrs. H.C. Travers of Bloomfield, IA., Mrs. Susanna M.P. Nash and Miss Louise Preston of Amherst. Mrs. Lovina P. Stockwell of Stafford Springs, CT., Mrs. Dr. Noyes Barstow of Belchertown, Mr. Daniel Pierce of Bolton, Mrs. Newton S. Ball of Everett Street, Springfield, Otis S., James D., James N. and William F. Caldwell and Jonathan L. Preston, living in West Northfield; these being all descendants in the 8th generation from Peregrine White and ninth from the Pilgrims; besides a brother, Oscar V. Preston of Pittsford, and a sister of your correspondent, as well as your long-time contributor herself.'

Mrs. Annie A. Preston

West Northfield, (Mass.) December 29, 1875"
Published in the Springfield Republican?

Author's Note: October 31, 1995 Today I am in receipt of a letter from **Caroline Lewis Kardell, Historian General of the General Society of Mayflower Descendants**. The text of her letter reads as follows:

"Your Susannah White, daughter of John and Mary (Grover) White was born in Norton, MA. This town is next door to Mansfield.

The White family of Taunton, Norton and Mansfield probably all descend from **Nicholas and Ursilla (Macomber) White** of Taunton. They had sons **Nicholas and Matthew** both of whom settled in the area and probably others from this same White ancestor.

They do not appear to be Mayflower Whites. Mrs. Annie Preston was correct back to her great-grandparents, but erred in the next generation back in trying to tie them into the Mayflower line."

Further research will be required to ascertain whether the line does go back to the Mayflower. I have a line on a researcher who has been quite successful in searching for Mayflower relatives. Perhaps in time we might be able to prove the lineage, as of now we do not have the proof.

Following is information which seems to bear out what Ms. Kardell mentions in her letter as our White family line.

JOHN WHITE
  b. 1730 probably Norton, MA
  d. probably Norton, MA
  m. Sep. 5, 1751 at Norton, MA to
MARY GROVER
Children of John &Mary (Grover) White all born at Norton, MA

John	b. May 13, 1752
Mary	b. Oct. 17, 1753
Susannah	b. Aug. 11, 1755
John	b. Sep. 18, 1757

Abiel/Abial	b. Aug. 18, 1759
Rachel	b. Jul. 18, 1761
Azuba	b. May 23, 1763
Levine/Lavina	b. Jul. 11, 1765
Asa	b. Sep. 25, 1767
Lucy	b. Feb. 3, 1770

Descendants of: John White & Mary (Grover) White
JOHN FRENCH
  b.1756 at
  d. Apr. 1833 at Northfield, MA?
  m. 1775/1776 at Providence, RI to
SUSANNAH WHITE
  b. Aug. 11, 1755 at Norton, MA
  d. Nov., 1836 at Northfield, MA

Susannah was pledged to marry William French, who was killed at the battle of Bunker Hill. At the intercession of his mother, **she married his brother, John.** (see foregoing letter written by Annie A. Preston Dec. 29, 1875) They purportedly had eleven children. Have found information on four daughters and two sons listed as follows:

Children of John & Susanna (White) French

Susanna	m. to Aaron Beale and at his death to a Mr. Lovejoy both of New Hampshire
Polly	m. to John Caldwell
Lovina	m. to James Caldwell
Achsah	m. to Aaron Presson (Preston)
John	
Otis (Sgt)	m. Jan. 5, 1813

PRESSON (PRESTON)
Descendants of: John French & Susanna (White) French
AARON PRESSON
  b. Jun. 26-27, 1791 at Dummerston, VT
  d. Jan. 11, 1872
  bur. West Northfield, MA
  married at Hollis, NH ? to
ACHSAH FRENCH
  b. 1792
  d. Dec. 9, 1859
  bur. West Northfield, MA

Children of Aaron & Acsah (French) Presson
    (all born at Northfield, MA

George	b. May 25, 1810
Susan M.	b. Jun. 27, 1812
William B.	b. Sep. 16, 1813
Jonathan L.	b. Jan. 29, 1815
John E., Dr.	b. Dec. 3, 1816

Aaron O.	b. May 26, 1818
Acsah Lovina	b. Jun. 3, 1821
Emily Louise?	b. Jul. 25, 1824
Charles B.	b. May 22, 1826

Descendants of: Aaron Preston & Achsah (French) Preston

SAMUEL AUSTIN STOCKWELL
   b. Feb. 16, 1825 at Erving, MA
   d. Jun. 18, 1899 at Belchertown, MA
   bur. at Mount Hope Cem., Belchertown, MA
   m. May 6, 1846 at Guilford, VT to
ACHSAH LOVINA PRESTON (PRESSON)
   b. Jun. 3, 1821 at Northfield, MA
   d. Feb. 10, 1891 at Belchertown, MA
   bur. at Mount Hope Cem.., Belchertown, MA

Children of Samuel A. Stockwell & Achsah L. (Preston/Presson) Stockwell
Louise (Lydia) Lavina	b. Jul. 3, 1848 at Amherst, MA
Martha M.	b. Sep. 2, 1849 at Amherst, MA
Wesley Wright	b. May 28, 1851 at Amherst, MA

Descendants of: Samuel A. Stockwell & Achsah L. (Presson) Stockwell

HENRY ALBERT PAINE (GEN. VIII, Paine Family)
   m. Mar.30, 1869 at Belchertown, MA to
LOUISE L. STOCKWELL
   b. Jul. 31, 1848 at Amherst ,MA

Children of Henry A. & Louise L. (Stockwell) Paine
Merton Kingsley	b. Jul. 6, 1870 at Belchertown, MA
George Austin	b. Jun. 27, 1872 at Springfield, MA
Herbert D.	b. Jan. 26, 1876

MERTON KINGSLEY PAINE (GEN. IX, Paine Fam.)
   m. Jan. 7, 1891 at Springfield, MA to
ELLA GORDON FRENCH (GEN. II, French Fam.)
   d. Mar. 28, 1957 at Avon, CT

See Chapter One this book for Descendants of Merton Kingsley & Ella Gordon (French) Paine.

CHAPTER SEVEN
THE OTHER SIDE OF THE COIN

This chapter will reflect information on genealogy of spouses of the Paine descendants and unless otherwise specified contains materials obtained from the families themselves.

SPOUSES OF GENERATION X

HADSELL
DELMAR A. HADSELL
  b. 1868 at Avon, CT,
  d. May 1928
  m.to
MARY MOSES
  b. 1870
  d. 1948

Children of Delmar A. & Mary (Moses) Hadsell
  Grace
  Mary   b. Apr. 25, 1898, Avon, CT
                               d. Jan. 4, 1992 at Simsbury, CT

  Edith

MARY HADSELL
  m. Apr. 2, 1917 at Avon CT to
ALBERT I. PAINE (GEN. X, Paine Family)

WEED
JAMES WEED-came to America from England settled in Stamford, CT

Child of James Weed
  Ebenezer   no available record of birth, or death.

EBENEZER WEED-built farmhouse ca 1770 in section of Danbury, CT
                 (now called Bethel, CT)

Child of Ebenezer Weed
James   b. 1726
                               d. l789 at Wethersfield, CT

JAMES WEED-Sgt. in Capt. Benedict's Co. 1776
  m. to
KETURAH BALDING
  b. 1728
  d. 1787

Child of James & Keturah (Balding) Weed
Solomon   b. 1757
                                 d.1826

SOLOMON WEED
  m. 1779 to
RACHAEL DIBBLE
  b. 1755
  d. 1850

Child of Solomon & Rachael (Dibble) Weed
Ammon   b. 1799
                                 d. 1872

AMMON WEED
  m. Dec. 31, 1829 to
ELIZABETH (Betty, Betsey) M. BENEDICT
  b. 1803
  d. 1889

Child of Ammon & Betsy M. (Benedict) Weed
Frederick Augustus   b. unk.
                                 d. unk.

FREDERICK AUGUSTUS WEED
  m. Oct. 25 1871 or 1874 at Bethel, CT to
MARY A DAVIS

Authority: Book entitled "Advice to a Married Couple" filled out with marriage date (year 1871 or 4) and presented to the couple by their--Pastor at the Congregational Church, Robert C. Bell.

Child of Frederick A. & Mary A. (Davis) Weed
Frederick Davis   b. 1876
                                 d. May 19, 1964 at Danbury, CT

<u>BOERUM</u>
WILLIAM WOOD BOERUM
  m. to
REBECCA GREGORY

Child of William Wood & Rebecca (Gregory) Boerum
Ada Louise   b. Jul. 15, 1872 at Bridgeport, CT
                                 d. Apr. 11, 1968

FREDERICK DAVIS WEED
  m. to
ADA LOUISE BOERUM

Child of Frederick Davis & Ada Louise (Boerum) Weed
William Boerum   b. Apr. 18, 1904 at Bethel, CT

WILLIAM BOERUM WEED
  d. Feb. 10, 1970 at Denver, CO
  m. Aug. 20, 1927 at Simsbury, CT to
MATTIE PAINE (GEN. X, Paine Family)

GLAZIER
WILLIAM GLAZIER
b. Gloucester, England

William accompanied Governor Wolcott to Wolcott and surveyed the Gov. Wolcott Turnpike from Tolland to Ashford. At one time William owned 900 acres in Willington, CT

SILAS GLAZIER, son of William, was a soldier in the Revolutionary War.
He received a pension in later years.
  m. to
HOLT

DAVID GLAZIER son of Silas

ALDEN GLAZIER son of David
  b. Willington, CT
  d. 1963 at Somers, CT

DWIGHT J. GLAZIER son of Alden
  b. Feb. 14, 1837 at Willington, CT

HERBERT ASA GLAZIER son of Dwight
  m. Nov. 21, 1893 at West Stafford, CT to
C. JOSEPHINE DIMMOCK

Child of Herbert Asa & C. Josephine (Dimmock) Glazier
  Dimock Burdette   b. Apr. 15, 1897 at Stafford, CT
                             d. Mar. 8, 1979 at Simsbury, CT

DIMOCK BURDETTE GLAZIER
  m. Feb. 18, 1925 at Simsbury, CT to
MABEL PAINE (GEN. X, Paine Family)

STOUTENBURGH
The ancestry of the Stoutenburgh Family was obtained in large part from the Stoutenburgh-Teller Association of Hyde Park, New York. A large portion of the acreage now called Hyde Park, was in early years called Stoutenburgh Village and much of that acreage was owned by the Stoutenburgh family. Proof of this is borne out in land records of that area. **Direct ancestors** pertinent to **Eldora van Ness Stoutenburgh,** my mother, will be given here. The work is too extensive to include in this book and will, I hope, be printed in a book under separate cover in the future.
The Netherlands ancestry is traced back to Eemland, (3 miles outside of Amersfoort) Holland, where **Wouter, Lord of Stoutenburg** founded the City of Stoutenburg in 1252. The castle was

destroyed, rebuilt, and destroyed again. The building now standing nearby is in use as a Franciscan meeting center

We then have an ancestry gap until Gerard and his wife, Deliana who were the parents of Johan van Olden Barneveldt. Von and van seem to be used interchangeably. (perhaps by searchers who misspelled along the way?)

GERARD von OLDEN BARNEVELDT (BARNEVELD)
   m. to
DELIANA von WEEDE von STOUTENBURG

Child of Gerard (von Stoutenburgh) von Olden Barneveld and
            Deliana (von Weede) von Olden Barneveld
   Johan van Olden Barneveldt   b. Sep.14, 1547 at Amersfoort,
                                           Province of Utrecht, Holland
                                        d. May 13, 1619 at Riderqaal,
                                           Knights Hall, Binnenhof, The Hague

JOHAN van OLDEN BARNEVELD, LORD OF STOUTENBURG
   m. to
MARIA van UTRECHT

Johan studied law at Louvain, at Bourges and at Heidelburg. He had a law practice in the courts at The Hague. In 1576 he became pensionary of Rotterdam. A statue of JVO can be seen there in front of the Stadhuis. In 1586 he was appointed Lord Advocate of Holland and rapidly became the leading statesman of the united provinces. He took an active part in the founding of the Dutch East India Company.

A noted American Historian, John Lothrop Motley, was fascinated with the history of the Dutch Republic and wrote volumes in regard to its history, including a two volume biography entitled "The Life and Death of John of Barneveld" whom he considered to be the greatest statesman of Europe, during that time.

Johan served William, The Silent as well as William's son, Prince Maurice of Nassau and of Orange; and his beloved country in every office of importance with unselfish devotion for more than forty years. A conflict arose between Maurice of Nassau and Johan van Olden Barneveldt mostly due to religious differences. Through his dictatorial power Maurice had Johan imprisoned in August of 1618. Maurice then formed a special court, mostly of Johan's enemies and allowed no facilities for John's defense. He was found guilty of treason, and on May 13, 1619, he was beheaded in front of the entrance to the Riddeqaal, *the Knights Hall,* of the Binnenhof in The Hague. (A statue of Barneveld stands there today.) The family holdings and titles were stripped away.

Children of Johan van Olden Barneveld & Maria van Utrecht
   Reinier, Lord of Groeneveld
                           d. May 28, 1623 (beheaded)
   Jan (died young)
   Willem, Lord of Stoutenburg
                           d. place believed to be Brussells

WILLEM van OLDEN BARNEVELDT
   m. to
WALBURG De MARNIX

William, up to the time of his father's death, a brilliant cavalry officer in the Army of Prince Maurice, tried to obtain justice and redress for the ruin of his father's and mother's family names and holdings. Failing that, he organized a conspiracy against the life of Maurice, which almost succeeded. He was caught out and fled to Spain. After wandering for a few years, he entered the military service of Spain. His brother, Lord Groeneveld and the others involved in the conspiracy were all caught and condemned to death and were beheaded.

Walburg, daughter of Marnix of Sainte-Aldegonde had endured poverty, obscurity and unmerited scorn, which had become the fate of Johan's family after his tragic end, but she came of a race that would not brook dishonour. When her husband Willem's conspiracy against Prince Maurice was discovered, she left Holland taking her young son, Pieter, and a daughter with her to France and had no further contact with Willem.

Children of Willem van Olden Barneveldt, Lord of Stoutenburg & Walberg de Marnix
Pieter   b.1613 at Holland
                                           d. Mar. 9, 1698/1699 at New York City
                                                   (formerly New Amsterdam)
                                           bur. New York City
Daughter   b. unknown

PIETER van OLDEN BARNEVELDT came to New Amsterdam, America in 1635 on the same ship bringing Governor Kieft, a new Governor for New Amsterdam. When emerging on the New Amsterdam scene Pieter took the name of his father's Netherlands estate "**STOUTENBURG**" for purely political reasons. At this time in Dutch history he probably still felt that the name of van Olden Barneveldt was held in disrepute. That is how the present families in America came to use the surname of Stoutenburgh, Stoutenburg, Stoutenboro, or Stoutenborough. All are believed to be direct descendants of the Netherlands great statesman Johan van Oldenbarneveldt, Lord of Stoutenburg.

PIETER STOUTENBURG
  m. to
AEFJE (Eva) van TIENHOVAN

Child of Pieter Stoutenburg & Eva van Tienhovan
Tobias   Christened Jan. 18, 1660

TOBIAS STOUTENBURG
  m. to
ANNEKE A. ROLLIGOOM

Child of Tobias & Anneke A. (Rolligoom) Stoutenburgh
Jacobus   Chr. June 7, 1696 at New Dutch Church, NYC, NY
                                           d.1772, New York

JACOBUS STOUTENBURG
  m. May 24, 1717 at NYC, NY to
MARGARET TELLER
  b. Feb. 2, 1696
  d. Feb.23, 1789, New York

Child of Jacobus & Margaret (Teller) Stoutenburgh
Lucas (Luke)   b. Chr. June 5, 1736 at Phillipsburgh, NY
                                    d. Dec. 21, 1789, NY

LUCAS (LUKE) STOUTENBURGH
  m. Aug. 2, 1762 to
RACHEL TELLER
  b. unknown
  d. on or about 1761

Child of Lucas (Luke) & Rachel (Teller) Stoutenburgh
Jason Lucas   b. Mar. 27, 1764
                                  d. Dec. 16, 1831

JASON LUCAS STOUTENBURGH
  m. to
SARAH MORRIS
  b. June 1774
  d. Mar. 1846 at Pleasant Valley, NY

Child of Jason L. & Sarah (Morris) Stoutenburgh
William Isaac   b. June 12, 1804, Dutchess Co., NY
                                  d. Feb. 14, 1882, New York

WILLIAM ISAAC STOUTENBURGH
  m. to
CAROLINE ALLEN

Child of William I. & Caroline (Allen) Stoutenburgh
William Jackson   b. Sept. 20, 1833, NY?
                                  d. Detroit, MI

WILLIAM JACKSON STOUTENBURGH, REV.
  m. to
CELESTE van NESS

Child of Rev. William J. & Celeste (van Ness) Stoutenburgh
George Alfred   b. Feb. 23, 1861, NYC, NY
                                  d. Nov. 25, 1910 at Waterbury, CT
                                  bur. Pine Grove Cem., Waterbury, CT

GEORGE ALFRED STOUTENBURGH
  m. (1) to
LYDIA ZORTMAN
  m. (2) to
IDA MABEL KENDALL, Widow of George Johnson
  b. Jan. 6, 1868 at East Kingston, NH
  d. Apr. 26, 1915 at Plainville, CT
  bur. West Cem., Plainville, CT

Child of George A. & Ida M. (Kendall) Stoutenburgh
Eldora van Ness   b. Dec. 3, 1897 at Brooklyn, NY
                             d. Sep. 23, 1959 at Burlington, CT
                             bur. Curtiss Cem., Simsbury, CT

ELDORA van NESS STOUTENBURGH
   m. Sept. 30, 1927 to
ARCHIE WILLIAM PAINE (GEN. X, No. 632, Paine Family)

SPOUSES OF GENERATION XI

<u>McLAUGHLIN</u>
J. HENRY McLAUGHLIN
   b. Feb. 13, 1894 at Hamilton, MA
   d. May 2, 1987 at Avon, CT
   bur. West Avon Cem., Avon, CT
   m. to
HANNAH B. (UNKNOWN)
   b. Aug. 20, 1888 at Buckland, CT
   d. Apr. 8, 1964 at Avon, CT
   bur. West Avon Cem., Avon, CT

Child of J. Henry & Hannah B. McLaughlin
Mabel Inez   b. Jun. 26, 1920 at Hartford, CT

MABEL INEZ McLAUGHLIN
   m. Jun 26, 1940 at Avon, CT to
FERDINAND RUDOLPH AUGUST, JR. (Gen. XI, Paine Family)

<u>THOMPSON</u>
ALBERT RICHARD THOMPSON
   b. Jul. 5, 1891 at Warren, CT
   d. Nov. 22, 1977 at Avon, CT
   bur. West Avon Cem., Avon, CT
   m. to
ANNIE VESTA MARJORIE LOURIE
   b. Jul. 29, 1899 at Olinville, New Brunswick, Canada
   d. Aug. 7, 1982 at Avon, CT
   bur. West Avon Cem., Avon, CT

Child of Albert R. & Annie V.M. (Lourie) Thompson
Gladys Eleanor   b. Oct. 31, 1921 at Avon, CT

GLADYS ELEANOR THOMPSON
   m. June 26, 1948 at Avon, CT to
ROBERT BURTON AUGUST (Gen. II, Paine Family)

KELLY
EDWARD LAWRENCE KELLY
   b. Apr. 16, 1899 at Elizabeth, NJ
   d. Feb. 12, 1995 at Tariffville, CT
   bur. St. Bernard's Cem., Tariffville, CT
   m. to
ROSE POPELLER
   b. Aug. 21, 1900
   d. Aug. 10, 1977 at Tariffville, CT
   bur. St. Bernard's Cem., Tariffville, CT

Child of Edward L. & Rose (Popeller) Kelly
Edward Lawrence, Jr.   b. Aug. 13, 1929 at Tariffville, CT

EDWARD LAWRENCE KELLY, JR.
   m. Sep. 19, 1953 at St. Bernard's Ch., Tariffville, CT to
GLADYS ELIZABETH PAINE (Gen. XI, Paine Family)

TOOLE
ALBERT TOOLE
   b. Aug. 10, 1892 at Holyoke, MA
   d. Apr. 24, 1973 at Holyoke, MA
   m. to
EVELYN HOGAN
   b. Jul. 4, 1891 at Holyoke, MA
   d. Jul. 16, 1972 at Holyoke, MA

Child of Albert & Evelyn (Hogan) Toole
Charles John   b. Dec. 3, 1923 at Holyoke, MA

CHARLES JOHN TOOLE
   m. Nov. 6, 1948 at St. Mary's Ch., Westfield, MA to
ELEANOR GRACE SEIBERT (Gen. XI, Paine Family)

MacWILLIAMS
HAROLD MacWILLIAMS
   b. Worcester, MA
   d. Feb. 19, 1948 at Enfield, CT
   bur. Enfield Cem., Enfield, CT
   m. to
EDNA ELIZABETH JOLIE
   b. Apr. 29, 1909
   d. Dec. 20, 1972 at Enfield, CT
   bur. Enfield Cem., Enfield, CT

Child of Harold & Edna E. (Jolie) MacWilliams
Mae Elizabeth   b. May 24, 1929 at Springfield, MA

MAE ELIZABETH MacWILLIAMS
  m. Apr. 18, 1949 to
LEONARD LEROY SEIBERT (GEN. XI, Paine Family)

MURPHY
STEPHEN HENRY MURPHY
  b. Aug. 12, 1901 at Newport, VT
  d. Jan. 6, 1964 at Hartford, CT
  bur. Bloomfield, CT
  m. to
BARBARA BICKFORD
  b. Jun. 5, 1906 at Hartford, CT
  d. Oct. 13, 1974 at Bloomfield, CT
  bur. Bloomfield, CT

Child of Stephen H. & Barbara (Bickford) Murphy
  Alice Theresa   b. Nov. 1, 1932 at Hartford, CT
                             d. Aug. 31, 1971 at Southwick, MA

ALICE THERESA MURPHY
  m. Mar. 21, 1952 at Suffield, MA to
MERTON GEORGE SEIBERT (Gen. XI, Paine Family)

EDWARDS
MINOT RUDYARD EDWARDS
  b. Nov. 19, 1887 at Arlington, MA
  d. Dec. 1966, at Houston, TX
  bur. Houston, TX
  m. to
ALICE LOUISE WALLACE
  b. Oct. 6, 1899 at Somerville, MA
  d. Apr. 30, 1983 at Lemark, TX
  bur. Houston, TX

Child of Minot R. & Alice L. (Wallace) Edwards
  Ruth Eleanor   b. July 13, 1936 at Braintree, MA

RUTH ELEANOR EDWARDS
  m. (l) to
McNAMARA

  m. (2) April 4, 1973 at Southwick, MA to
MERTON GEORGE SEIBERT (Gen. XI, Paine Family)

Children of Ruth E. (Edwards) McNamara
  Christine Alice   b. Apr. 13, 1965 at Hartford, CT
  Joseph Edward   b. Sep. 2, 1967 at Hartford, CT
  Bobbi Jo   b. Aug. 9, 1970 at Springfield, MA

FORLINGIERI
RAPHAEL FORLINGIERI
  b. Italy
  d. Providence, RI
  m. to
LUCIA TOMASELLI
  b. Italy
  d. Providence, RI

Both were born in Italy, one in the vicinity of Naples and the other in the vicinity of Rome, not known exact location of either. Spelling of last name was changed after they came to the United States.

Child of Ralph & Lucia (Tomaselli) Forlingieri
Thomas	b. Aug. 28, 1923 at RI
	d. Jan. 6, 1949

THOMAS FERLINGERE
  m. Jan. 6, 1949 at Seekonk, MA to
BERTHA MAE WEED (Gen. XI, Paine Family)

SUTHERLAND
THOMAS SUTHERLAND
m. to
PEARL RENGAL TRUDELL
  d. Chicago, IL
bur. Chicago, IL

Child of Thomas & Pearl R. (Trudell) Sutherland
Mack Horice	b. Jan. 2, 1919 at Oxford, MS
	d. Apr. 25, 1987 at Boulder, CO

MACK HORICE SUTHERLAND
  m. Feb. 19, 1949 at Denver, CO to
LOIS MATTIE WEED (Gen. XI, Paine Family)

LOWE
FRED STANDING ARROW LOWE
  b. 1893 at Cochise Apache Reservation, AR
  d. Jul 19, 1942 at Denver, CO
  bur. Crown Hill, Denver, CO
  m. to
EDITH BERTHA LITTLEDOVE
  b. Dec. 9, 1895 at Cochise Apache Reservation, AR
  d. Oct. 26, 1990 at Denver, CO
  bur. Crown Hill, Denver, CO

Child of Fred Standing Arrow & Edith B. (Littledove) Lowe
Evelyn Bertha	b. Dec. 6, 1921 at Fruita, CO
	d. Oct. 26, 1987 at Attica, KA

EVELYN BERTHA LOWE
  m. to
FRANK MONTE TAYLOR
  b. June 6, 1901
  d. Sep. 3, 1956 at Denver, CO
  bur. Denver, CO

Child of Frank M. & Evelyn B. (Lowe) Taylor
  Ronald Leo   b. May 14, 1937 at Denver, CO

RONALD LEO TAYLOR
  m. (l) to
PATRICIA ANN TRIGONING
  b. Jul. 11, 1942 at Sacramento, CA

  m. (2) Aug.2, 1975 at Colorado Springs, CO to
LOIS MATTIE WEED (Gen. XI, Paine Family)

Children of Ronald L. & Patricia A. (Trigoning) Taylor
  Ronald Anthony   b. June 21, 1958 at Denver, CO
  Deborah Lynn   b. Feb. 9, 1960 at Denver, CO
  Dennis Ray   b. Mar. 17, 1962 at Denver, CO
  Andrew Monty   b. Mar. 28, 1964 at Denver, CO
  Rebecca Christine   b. Aug. 22, 1972 at Denver, CO

REBECCA CHRISTINE TAYLOR
  m. to
TIMOTHY CHAMBERS

BERRY
ALEXANDER JACOB BERRY
  b. 1862
  d. 1926
  m. to
ANN Mac CANN
  b. 1872
  d. 1923

Child of Alexander J. & Ann (Mac Cann) Berry
  (Joe) Dolson   b. Jun 23, 1905 at Walla Walla, WA
                            d. Dec. 27, 1992 at Riverside, CA

GOODMAN
WILLARD GOODMAN
  b. Jan. 29, 1868 at Jonesboro, Union, IL
  d. Apr. 10, 1927 at Riverside, CA
  m. to
DELLA HOLLAND SHAW
  b. Oct. 5, 1872 at Birwick, Kings, NS, CA
  d. Oct. 12, 1909

Child of Willard & Della H. (Shaw) Goodman
Helen Elizabeth b. Jun 17, 1908 at Redland, CA

(JOE) DOLSON BERRY
  m to
 HELEN ELIZABETH GOODMAN

Children of Joe Dolson & Helen E. (Goodman) Berry
Jo Donna b. Dec. 5, 1935 at Riverside, CA
d. Dec. 17, 1993 at Cottonwood, AZ
bur. Cottonwood, AZ
Alberta Ruth b. Jan. 6, 1939 at Walnut, CA

JO DONNA BERRY
  m. Apr. 22, 1956 at Yuma, AZ to
FREDERICK DAVIS WEED, II (Gen. XI, Paine Family)

ALBERTA RUTH BERRY
  m. June 16, 1956 at Escondido, CA to
WILLIAM BOERUM WEED, JR. (Gen. XI, Paine Family)

LONG
AMOS HEZEKIAH LONG
  b. Jul. 9, 1881 at Effingham, IL
  d. Mar. 5, 1939
  m. Feb. 1, 1905 to
SARA CORDELIA JANE BOATMAN
  b. Oct. 11, 1884 at Arcadia, IL
  d. Dec. 22, 1961

Child of Amos H. & Sara C.J. (Boatman) Long
Joe Clifford b. Sep. 2, 1921 at Arnezville, IL
d. Sep. 2, 1976
JOE CLIFFORD LONG
  m. Mar. 1, 1941 to
RUTH LOUISE BAPTIST
  b. May 26, 1923 at Jacksonville, IL

Child of Joe C. & Ruth L. (Baptist) Long
Ruth (Ruthie) Elaine b. Dec. 13, 1941 at Jacksonville, IL

RUTH (RUTHIE) ELAINE LONG
  m. (1) 1960 to
LARRY HAGEN

  m. (2) Sep. 2, 1995 at Sedona, AZ to
FREDERICK DAVIS WEED, II (Gen. XI, Paine Family)

Children of Ruthie E. (Long) & Larry Hagen
Jeffrey Christian b. Jul. 22, 1961 at Jacksonville, IL
Kirk Lawrence b. Mar. 28, 1965 at Jacksonville, IL

JEFFREY CHRISTIAN HAGEN
  m. Jun. 21, 1986 to
ANNA LOUISE PIFER
  b. May 20, 1965 at Pasadena, CA

Children of Jeffrey C. & Anna L. (Pifer) Hagen
  Beth Leigh   b. Sep. 18, 1990 at Champaign-Urbana, IL
  Cory Jefferson   b. Jul. 15, 1992 at Champaign-Urbana, IL

KIRK LAWRENCE HAGEN

Child of Kirk M. Hagen
  Kaleb Matthew Smith   b. Nov. 28, 1990 at Champaign-Urbana, IL

<u>MARTINOLI</u>
GIOVANNI MARTINOLI
  b. Jun 23, 1799 at Sondrio, Italy
Possible relative.

JOSEPH MARTINOLI
  b., Sondrio(?), Italy
  m. to
MADELINE
  b. Italy

Child of Joseph & Madeline Martinoli
  John   b. Feb. 6, 1877/1878, Sondrio, Italy

<u>SCANELLI</u>
JOSEPH DOMINIC SCHNELLI/SCANELLI
  b. Italy
  m. to
MARY FERARI
  b. Italy

Child of Joseph Dominic & Mary (Ferari) Schnelli/Scanelli
  Lena   b. Feb. 11, 1879 at Pianello, Italy

JOHN MARTINOLI
  b. Feb. 6, 1877/1878, Sondrio, Italy
  d. Apr. 17, 1938 at Hartford, CT
  m. Oct. 25, 1898 at Windsor Locks, CT to
LENA SCHNELLI/SCANELLI
  b. Feb. 11, 1879 at Pianello, Italy
  d. Oct. 20, 1972 at Hartford, CT

Authority: Marriage Lic. Windsor Locks, CT, Social Security record,
Death Certs. Hartford, CT
Author's Note: Schnelli and Scanelli were both used in various vital records as well as
Joseph /Dominic Schnelli and Scanelli.

Child of John & Lena (Schnelli/Scanelli) Martinoli
Joseph Edward   b. Oct. 1, 1899 at Hartford, CT

Authority: Death Record, Hartford, CT (also shows date of birth)

BROWN
JAMES BROWN
  b. Ireland (
  d. Richford, VT?
  m. to
NANCY LARKIN
  b. Richford, VT
  d. Richford, VT?
  Info. Birthplaces of James & Nancy (Larkin) Brown ob. from death cert. of Aug. Brown.

Child of James & Nancy (Larkin) Brown
  Augustine (Gustine)   b. Dec. 10, 1880 at Mansonville/Sutton, Quebec, Canada

JOHNSON
GEORGE WASHINGTON JOHNSON
  b. Ab 1852 at Dunham, Prov. Quebec, Canada
  m. to
ELIZA LAVERY
  b. Christening - 1856 - Dunham, Prov. Quebec, Canada

Children of George & Eliza (Lavery) Johnson
  Elizabeth Almida (Lizzie)   b. Mar. 24, 1876 at Dunham, Quebec, Canada
                                    Chr. June 18, 1876 at St.Croix, R.C., Dunham, Canada
  Frances Ellen   b. Sep. 12, 1878 at Dunham, Prov. Quebec, Canada
                                    d. Oct. 21, 1971 at Newport, Orleans, VT
                                    bur. Oct. 21, 1971 at Hillside Cem., Richford, VT

AUGUSTINE (GUSTINE) BROWN
  d. Feb. 18, 1947 at Newport, Orleans, VT
  bur. Glen Sutton, Quebec, CA
  m. Sept. 16, 1891 at St.Croix, R.C., Dunham, Quebec, Canada to
ELIZABETH ALMIDA (LIZZIE) JOHNSON
  d. Mar. 29, 1971, at Hartford, CT
  bur. Rose Hill Mem. Cem., Rocky Hill, CT

Authority: Marriage Copy, Ste-Croix, Dunham, (Quebec) Superior Court Records; Death Copy; (for Gustine Brown) Vitals Records, Newport, VT. Book 30 pg. 14; Burial Permit copies show. trans. from East Side Cem. Newport, VT vault to Cem. in Glen Sutton, Que, Canada for burial.

Child of Augustine & Elizabeth A. (Johnson) Brown
  Edith Elizabeth   b. Mar. 11, 1900 at Richford, VT

Authority: Birth record, Richford, VT. Bk. 1897-1917 pg. 1900

EDITH ELIZABETH BROWN
  d. Jan. 10, 1955 at Hartford, CT
  bur. Mt. St. Benedict Cem. Bloomfield, CT
  m. Nov. 11, 1922 at St. Joseph's Cath., Hartford, CT to
JOSEPH EDWARD MARTINOLI
  d. Sept. 21, 1975 at Hartford, CT
  bur. Mt. St. Benedict Cem., Bloomfield, CT

Authority: Death Records- Hartford, CT

Children of Joseph E. & Edith E. (Brown) Martinoli

Earl Marshall	b. Apr. 25, 1924 at Hartford, CT
	d. Dec. 23, 1981 at West Haven, CT
	bur. Mt. St. Benedict Cem., Bloomfield, CT
John Joseph	b. Aug. 19, 1929, at Hartford, CT
Joseph Edward, Jr.	b. Nov. 5, 1934 at Hartford, CT
	d. Jul 22, 2000 at Waterbury, CT
	bur. Mt. St. Benedict, Cem, Bloomfield, CT

Authority: Death Record for Earl, West Haven, CT

JOHN JOSEPH MARTINOLI
  b. Aug. 19, 1929 at Hartford, CT
  d. Dec. 20, 1990 at New Haven, CT
  bur. Ashes strewn at Naugatuck State Forest
  m. April 30, 1949 to
BEVERLY MARION PAINE (Gen. XI, Paine Family)

Authority: Birth Record, (for both John & Beverly) Htfd. CT; Marriage Record, Simsbury, CT; & Death Record (for John) New Haven, CT

FULOP
JOHN FULOP
  b. Jul. 24, 1904 at Torrington, CT
  d. Jul. 2, 1945 at Torrington, CT
  m. at Torrington, CT
RUTH MARY DOUYARD
  b. May 29, 1906 at Unionville, Farmington, CT
d. Torrington, CT

Children of John & Ruth M. (Douyard) Fulop

John A.	b. Mar.11, 1927 at Torrington, CT
	d. Nov. 1995 at Torrington, CT
James B.	b. May 20, 1928 at Torrington, CT
Elizabeth Ann	b. Oct. 13, 1929 at Torrington, CT
Edward G.	b. Nov. 19, 1931 at Torrington, CT
Thomas F.	b. Oct. 24, 1933 at Torrington, CT
Doris M.	b. Jul. 18, 1940 at Torrington, CT
Roger	b. Feb. 23, 1942 at Torrington, CT

ELIZABETH ANN FULOP
  m. (1) Apr. 7, 1949 at Torrington, CT
ARCHIE W. PAINE (Gen. XI, Paine Family)

  m. (2) Aug. 17, 1957 at Collinsville, CT to
DAVID C. HOLLOWAY

HOLLOWAY
ROBERT BENFIELD HOLLOWAY
  b. Apr. 16, 1907 at Chicago, IL
  d. 1965 at St. Petersburg, FL
  bur. Tampa, FL
THELMA LOUISE CAMPBELL
  b. Sep. 15, 1911 at Grand Rapids, MI
  d. Odessa, TX
  bur. Odessa, TX

Child of Robert B. & Thelma L. (Campbell) Holloway
  David Carl   b. Apr. 16, 1934 at Grand Rapids, MI

DAVID CARL HOLLOWAY
  m. Aug. 17, 1957 at Collinsville, CT to
ELIZABETH ANN FULOP

Children of David C. & Elizabeth A. (Fulop) Holloway
  Dennis John   b. Nov. 7, 1959 at Torrington, CT
  Tracy Elizabeth   b. Aug. 18, 1967 at Honolulu, HI

GEORGE EVERETT HUFTEN
  b. Apr. 22, 1908 at Elizabeth, NJ
  d. Oct. 1988 at Foley, AL
  m. to
GIZELLA KUSCHKA
  b. Mar. 13, 1908 at Budapest, Hungary
  d. Dec., 1987 at Foley, AL

Children of George E. & Gizella (Kuschka) Huften
  Dorothy Margaret   b. July 10, 1932 at Hartford, CT
  George Everett, Jr.   b. Dec. 21, 1935 at Hartford, CT
  Donald David   b. Nov. 16, 1936 at Winsted, CT
  Grace   b. Jul. 27, 1944 at Winsted, CT
  Helen   b. Jul. 12, 1945 at Winsted, CT

DOROTHY MARGARET HUFTEN
  m. May 9, 1954 at Winsted, CT to
ARCHIE WILLIAM PAINE, JR. (Gen. XI, Paine Family)

BARNUM

ALLEN BARNUM
 b. Oct. 9, 1900 in CT
 d. June 5, 1970 at Bristol CT
 m. to
CORA BELLE EATON RIDER
 b. 1903 at Coventry, CT
 d. Aug. 2, 1957 at Bristol CT

Child of Allen & Cora B. E. (Rider) Barnum
 Barbara Ann   b. Mar. 3, 1935 at Bristol, CT

BARBARA ANN BARNUM
      m. Jan. 29, 1963 at City Hall, Hartford, CT to
PHILLIP IRVING PAINE (Gen. XI, Paine Family)

KEANE

MICHAEL JOSEPH KEANE
 d. 1926
 m. Oct. 16, 1893 to
MARGARET BRIDGET DALY
 b. Feb. 2, 1869
 d. Jan. 28, 1949

Child of Michael J. & Margaret B. (Daly) Keane
 James Louis   b. Jan. 9, 1896
                                    d. Mar. 1970

O'CONNELL

FERGUS A. O'CONNELL
 m. to
ANNIE FIORE

Children of Fergus A. & Annie (Fiore) O'Connell
 Annie Veronica   b. Jan. 13, 1908 at London, England
                                    d. Aug. 2, 1990 at Avon, CT

 Vincent

JAMES LOUIS KEANE
 m. to
ANNIE VERONICA O'CONNELL
Child of James L. & Annie V. (O'Connell) Keane
 James Michael   b. Jul. 27, 1932 at Hartford, CT

JAMES MICHAEL KEANE
 m. Sep. 10, 1955 at Newington, CT to
NANCY JOAN PAINE (GEN. XI, Paine Family)

BISHOP
WALTON BURREL BISHOP
  b. Aug. 25, 1917 at LeRoy, IL
  m. to
MARJORIE NELLE HANSEN
  b. Aug. 2, 1917 at Normal, IL
  d. Aug. 18, 1995 at Acton, MA
  bur. Paxton, IL

Child of Walton B. & Marjorie N. (Hansen) Bishop
  Gregory James   b. Oct. 14, 1941 at Chelsea, MA

GREGORY JAMES BISHOP
  m. Jun. 3, 1967 at Congregational Church, Collinsville, CT to
CLAUDIA ANN PAINE (Gen. XI, Paine Family)

SPOUSES OF GENERATION XII

LLEWELLYN
HAROLD JONES LLEWELLYN
  b. Jun. 7, 1900 at Plymouth, PA
  d. Jul. 7, 1961 at Wilkes-Barre, PA
  bur. Dallas, PA
  m. to
BEULAH MAY JOHNSON
  b. Jun. 16, 1910 at PA
  d. Nov. 7, 1992 at Avon, CT
  bur. Dallas, PA

Child of Harold Jones & Beulah May (Johnson) Llewellyn
  Virginia   b. Sep. 25, 1945 at Wilkes-Barre, PA

VIRGINIA LLEWELLYN
  m. Mar. 21, 1970 at Wilkes-Barre, PA to
NORMAN FREDERICK AUGUST (Gen. XII, Paine Family)

PAGE
MERTON McARTHUR PAGE
  b. Mar. 25, 1910 at New Bern, NC
  d. Aug.9, 1984 at New Bern, NC
  m. to
OLIVIA EDWARDS
  b. Aug. 8, 1911 at New Bern, NC
  d. May 26, 1984 at New Bern, NC

Child of Merton McArthur. & Olivia (Edwards) Page
  Janice Faye   b. Jul. 1945 at Portsmouth, VA

JANICE FAYE PAGE
   m. Nov. 26, 1966 at Havelock, NC to
JAMES ALBERT AUGUST (Gen. XII, Paine Family)

TELLIER
RAYMOND ADRIEN TELLIER
   b. May 17, 1921 at Manchester, NH
   d. Aug. 3, 1994 at Interlachen, FL
   bur. Memorial Gardens, Palatka, FL
   m. to
SIMONE LAVIGNE
   b. June 15, 1922 at Manchester, NH

Child of Raymond A. & Simone (Lavigne) Tellier
   Jacqueline Yvette   b. Nov. 18, 1945 at Simsbury, CT

JACQUELINE YVETTE TELLIER
   m. Jan. 31, 1969 at Simsbury, CT to
LARRY STRONG AUGUST (Gen. XII, Paine Family)

BALL
R. EDWIN BALL
   d. Bloomsburg, PA
   m. to
HELEN MAXINE SHOLES
   b. Mar. 4, 1920 at Lafayette, CO
   d. Jul. 31, 1969 at Lafayette, CO
   bur. Crown Hill Cem., Denver, CO

Child of R. Edwin & Helen M. (Sholes) Ball
   Jane Ellen   b. June 22, 1948 at Denver, CO

JANE ELLEN BALL
   m. Dec. 20, 1969 at Lafayette, CO to

MICHAEL JAY AUGUST (Gen. XII, Paine Family)

BIRINGER
WALTER CONRAD BIRINGER
   b. Jul. 5, 1902 at New York, NY
   d. Aug. 31, 1986 at Bristol, CT
   bur. West Cem., Bristol, CT
   m. to
ALICE E. MINOR
   b. May 6, 1914 at New York, NY

Child of Walter C. & Alice E. (Minor) Biringer
  Samuel   b. Jul. 25, 1943 at New Britain, CT

SAMUEL BIRINGER
  m. Jul. 31, 1971 at Avon, CT to
SHARYN ELIZABETH AUGUST (Gen. XII, Paine Family)

BRISTOL
STUART WILLIAM BRISTOL
  m. to
MARGARET JOHNSON

Child of Stuart W. & Margaret (Johnson) Bristol
  Arthur   b. Dec. 17, 1921 at Hartford, CT

WILDER
FRANK EARL WILDER
  m. to
AHLENE GIBBONS

Child of Frank E. & Ahlene (Gibbons) Wilder
  Joyce   b. May 13, 1924 at Collinsville, CT

ARTHUR BRISTOL
  m. to
JOYCE WILDER

Child of Arthur & Joyce (Wilder) Bristol
  Janice Anne   b. Mar. 20, 1950 at Hartford, CT

JANICE ANNE BRISTOL
  m. Sep. 13, 1975 at Collinsville, CT to
JOHN EMERSON GANGELL (Gen. XII, Paine Family)

STAGG
LESTER P. STAGG
  b. 1935 at Eunice, LA
VELMA PETIGO
  b. 1937 at Eunice, LA

Child of Lester P. & Velma (Petigo) Stagg
  Duane James   b. Mar. 26, 1955 at Eunice, LA

DUANE JAMES STAGG
  m. Jun. 24, 1988 at Simsbury, CT to
SUSAN GAIL PAINE (Gen. XII, Paine Family)

CROMBEZ
RENE TERRENCE CROMBEZ
   b. Mar. 15, 1943 at Monroe, MI
   m. to
MELINDA LEE SCHWARTZ
   b. Apr. 21, 1943 at Tecumseh, MI

Child of Rene T. & Melinda L. (Schwartz) Crombez
   Sean David   b. Dec. 13, 1968 at Tecumseh, MI

SEAN DAVID CROMBEZ
   m. Nov. 25, 1996 at Simsbury, CT to
DONNA JOY PAINE (Gen. XII, Paine Family)

OUIMET
DAVID OUIMET
   b. Jun 23, 1912 at Montreal, CANADA
   m. to
YVETTE DESHAMPS
b. Dec. 18, 1920 at Montreal, CANADA

Child of David & Yvette (Deshamps) Ouimet
   Roger Denis   b. Feb. 23, 1944 at Montreal, Canada

ROGER DENIS OUIMET
   m. to
ANNE MARIE TOOLE (Gen. XII, Paine Family)

SHAW
JOHN SHAW
   m. to
BLANCHE

Child of John & Blanche Shaw
   Charles Henry   b. Sep. 18, 1950 at Norwood, MA

CHARLES HENRY SHAW
   m. Aug. 15, 1987 at Amherst, MA to
VIRGINIA ROSE TOOLE (Gen. XII, Paine Family)

SCOTT
COPLEY HILDRETH SCOTT
   b. Sep. 18, 1923 at Lowell, MA
   m. to
DOROTHY ELIZABETH WELCH
   b. Dec. 30, 1923 at Northampton, MA

Child of Copley H. & Dorothy E. (Welch) Scott
   Richard Copley   b. Oct. 10, 1945 at Northhampton, MA

RICHARD COPLEY SCOTT
  m. Aug. 24, 1985 at Granby, MA to
ALICE MADELEINE TOOLE (Gen. XII, Paine Family)

BENOIT
CHARLES EDWARD BENOIT
  b. Jun. 6, 1915 at Springfield, MA
  m. to
CAROLYN GOODES
  b. Oct. 18, 1914 at Palmer, MA

Child of Charles E. & Carolyn (Goodes) Benoit
  Richard Edgar   b. Nov. 14, 1944 at Springfield, CT

RICHARD EDGAR BENOIT
  m. Feb. 18, 1959 at Huntington, MA to
CHERYL ANNE SEIBERT (Gen. XII, Paine Family)

COWLES
HARRY ANDREW COWLES
  b. May 10, 1881
  d. Jan. 14, 1976
  m. to
EDNA QUANCE
  b. Sep. 22, 1885
  d. Sep.23, 1930

Child of Harry A. & Edna (Quance) Cowles
  Richard Harry   b. Nov. 7, 1919 at Westfield, MA

CORCORAN
MICHAEL CORCORAN
  m. to
HELEN GOODE

Child of Michael & Helen (Goode) Corcoran
  Helen Barbara   b. Feb. 2, 1920 at Boston, MA

RICHARD HARRY COWLES
  m. to
HELEN BARBARA CORCORAN

Child of Richard H. & Helen B. (Corcoran) Cowles
  Richard   b. Jan. 31, 1946 at Westfield, MA

RICHARD COWLES
  m. May 20, 1972 at Southwick, MA to
LYNNE CAROL SEIBERT (Gen. XII, Paine Family)

BERESFORD
HOWARD JOHN BERESFORD
b. Nov. 3, 1917
d. Jan. 25, 1994 at Enfield, CT
bur. West Suffield, CT
m. to
JESSIE STILES
b. Jul 4, 1919 at Springfield, MA

Child of Howard J. & Jessie (Stiles) Beresford
Daniel Paul   b. Sep. 4, 1959 at Hartford, CT

DANIEL PAUL BERESFORD
m. Oct. 27, 1990 at Southwick, MA to
LAURIE DEE SEIBERT (Gen. XII, Paine Family)

BLAIR
ARTHUR BLAIR
b. May 16, 1931 at Richford, VT
m. to
THELMA COUSENS
b. Jun. 20, 1934 at Montreal, CANADA

Child of Arthur & Thelma (Cousens) Blair
Gregory Arthur   b. Apr. 13, 1956 at Granby, CT

GREGORY ARTHUR BLAIR
m. Sept. 11, 1976 at Granby, CT to
PATRICIA ANN SEIBERT (Gen. XII, Paine Family)

BAKEWELL
THOMAS OLIVER BAKEWELL
m. to
NELDA JEAN
Child of Thomas O. & Nelda J. Bakewell
Loyd Thomas   b. Feb. 22, 1942 at Salt Lake City, UT

The family homesteaded in Wyoming.

LOYD THOMAS BAKEWELL
m. Jan. 31, 1970 at Denver, CO to
VALERIE MAE FERLINGERE (Gen. XII, Paine Family)

RICE
JAMES ROBERT RICE
 m. to
FLOY LOUISE MARKHAM
 d. prior to 1985

Child of James R. & Floy L. (Markham) Rice
 Sharon Ann　　　　　　　b. Nov. 8, 1951 at Green Bay, WI

SHARON ANN RICE
 m. Jan. 15, 1971 at Green Bay, WI to
THOMAS SCOTT FERLINGERE (Gen. XII, Paine Family)

CIPRIANO
FRANK JOSEPH CIPRIANO
 b. May 30 at IL
 m. to
ELIZABETH ANN SCHUMACHER
 b. Mar. 1 at Elmhurst, IL

Child of Frank J. & Elizabeth A. (Schumacher) Cipriano
 Elizabeth Ann　　　　　　b. Dec. 5, 1967 at El Paso, TX

ELIZABETH ANN CIPRIANO
 m. Aug. 13, 1988 at Aspen, CO to
WYLIE CHRISTOPHER DUKE (Gen. XII, Paine Family)

LEONARDI
ALDO RUDOLPH LEONARDI
 b. June 24, 1925 at Hudson, WY
 d. Nov. 6, 1991 at Ogden, UT
 m. to
MARGARET IRENE YARDAS
 b. Nov. 24, 1924 at Superior, WY
 d. May 13, 1988 at Ogden, UT

Child of Aldo R. & Margaret I. (Yardas) Leonardi
 David Michael　　　　　　b. May 7, 1968 at Ogden, UT

DAVID MICHAEL LEONARDI
 m. June 22, 1981 at Ogden, UT to
DAWN TERRI SUTHERLAND (Gen. XII, Paine Family)

GREGG
JACOB LEE GREGG
 b. Aug. 3, 1925 at Ogden, UT
 d. Jan. 1964, at Phoenix, AZ
 m. to
LaRITA FRANCES WILSON
 b. Aug. 30, 1926 at Broken Bow, NE

Child of Jacob L. & LaRita F. (Wilson) Gregg
  Steve   b. Jan. 19, 1951 at Longview, WA

STEVE GREGG
  m. Mar. 31, 1986 at Longview, WA to
DAWN TERRI SUTHERLAND (Gen. XII, Paine Family)

KNIGHT
McCONNELL EARL KNIGHT
  m. to
BETTY ROTH

Child of McConnell E. & Betty (Roth) Knight
  McConnell Earl, Jr.   b. Sep. 10, 1951

McCONNELL EARL KNIGHT, JR.
  m. Mar. 18, 1978 at Pasadena CA to
ROSEMARIE NINA WEED (GEN. II, Paine Family)

CATO
ARTHUR LEONARD CATO
  b. June 10, 1917 at London, England
m. to
INGEBORG FISCHER
  b. Jul. 15, 1927 at Dortmund, Germany

Child of Arthur L. & Ingeborg (Fischer) Cato
  Colin Alexander   b. Nov. 1, 1946 at London, England

COLIN ALEXANDER CATO
  m. (1) to July, 1971 to
ELIZABETH MARIE RAU
  b. Dec. 5, 1947 at Brugge, Belgium

  m. (2) Feb. 10, 1985 at Pasadena, CA to
ROSEMARIE NINA WEED (Gen. XII, Paine Family)

Children of Colin A. & Elizabeth M. (Rau) Cato
  Karen Elizabeth   b. Jun 17, 1972 at Radlett, England
  Mark Alexander   b. May 30, 1974 at Dusseldorf, Germany

KAREN ELIZABETH CATO
  m. Sept. 4, 1994 at Riverside, CA to
LLOYD WILLIAM SULLINS
  b. Jan. 25, 1970 at Evanston, IL

MARK ALEXANDER CATO
  m. Aug. 22, 1993 at Las Vegas, NV to
CHRISTI IRENE SCAFANI
  b. Oct. 23, 1973 at March Air Base, Riverside, CA

Child of Mark A. & Christi I. (Scafani) Cato
  Christopher Fredrick Louis b. June 24, 1995

MURPHY
JOHN WILLIAM MURPHY
  b. Oct. 13, 1932
  m. May 1, 1950 at Manchester, CT to
MARLENE MAY MAGNELL
  b. Feb. 21, 1931
  d. Feb. 15, 1994 at Hartford, CT
bur. West Hartford, CT

Child of John W. & Marlene M. (Magnell) Murphy
  Janice Eileen   b. Nov. 12, 1952 at Manchester, CT

JANICE EILEEN MURPHY
  m. Dec. 31, 1988 at Bradford, VT to
GEORGE ALOYSIUS POIRIER, JR. (Gen. XII, Paine Family)

HELLER
JOHN RAYMOND HELLER
  b. May 5, 1934 at New Britain, CT
  m. Sept. 29, 1956 at Manchester, CT to
SUSAN JANES
  b. Feb. 14, 1937 at Hartford, CT

Child of John R. & Susan (Janes) Heller
  John Raymond, Jr.   b. Apr. 12, 1958 at Hartford, CT

JOHN RAYMOND, HELLER, JR.
  m. Jun. 3, 1978 at North Church, Granby, CT to
DALE ELLA GLAZIER (Gen. II, Paine Family)

LOFTUS
ANTHONY LOFTUS
  m. to
ANNA BARRETT

Child of Anthony & Anna (Barrett) Loftus
  Anthony Francis   b. Mar. 13, 1869

McMANUS
M. McMANUS
  b. Ireland
  m. to
MARGARET NOLAN
b. Ireland

Child of M. & Margaret (Nolan) McManus
  Katharine   b. Jan. 1, 1881 at Hudson, PA

ANTHONY FRANCIS LOFTUS
  d. July 15, 1943
  m. to
KATHARINE McMANUS
  d. June 2, 1965
Child of Anthony F. & Katharine (McManus) Loftus
  Thomas Michael   b. Oct. 2, 1918 at Hudson, PA

BRANNIGAN
FELIX BRANNIGAN
  b. Co. Mayo, Ireland
  m. to
MARY GALLAGHER
  b. Co. Mayo, Ireland

Child of Felix & Mary (Gallagher) Brannigan
  John Felix   b. Aug. 21, 1881

GALLAGHER
DOMINICK GALLAGHER
  b. Ireland
  m. to
SUSAN GALLAGHER
  b. Ireland

Child of Dominck & Susan Gallagher
  known as Patrick aka Pappy b. Ireland

PATRICK GALLAGHER
  m. Sep. 9, 1847 to
BRIDGET GOUGHAN
  b. Ireland?

Child of Patrick & Bridget (Goughan) Gallagher
  Mary   b. Co. Mayo, Ireland

HOGAN
PHILIP HOGAN
  b. Co. Mayo, Ireland

Child of Philip Hogan
  Patrick   b. Co. Mayo, Ireland

PATRICK HOGAN
  m. to
MARY BROGAN
  b. Cross Molino, Ireland
  d. Oct. 13, 1917

Child of Patrick & Mary (Brogan) Hogan
Bridget Angela   b. Jul. 18, 1876

JOHN FELIX BRANNIGAN
  b. Aug. 21, 1881
  d. Sep. 6, 1965
  m. Aug. 17, 1909 to
BRIDGET ANGELA HOGAN
  b. Jul. 18, 1876
  d. Feb. 24, 1956

Child of John F. & Bridget A. (Hogan) Brannigan
Margaret Louise   b. Oct. 21, 1917 at Plains, PA

THOMAS MICHAEL LOFTUS, M.D.
  b. Oct. 2, 1918 at Hudson, PA
  d. Jan. 13, 1993
  m. to
MARGARET LOUISE BRANNIGAN
  b. Oct. 21, 1917 at Plains, PA

Child of Thomas M. & Margaret L. (Brannigan) Loftus
  Kathryn Laboure Margaret b. Jul. 10, 1950 at Philadelphia, PA

KATHRYN LABOURE MARGARET LOFTUS
  m. May 6, 1972 at Philadelphia, PA to
JOHN JOSEPH MARTINOLI, JR. (Gen. XII, Paine Family)

DeFELICE
JOSEPH S. DeFELICE
  m. to
GIOVANNA (JENNY) PERGOLA

Child of Joseph S. & Jenny (Pergola) DeFelice
  Joseph Anthony   b. Dec. 14, 1952 at Derby, CT

JOSEPH A. DeFELICE
  m. (1) to **ALYCE THOMAS**
  m. (2) **JILL ELIZABETH MARTINOLI MARINO (Gen. XII, Paine Family)**

Child of Joseph A. & Alyce (Thomas) DeFelice
  Paul Joseph   b. Dec. 17, 1978 at Derby, CT

TENNETT
RONALD EUGENE TENNETT
  b. Jul. 7, 1940 at Providence, RI
  m. to
HARRIET PAULINE HOULE
  b. Jul. 3, 1942 at W. Warwick, RI

Child of Ronald E. & Harriet P. (Houle) Tennett
   Karen Linda   b. Mar. 22, 1963 at Providence, RI

KAREN LINDA TENNETT
   m. Jun. 10, 1995 at Warwick, RI to
ARCHIE WILLIAM (PAINE) HOLLOWAY (Gen. XII, Paine Family)

JAMES MURRAY ROONEY
   b. Jul. 10, 1924 at Brighton, MA
   m. Jan. 10, 1948 at Watertown, MA to
AGNES LILLIAN PITTS (PETTIPAS)
   b. Jan. 10, 1928 at Watertown, MA
 James is the eldest of ten children. Agnes (Lil) is the third youngest of nineteen children. The family came down from Canada. When emigrating from Canada to the U.S. they changed their name from Pettipas to Pitts

Child of James M. & Agnes L. (Pitts) Rooney
   Marian Ellen   b. Jul. 7, 1954 at Boston, MA

MARIAN ELLEN ROONEY
   m. Nov. 12, 1971 at Warwick, RI to
DAVID ALAN (PAINE) HOLLOWAY (Gen. XII, Paine Family)

REID
ROBERT C. REID
   b. Aug. 7, 1944, Fitchburg, MA
   m. to
BEVERLY A. CHASTAIN
   b. Oct. 22, 1943 at Fitchburg, MA

Child of Robert C. & Beverly A. (Chastain) Reid
   Melanie Rae   b. Jan. 22, 1971 at Fitchburg, MA

MELANIE RAE REID
   m. Sep. 18, 1993 at Fitchburg, MA to
DAVID ALAN PAINE HOLLOWAY (Gen. XII, Paine Family)

FISKE
EARL FISKE, SR.
   b. Feb. 20, 1905 at Providence, RI
   d. Nov. 4, 1962 at Providence, RI
   bur. Gate of Heaven, Barrington, RI
   m. to
RITA L. CONWAY
   b. Mar. 19, 1919 at Providence, RI
   d. May 7, 1988 at Providence, RI
   bur. Gate of Heaven, Barrington, RI

Child of Earl L. Sr. & Rita L. (Conway) Fiske
   Barbara Margaret   b. June 3, 1949 at Cranston, RI

BARBARA MARGARET FISKE
  m. Aug. 17, 1986 at Providence, RI to
DENNIS JOHN HOLLOWAY

<u>**HOLLOWAY**</u>
TRACY ELIZABETH HOLLOWAY
  b. Aug. 18, 1967 at Honolulu, HI
  m. (1) Jul. 12, 1996 at East Providence, RI to
MARK GEMMELL

  m. Aug. 16, 2003 at Warwick, RI to
LAWRENCE VINCENT D'ALESSIO

Children of Tracy Holloway
Lauren Elizabeth	b. Apr. 1, 1984 at Warwick, RI
David Carl, II	b. Apr. 21, 1991 at Warwick, RI

Children of Mark & Tracy E. (Holloway) Gemmell
Brandon Mark	b. Jul. 7, 1996 at Warwick, RI
Elizabeth Tracy	b. Jul. 10, 1997 at Warwick, RI

<u>**SYMONDS**</u>
WILLIAM SYMONDS
m. to
MARY PATRICIA KEANE

Child of William & Mary P. (Keane) Symonds
Patricia	b. Aug. 1, 1949 at New Britain, CT

PATRICIA SYMONDS
  m. (1) to
JOHN RICHARD MINER, JR

  m. (2) Mar. 4, 1989 at Farmington, CT to
GREGORY KEANE (Gen. XII, Paine Family)

Children of John R. Jr. & Patricia (Symonds) Miner
Ryan Patrick	b. Mar. 31, 1973 at Hartford, CT
Aubrey Kathleen	b. Nov. 10, 1975 at Hartford, CT

<u>**SCHRIJN**</u>
JEAN EUGENE SCHRIJN
  b. Sep. 20, 1923 at Bogor, Indonesie
  m. to
JOSEPHA MARTINA
  b. Aug. 2, 1933 at Magelang, Indonesie

Child of Jean Eugene & Josepha (Martina) Schrijn
James Udo	b. Oct. 24, 1960 at Hartford, CT

JAMES UDO SCHRIJN
  m. Oct. 21, 1995 at Collinsville, CT to
THERESA MARIE KEANE (Gen. XII, Paine Family)

CARRON
MICHAEL JOSEPH CARRON
  m. to
ANN LUISE WILLEY

Child of Michael J. & Ann L. (Willey) Carron
  Mark   b. Jul. 8, 1962 at Springfield, MA

MARK CARRON
  m. Dec. 17, 1994 at Southbridge, MA to
CYNTHIA MARGARET KEANE (Gen. XII, Paine Family)

Child of Mark Carron
  Allison   b. May l, 1989

SPOUSES OF GENERATION XIII

MULKEY
RICKEY MULKEY
  m. to
APRIL

Child of Rickey & April Mulkey
  April Nicole   b. 1974

APRIL NICOLE MULKEY
  m. to
TODD J. AUGUST (Gen. XIII, Paine Family)

DUNN
HOWARD WILLIAM DUNN
  m. to
DOROTHY JEAN HOUSE

Child of Howard W. & Dorothy J. (House) Dunn
  Jane Diane   b. Oct. 12, 1954 at Anadarko, OK

JOHNSTON
DONALD RAY JOHNSTON
  b. Sep. 19, 1951 at Anadarko, OK
  m. to
JANE DIANE DUNN

Child of Donald R. & Jane D. (Dunn) Johnston
  Jennifer Dawn   b. Mar. 13, 1973 at Weatherford, OK

JENNIFER DAWN JOHNSTON
  m. to
JONATHAN D. BAKEWELL (Gen. XIII, Paine Family)

DAVIS
GEORGE A. DAVIS, SR.
  m. to
EDNA MILDRED YLITALO
  b. Connaut, OH
  d. Jul 1974 at Ashtabula, OH

Child of George A. Sr. & Edna M. (Ylitalo) Davis
  Richard C.   b. Jun. 7, 1937 at Ashtabula, OH

DANIELS
FRANK J. DANIELS, SR.
  d. Oct. 1980 at Buffalo, NY
  m. to
ROSE A. BAMBINO

Child of Frank J., Sr. & Rose A. (Bambino) Daniels)
  Rose A.   b. Jul 27, 1940 at Ashtabula, OH

RICHARD C. DAVIS, SR.
  m. Jul 11, 1959 at Ashtabula, OH to
ROSE A. DANIELS

Child of Richard C. Sr. & Rose A. (Daniels) Davis
  Michael Scott   b. Nov. 1, 1966 at Ashtabula, OH

MICHAEL SCOTT DAVIS
  m. (1) to
KIM GIDDINGS GIRARO
  m. (2) to
CELLINA L. FERLINGERE (Gen. XIII, Paine Family)

DUNN
JACK DUNN
  m. to
MARYELLEN FANNING

Child of Jack & Maryellen (Fanning) Dunn
  Timothy Fanning   b. Aug. 4, 1971 at Washington, D.C.

TIMOTHY FANNING DUNN
  m. Apr. 29, 2000 at Oxford, CT to
MEEGAN ANGELA MARINO (Gen. XIII, Paine Family)

GLENNON
ROBERT GLENNON

m. to
MARGARET McGRATH

Child of Robert & Margaret (McGrath) Glennon
Megan Ann   b. Oct. l, 1978 at Bridgeport, CT

MEGAN ANN GLENNON
m. Mar 12, 2005 at North Haven, CT to
PAUL J. DeFELICE

BRISTOW
JOHN GREGORY BRISTOW
m. to
JOAN SIGLER ECKER

Child of John G. & Joan S. (Ecker) Bristow
Joanne Latham   b. Nov. 9, 1974 at Bryn Mawr, PA

JOANNE LATHAM BRISTOW
m. Sep. 24, 2004 at Wyncote, PA to
JOHN D. MARTINOLI (Gen. III, Paine Family)

KENNEY
WILLIAM KENNEY
m. to
CHRISTINE McTAGUE

Child of William and Christine (McTague) Kenney
Joseph Patrick Kenney   b. Mar. 30, 1978 at Philadelphia, PA

JOSEPH PATRICK KENNEY
m. May l, 2009 at Media, PA to
SUSAN ELIZABETH MARTINOLI (Gen. III, Paine Family)

PERKINS
JERRY PERKINS, JR
m. to
PAMELA MILLER

Child of Jerry & Pamela (Miller) Perkins,Jr.
Savhanna   b. Nov. 15, 1987 at Bridgeport, CT

CARR
ROBERT ARTHUR CARR
m. to
BRENDA ANN DYER

Child of Robert Arthur & Brenda Ann (Dyer) Carr
Jeremy Jason   b. Sep. 18, 1975 at Toledo, OH

JEREMY JASON CARR
m. Sep. 21, 2003 at Eisenhower House, Newport, RI to
SARAH NICOLE HOLLOWAY (Gen. XIII, Paine Family)

CHAPTER EIGHT
CEMETERY RESEARCH

OAK GROVE CEMETERY, SPRINGFIELD, MA

Sept. 23, 1997 Archie, Nancy and I drove to Chicopee, MA today and picked up our cousin, Eleanor (Seibert) Toole. We visited Oak Grove Cemetery in Springfield, MA to look for graves of **French Ancestors.**

There we found the monument of our Great-grandfather **William Henry French** and his wife **Mary Dugan French**. It is located in Lot 444 Section 12. Also engraved on the monument is the name of their **son, Thomas J. French**, born 1866 and giving his date of death as 1888, aged 22 years. We checked back with the office there at the cemetery. The record shows that the **full date of death** was **November 15, 1888**. There are also **two metal plaques** in the ground beside the monument - one stating that a **Union Defender** is buried there and another stating that a **Veteran of Foreign Wars** is buried there. Various articles and the obituary of William H. French recorded elsewhere in this book bear out the information that he was both a Union Defender and a Veteran of Foreign Wars.

According to records at the cemetery office the following persons were also buried in the same plot:

Mae Emmaline French	May 11, 1940 - Age 55
Anna B. French	Mar. 23, 1943 - Age 75 yrs. 8 mos.
Mildred French	Jul. 14, 1962 - Age 64 yrs.
Willie French	Dec. 21, 1908 - Age 42 yrs.
Baby George E.	Dec. 21, 1908 - Age 3 days

We found no monuments or headstones so don't know how they tie in.

Cemetery records also show that **Wilberta (Fryer) Taylor**, her husband **Clarence Taylor** and their son **Roy** are buried in Lot 2345, Section 19. Although we walked the Section, we were unable to locate a monument or headstones. **Wilberta** was the **daughter** of **Mary (Dugan) Fryer French**. Mr. Fryer (Frier) died before Wilberta's birth in 1862. Mary Dugan married William H. French in 1865 right after the close of the Civil War.

OLD BURYING GROUND, LUDLOW, MA
EAST CEMETERY/LIBERTY CEMETERY
LUDLOW & BELCHERTOWN, MA

After lunch in Ludlow, MA, we started looking for graves of some of the **PAINE ANCESTORS.** We had asked directions to the oldest cemetery that one of the waitresses knew of in Ludlow. She directed us to First Church of Ludlow on Route 21, which has a cemetery beside it. There is also another cemetery on the opposite side of the road but closer to the interstate.

At First Church, Nancy and I went in to the offices, as there were cars in the parking lot. We met a group of folks who had been working on mailing their monthly newsletter to parishioners. They were just finishing up and getting ready to leave. We introduced ourselves and asked them about Paine graves. One of the older couples mentioned that there was a Paine Rd. and a Paine Farm in another part of town and also a cemetery in that vicinity. They suggested that Town Hall could perhaps supply us with a map.

After checking out the cemetery at First Church and coming up blank we took their advice and proceeded to the Town Hall. Nancy and I went in and asked them to check for death records on **David Paine and Abigail Shepard Paine** of whom we had information from Clara Paine Ohler's book that they were buried in Ludlow at the **"Old Burying Ground"** Ludlow's Vital Records showed no mention of either name. They did however sell us a map of Ludlow and point us in the direction of Paine Ave., an unpaved road.

We then proceeded to Paine Ave., a dead end road off Poole St. Turning onto that road we passed a ranch house and reached an old Farm House at its end. There was an old truck parked in front with a sign painted on the door indicating "Paine Farm". Although there was plenty of equipment in open sheds, the house itself looked unoccupied. Archie spoke with a truck driver who was exiting from a pasture behind the barn. The man did not seem familiar with the area and was apparently there for delivery and pick up. We turned around in the yard and headed back to stop at the ranch house. I knocked but no one answered the door. We went back to Poole St. and continued up the road until we found a cemetery. We wandered around reading the names on monuments, finding any number of Paine graves but not the ones we were looking for.

We noted a herd of Herefords across the street in the pasture. Shortly after we got out of our car, a lady arrived to ask if we might be Paine cousins. She had seen activity on the hill and was concerned that someone was in the pasture with the herd so came to investigate. Her name was Mary A. Paine, her husband being Merrill Bailey Paine. They live in the ranch house on Paine Ave. She was at home when we stopped there, but did not hear me knock. She'd recently come home from the hospital and her illness had resulted in a loss of hearing. She did not seem to be too strong, but certainly enjoyed visiting with us. She showed us where **David and Abigail's graves** are located in the **Old Burying Ground Section** of what is now known as **East Cemetery**, Poole St., Ludlow, MA. **East Cemetery** inside the **Ludlow** town line becomes the **Liberty Cemetery** on the **Belchertown** side of the line although it is one continuous burial ground. David's stone is not very legible. Abigail's is quite clear by comparison. We were able to get a picture of both and David's epitaph reads as follows:

"Mr. David Paine/ departed this life July 2nd/1807 (by a cart/ wheel running across/ his brest he expired/ instantly) AED 70/ He was a friend/ of Religion &/ Piety. (actual spelling)

We chatted with Mary a good while finding out about the various Paine farms in the area. She mentioned that the Power Company had taken some of the Paine Farmhouses and outbuildings when putting a new power line through. One of the homes razed was their own place and another was the farm known as the A.K. Paine (Alfred Kingsley) homestead. Mary also mentioned that there had been another Paine Farm just over the line on Poole St. in Belchertown. She did not know the name of the Paine family who owned that one. We think it was **possibly** at one point in time the **home of Henry A. Paine**, our great grandfather. Perhaps research into the land records will bear that out. While we were chatting, Mary's husband, **Merrill Bailey Paine** came along. He pulled over and we introduced ourselves to him. He parked his van and came to talk with us. Merrill has a picture of the Belchertown house with a lady in a long dress standing in front of it. The lady is not identified. Merrill told us that the house was very dilapidated and was leveled some time ago.

It turns out that **Merrill's grandfather, Alfred Kingsley Paine** was **brother** to our great-grandfather, **Henry A. Paine.** So that would make **Merrill first cousin to Grandpa, Merton K. Paine**. Merrill remembered being in the house up the road in Belchertown. He told us how run down it was. He also mentioned the narrow winding stair to the second floor. Mary remarked that she never could understand how ladies in wide skirts got themselves up or down those stairs without falling.

POOLE STREET ONCE KNOWN AS BURYING GROUND HILL

The section of Poole St. where the cemetery is located was known as Burying Ground Hill in the old days. According to Merrill, **David was traveling over Burying Ground Hill** coming home from the mill, when he was jolted off his cart and run over by one of the cartwheels. As I mentioned earlier the epitaph on his gravestone indicates this as the cause of his death. There is a picture of David's gravestone in the book by Clara (Paine) Ohler showing the location of the gravestone in a cemetery at Ludlow, Mass. along with a quote of his epitaph.

We had a wonderful, informative day. We hope to return to Ludlow and Belchertown next summer to do more research, and hopefully get in a longer visit with Mary and Merrill Paine.

Sept. 24, 1997

I called Merrill today as I had more questions. Merrill's father, **Herman Chester Paine**, was one of the nine children of Alfred Kingsley and Minnie (Olds) Paine. Herman's wife had Merrill Bailey and Chester Maurice. Merrill's brother Chester M. is retired and lives on the West Coast.

Merrill's uncle, **Maurice Stanley Paine**, (brother of Herman C. Paine) has a daughter, Marilyn, who lives in Florida. Of the nine children only Herman and Maurice had children. Merrill's grandparents, **Alfred Kingsley Paine** and **Minnie (Olds) Paine** are also buried at this cemetery. Reference may be found in the Clara (Paine) Ohler book as to Herman, Maurice and their other siblings.

Our great-great grandfather **David Kingsley Paine** and his wife **Marcia (Fuller) Paine** are both buried at this cemetery also.

DIRECT ANCESTRY BURIED THERE

> David Paine/Abigail Shepard
> Jonathan Paine/Sally (Hayden) Paine
> David K.(Kingsley) Paine/Marcia (Fuller) Paine

The above named are also direct kin of Merrill Bailey Paine of Ludlow.

Also buried there is Herbert N. Paine and Henrietta C. Boutelle, his wife. He was the brother of Alfred K. and Henry A. Paine.

JULY 10, 1998   TO LUDLOW AGAIN

Today Archie and I took our cousin, Bertha (Weed) Duke, who was visiting from Colorado to Massachusetts. Again we picked up our cousin Eleanor (Seibert) Toole in Chicopee, and continued on to Ludlow and Belcherton to visit and try to locate other burial sites of Paine ancestors.

Our first stop was at Ludlow to allow cousin Bertha to walk around the area to see the monuments and headstones of the many relatives buried there. We then proceeded to see our cousin Merrill Bailey Paine who lives nearby. Had a good visit with him and met his son, John. Bertha was pleased to meet them too.

SEARCH FOR FAMILY BURIAL PLACE IN BELCHERTOWN, MA

We then proceeded to Belchertown, MA which is located next door to Ludlow, to ascertain whether or not we could locate the cemetery where **Henry A. Paine** and his wife **Louise (Stockwell) Paine** were buried. We stopped in at the Town Hall there and did some inquiring. They directed us to the Congregational Church that is located right on the green. It was there at **Mount Hope Cemetery** adjacent to the Congregational Church that we were able to locate their monument and headstones. The monument reads as follows:

PAINE
HENRY A. PAINE
1846 – 1919
LOUISE STOCKWELL, HIS WIFE
1848 – 1922

Their headstones read H.A.P. & L.S.P.

Also located there in the same plot were headstones for **Samuel A. Stockwell** (SAS) and for **Achsah Lovina (Presson) Stockwell** (L.A.S.), the parents of **Louise Stockwell Paine**. There are only initials on their stones; no dates of birth or death. Information obtained elsewhere indicates that Belchertown, MA was the place of death for both of them. So, one must assume until learning otherwise that these stones are theirs. **Achsah** also went by her middle name of **Lovina**, and was perhaps better known by that name as her stone's initials are **LAS** rather than **ALS**.

It was both a day of discovery and reunion.

Henry A. Paine and Louise S. Paine Belchertown, just over the line from Ludlow, beyond East Cemetery/Liberty Cemetery.

CHAPTER NINE

THE USS CONSTELLATION

The story told by Great Grandfather, William H. French, relating to his three and a half year adventures aboard *Constellation*, during her period of chasing down slave trading ships along the African coast, is found in the chapter on the French Family. Great Grandfather always labored under the impression that his *Constellation* was cut down from the original *1797 Constellation*.

Related here is the history of this 22 gun sloop-of-war, from her construction in 1854 to her current status.

The original frigate *Constellation* was born in 1797 at Harris Creek in Baltimore's Fells Point, one of six frigates built for the newly established United States Federal Navy. She was designed with a main battery of 38 guns and displaced 1,165 tons with a beam of 41 ft. and a length of 164 ft. 340 officers and men manned her. She differed from the sloop-of-war that succeeded her by having a square transom stern and mounting broadside guns on her upper-most deck. Thoroughly worn out, she was broken-up at the Gosport Navy Yard in Norfolk, Virginia in 1853 at the same time the sloop-of-war was being built.

The present *Constellation* was built as the largest sloop-of-war to that date. Her main battery of guns was mounted on one deck only and was comprised primarily of 8" muzzle loading guns, which fired exploding shells and four 32 pound cannons. She is 176 ft (some reports say 179 ft.) long, with a beam of 42 ft. and displaces 1,400 tons. She was manned by 240 officers and men. Unlike her predecessor, the sloop-of-war's spar deck (upper deck) completely covers the gun deck and ends in a rounded stern which came into fashion at the time. The rounded stern is significantly stronger than the square transom. A period newspaper article states that 8 timbers were taken from the frigate *Constellation* and placed in the new sloop-of-war. At this time the Museum has not found any physical proof to substantiate this story.

The sloop-of-war *Constellation* was designed by John Lenthall and incorporates many innovative features such as complex wrought iron spar fittings and 48 wrought iron water tanks holding 31,000 gallons of drinking water. *Constellation's* two pivot guns were mounted on the bow and stern of the ship. Hinged iron bulwarks folded down allowing the guns to turn and fire. She is the last all-sail powered warship built by the U.S. Navy and has fine lines below the water line, which gave her greater speed than earlier ships. *Constellation* is "ship" rigged: each of her three masts carries square sails with a fore'n aft sail or "spanker" on her mizzenmast. She set 20,000 square feet of sails.

Constellation was the flagship of the eight-ship US African Squadron, 1859 to 1861. She captured three slavers and saved a total of over 700 men, women and children from the defilement of slavery. One of the slavers, *Triton*, was the first naval capture of the War Between the States.
She spent 1862-1864 cruising the Mediterranean showing the flag and protecting American commerce.

After the war she saw various duties, carrying famine relief to Ireland and carrying precious American works of art to the Paris Exposition of 1878. She was used extensively as a training ship for Naval Academy midshipmen. She actively served as flagship for the US Atlantic Fleet (Adm. Royal E Ingersoll) from January-July, 1942.

In 1955, however her luck seemed to have run out. The Navy was preparing to scrap her when a group of determined people managed to have *Constellation's* dilapidated hull delivered to Baltimore in a U.S. Navy floating dry dock. Decommissioned by the Navy, she had been donated to a local non-profit foundation. With little money and no government support it was nearly a decade before she was restored enough to allow the public aboard. She was configured to resemble the 1797 frigate *Constellation* that was built in Baltimore. In 1968 she was installed in her present permanent berth in the Inner Harbor. She became the centerpiece of Baltimore's Inner Harbor, and has served as the crown jewel for the city's historic rebirth.

The height of the pavilions at Harbor place was dictated by the height of her jib boom. Since then over seven million people have crossed her decks and countless more have been photographed with her towering wooden hull as the backdrop.

Years of exposure to water and weather, along with a lack of funds to maintain her, had combined to bring *Constellation* perilously close to disaster. In 1994 her rigging was removed and she was closed to the public. A Navy survey showed her to be in an advanced state of deterioration.

The last surviving ship of the Civil War, everyone thought she'd last forever. So when the National Trust for Historic Preservation placed *U.S.S. Constellation* on their "Eleven Most Endangered List" in 1994, people sat up and took notice.

Baltimore's Mayor Kurt L. Schmoke immediately appointed a Blue Ribbon Committee to Save the *Constellation*. The Board of Directors of the U.S.S. *Constellation* Foundation resigned in favor of the Mayor's Committee. The Committee formed the nucleus of a renewed and renamed *Constellation* Foundation, Inc. with Louis Linden as its Executive Director.

The state of Maryland has committed $3 million dollars to the restoration from state bond proceeds and Mayor Schmoke has supported the effort since the beginning. His fiscal year 1997 budget committed 3 million dollars to the project.

It remains for the Foundation to raise the balance through donations from private businesses, foundations, and individual contributors.

Starting the Restoration
In November 1996, *Constellation* left the Inner Harbor for the first time since 1982 and was escorted down the harbor for 2 1/2 years of repair work at the Fort McHenry Shipyard on Locust Point. Her walking-speed voyage, powered by a tugboat took one hour and 48 minutes. Calm water and light winds allowed her to proceed without serious incident to a wharf in front to the shipyard's Dry Dock No.5. She spent several weeks there, off-loading 250 tons of ballast and 40 years of accumulated maritime junk before entering the dry dock.

Some of the *junk* removed turned out to be a treasure trove of iron fittings such as mast hoops, lifeline stanchions, hammock irons and more, believed to date from the 1850s. Project Engineer Powichroski believed that they were removed and stored below during one or more of several repair periods in the 1960s and 1970s, when the ship was altered in a misguided effort to make her look more like the 1797 frigate. The iron fittings that have emerged from the bilge and the orlop deck were saved. Some were used in the restoration. Others were copied. Those that were not of the proper vintage were not retained. Those included two 18th- century iron cannon and a smaller carronade, which were returned to the Naval Historical Center in Washington, D.C. Other items not authentic were scrapped, sold, or given away.

Twenty men and women tugged her into dry dock, on December 29th. No mean feat, since she had to be pulled in dead center to land perfectly on the pilings built to match her keel once the water drained from the dry-dock basin.

She had been neglected and improperly altered over the years. All of that was changed. Nationally renowned Shipwright G. Peter Boudreau, ship builder and restoration expert and builder of *Baltimore Pride II*, was Chief of *Constellation's* restoration. Her rotten lower planking was replaced with a rigid glued lamination never tried on a ship this big. Gravity is expected to straighten the 27-inch hogging in the ship's 142-year-old keel.

Rebuilding the ship using 19th century methods would have meant discarding seventy percent of the present timbers and planks at a cost of nearly thirty-five million. Mr. Boudreau used space-age lamination to make her healthy and watertight again for a quarter of that cost. The same technique was used on the gun deck. The ancient live-oak timbers stayed in place. More than just providing an antique atmosphere, the cold molded laminate process that was used to strengthen the hull saved the majority of the ship's remaining timbers. At this time, the ship possesses approximately 45-48% of its original 1854 historic fabric. As long as the laminate shell is maintained, this percentage should not decline. This is a remarkably high level of preservation relative to USS *Constitution* which is less that 20% original fabric. The laminate also helps the ship's curators explain the materials and technologies employed by the Gosport Naval Shipyard in Portsmouth, VA where *Constellation* was built.

If the hull and gun deck were completed by early 1998, Boudreau hoped to re-float the ship and move her to another site in the harbor. There, he would use conventional materials and techniques to complete the hull above the gun deck, build a new spar deck and add new masts and rigging.

The ship came out of the yard in 1999, looking just as she did in 1854, and without the hodge-podge of add-ons, alterations, and naval modernization's that occurred in the 20th century. Constellation Foundation, Inc. moved the ship back to the Inner Harbor in 1999.

John Wagner, president of Pacific Western Timbers Inc. was instrumental in finding a Douglas fir in the State of Washington, which was used, for deteriorated timbers on the ship's hull. The tree was an odd looking monster Douglas fir that perhaps because of its ungainly appearance, had sidestepped a near century of harvest. Its top had blown off long ago and a single fat branch reached skyward like a forgotten crippled sentry.

A crew of loggers employed by Crown Pacific Ltd. cut it from a stand of Crown's trees on Bear Creek that looked like toothpicks in comparison. Removing it took two and a half days and two logging trucks. Loggers sliced it down the center and loaded each half on the extendible back ends of the trucks.

Lumberyards don't stock what the ship required. Restoration teams searched worldwide to replace its ancient timbers and planks according to Lou Linden, then Executive Director, of *Constellation* Foundation, Inc. He said the Douglas fir tree was the real thing.

"The foundation is looking at preserving *Constellation* for the next 100 years and one of the ways you do that", he said, "is by finding the best wood possible." The ancient log, which some think was over two thousand years old, was milled into pieces 6 1/2 inches thick, 14 inches wide and 60 to 90 feet long.

Mr. Wagner who has gained a reputation for sleuthing special timbers, was also instrumental in supplying materials for the restoration of *U.S.S. Constitution*. He admits hurdles to meeting these kinds of orders since few huge trees remain. And current conditions place federal forest off limits. He seeks trees like Crown's, long ignored because of a blatant defect or so out of reach that harvest is too costly.

Mr. Linden said the restoration crews also used tropical woods from Guyana, custom laminate from domestic white oak for the beams and frames and tapped many other sources to replicate the original. The ships were originally built in a different era, one of huge, plentiful trees. Even the East Coast had a ready selection of massive live oak. Shipwrights designed their ships around the availability, one that no longer exists.

"For those of us who build and preserve ships, there's a certain ambivalence in taking a tree that's been growing since Columbus landed," Linden said. "But I can't think of a more noble purpose."

Funding for the Restoration
Coins were minted and are for sale to raise funds toward the cost of the restoration. The survey that ultimately confirmed the ship's identity was completed in 1991. Entitled *Fouled Anchors,* it was authored by Dana Wegner of the US Navy's David Taylor Research Center.

Peter Boudreau, restoration project manager stated that the survey was conducted with laser beams that compared the surface of the hull to the design drawn in 1853 by John Lenthall, the Navy's chief engineer, or constructor as he was then called. It was a perfect match. "It's the same ship. End of story," said Louis F. Linden, the foundation's executive director. "It's the first time she's been measured and compared."

The year, 1854, is emblazoned on the newly minted *Constellation* coin that was placed in the Knee (a support block) of the ship's stem, the forward post of the keel, July 29, 1997. Placed along side it was a Baltimore bicentennial coin and an 1854 half-dollar. One after the other, the coins were ceremoniously sealed into the bow at the cutwater.

Beyond observing a seafaring ritual meant to pay the way for drowned sailors across the mythical Underworld River Styx, the *Constellation* coin also has practical purposes. It is hoped that the coins will help to raise another $1 million dollars for the restoration. They will also serve as a lifetime pass to the ship.

Quoting Margherita Desy, former curator of USS Constitution Museum in Boston, "*Constellation* has a lot more of her undisturbed, as far as structure goes, than *Constitution. Constitution* was first. However, *Constellation* is the last of the old sailing navy. That in itself is important and for that reason she should be preserved and remembered".

On August 22, 1998, I traveled to Baltimore, Maryland with my brother, Archie W. Paine and my son, John J. Martinoli to see *Constellation* refloated from dry dock, her hull beautifully restored, making her seaworthy once more. Her mast must be stepped at another location as there is not enough room in dry-dock for the height needed.

It was an eventful day with sailors in old time dress singing sea shanties of the days of yore. Watching the crews move *Constellation* out onto the water was an experience, as they walked her out of the dock manning the hawsers along side her.

She was finally ready July 2, 1999 and returned to Baltimore's inner harbor. *Constellation* is the centerpiece of the USS Constellation Museum in Baltimore, MD

I was able to pay another visit to her in May of 2001, when I accompanied my daughter Jill and her husband Joe to Maryland for my granddaughter Meegan's commencement from Johns Hopkins. Christopher Rowsom, Executive Director of the USS Constellation Museum escorted us on a tour of *Constellation*. She has come a long way since I last visited her in 1998.

The plans now are for getting her furnished in a manner conforming to the days when she was sailing. The museum is searching for furniture of the period to purchase. Where that fails, replicas will be built.

Constellation celebrated her 150th Anniversary in 2004. On June 30, 2004 the US Postal Service unveiled a commemorative stamp that would be in circulation for one year.

Our great-grandfather, William H. French has his picture displayed in the Ship's Store alongside his remarks about his time aboard ship.

His picture and some of those remarks can also be found in two histories of *Constellation*.

The first book was written by Glenn F. Williams, and is entitled:

USS Constellation
A Short History of the Last All-Sail Warship Built by the U. S. Navy

Until recently Glen was Curator of the museum.

The second book was authored by Stephen R. Bockmuller and Lawrence J. Bopp and is entitled:

USS Constellation
An Illustrated History

Their book is a part of "The Civil War History Series."

Both books are beautifully illustrated and would be of great interest to us, his ancestors.

Anyone wanting more information on the **Museum** or the **Ship's Store** can reach them by
E-mail at www.constellation.org

or by writing them at:

USS Constellation Museum
Pier l, 301 East Pratt St.,
Baltimore, MD 21202-3134.

Addendum to **CHAPTER ON *CONSTELLATION***

I have recently been apprised of a wonderful journal donated to the USS Constellation Museum, by Paul Sweeney, the great grandson of William Ambrose Leonard. This journal was kept by William Leonard during his sojourn aboard the Constellation during her deployment patrolling the African Coast. Constellation was the Flag Ship of an eight-ship US African Squadron, 1859-1861. Their orders were to prevent slave ships from bringing any more human beings to be sold as slaves in America and other parts of the world. I received copies of several pages of the journal which mention our Great Grandfather, Wm. H. French.

It seems obvious that Mr. Leonard and Mr. French became quite good friends. Mr. Leonard tells of serving on the Captain's Gig with Great Grandfather French and four other crewmen. He names the six men who served as crew, their names, ages and weights as well as where they hailed from. He wrote of Great Grandfather, "Wm H French, a native of Philadelphia, Penn he is 25 years of age height 5 feet 6 inches and weighs 137 lbs." He says of himself, "Wm. A. Leonard, a native of Boston, Mass in height 5 feet 3 inches, weight 134 lbs, 23 years of age. I am the bowman" He goes on to say "The boat is a 12 oared boat but we only pull 6 oars, we pull single bank, a long side stroke, the oars being 17 feet long, the captain likes his boats crew, he gets us out of many a scrape." (Pages 302 and 303 of William Leonard's Journal)

Mr. Leonard also tells in his journal of the many dramas and musicals they performed aboard ship to the amusement of the crew and visitors from other ships and sometimes folks from the towns near where they anchored. Their performances were well received and certainly helped to relieve the boredom of patrolling day after day. Great Grandfather French and Mr. Leonard were actors in many of these skits, at times playing the parts of women, as there were obviously no females aboard ship in those days. Great Grandfather also performed in the minstrels, playing a banjo as well singing. (And I imagine doing some dancing too. According to his interviews in later years he really enjoyed entertaining.)

I hope one of these days that Mr. Sweeney or possibly the Constellation Museum can make available a copy of Mr. Leonard's entire journal for purchase. I'm sure we as ancestors of Wm. H. French would be very interested in obtaining a copy for our own records.

The History Channel aired a film on Feb. 10th, 2007 entitled "USS CONSTELLATION: Battling for Freedom" Mr. Leonard's journal was quoted quite extensively. It is the only personal journal that has ever come to light for that period of time in Constellation's history and is certainly a most wonderful addition to the Constellation Museum archives. The film was produced by **Indigo Films** of San Rafael, CA

The film also quoted our Great Grandfather William H. French's remarks made to the Springfield Daily Republican in an interview Sept. 16, 1924 entitled "Chasing Slavers with Old Wooden Navy" featuring his service on the "Constellation" suppressing slave trade off the African Coast.

On Saturday August 25, 2007 I had the pleasure of attending a Descendant Reunion aboard *Constellation* at the Inner Harbor in Baltimore, MD with my son Edward and his wife Carol. We were privileged to meet Paul Sweeney and his wife Kathe as well as Frederick Stam and his wife Barbara descendants of James Thompson who sailed aboard *Constellation* during the same time period. My cousin Dorothy (August) St. Pierre and her son Barry, his wife Sissy, her daughter Deborah Asaro and her husband Tony also attended.

CHAPTER TEN
THE CENSUS

Census reports were handwritten and subject to interpretation. Therefore sometimes spellings of names were misconstrued. The following are records I have located for **Paine Census Reports**. **Unless otherwise specified these are Direct Ancestors of Merton K. Paine, Ella Gordon (French) and their Descendants.**

PAINE FAMILY

1790 CENSUS
Paine, David (Gen. V, No. 94)
Son of Moses & Abigail (Adams) Paine
Page 53 & 60 of Paine Shepard Genealogy

Wife: Abigail Shepard
Home: Ludlow, MA (Hampden County)

Lists:
Free white males of 16 years and upward	2
Free white males under 16 years	3
Free white females (no age specified)	2

1800 CENSUS
Paine, David (Gen.V, No. 94)

Wife: Abigail Shepard
Page 53 & 60 of Paine Shepard Genealogy
Home: Ludlow, MA (Hampden County)

Lists:
Free white males of 16 to 26	2
Free white males of 45 and upward including heads of households	1
Free white females under 10 years	1
Free white females of 26 and under 45	1
Free white females of 45 and upwards	1

Note:
David Paine baptized 1737/8 at Braintree, MA died July 2, 1807 at Ludlow, MA

1840 CENSUS
Paine, Jonathan (Gen. VI, No. 112)
Son of David & Abigail (Shepard) Paine
Page 60 of Paine Shepard Genealogy

Wife: Sally Hayden
Home: Ludlow, Hampden, MA

Lists

Males in Household under 30		2
	under 60	1
Females	under 10	1
	under 15	2
	under 30	1
	under 60	1

Beginning in 1850, the Census began to list members of the household by name rather than just numbers in a certain age group.

1850 CENSUS
Paine, Jonathan (Gen. VI,No.112)
  Son of David & Abigail)Shepard) Paine
  Page 60 of Paine Shepard Genealogy
                Age 67 **Birthplace**: MA
                Farmer
Wife: Sally Hayden
                Born **Birthplace**: MA
Home: Ludlow, Hampden, MA

Children at Home

Louisa	Age 35
Sarah	Age 23
Harriet	Age 19
Caroline	Age 17

1850 CENSUS
Paine, David R. (Gen. VII, No 742) (Initial should be K for Kingsley)
  Son of Jonathan & Sally (Hayden) Paine
  Page 74 of the Paine Shepard Genealogy
                Age 33 **Birthplace**: MA
                Carpenter
Wife: Marcia A. Fuller
                Age 28 **Birthplace**: MA
Home: Ludlow, Hampden, MA

Child At Home
Henry A   Age 4 **Birthplace**: MA

Also listed with David's family
Daniels, Olds   Age 66 Farmer (probably hired hand)

Author's Note: Maiden names are given where known. Found in Paine-Shepard Genealogy. Census only lists them by married name.

1850 CENSUS
Paine, Chester (Gen. VII, No143)   <u>**Brother to David Kingsley Paine**</u>
  Son of Jonathan & Sally (Hayden) Paine
  Page 74 of the Paine Shepard Genealogy
              Age 31 **Birthplace**: MA
              Farmer
Wife: Hannah Whittemore
              Age 30 **Birthplace**: MA **(Act. Birth Aug.24,1823)**
<u>**Home: Ludlow, Hampden, MA**</u>

<u>Child at Home</u>
Rosetta E   Age 7 **Birthplace**: MA

1860 CENSUS
Paine, Jonathan (Gen. VI, No 112)
  Son of David & Abigail (Shepard) Paine
  Page No. 60 of the Paine Shepard Genealogy
              Age 76 **Birthplace**: MA
              Farmer
Wife: Sally Hayden
              Age 68 **Birthplace**: MA
<u>**Home: Ludlow, Hampden, MA**</u>

1860 CENSUS
Paine, David K (Gen.VII, No 142)
  Son of Jonathan & Sally (Hayden) Paine
  Page 74 of the Paine Shepard Genealogy
              Age 43 **Birthplace**: MA
              Farmer
Wife: Marcia A. Fuller
              Age 36 **Birthplace**: MA
<u>**Home: Ludlow, Hampden, MA**</u>

<u>Children at Home</u>
Henry A.   Age 14 **Birthplace**: MA
Alice A.   Age 9 **Birthplace**: MA
Herbert N.   Age 7 **Birthplace**: MA
Alfred K.   Age 4 **Birthplace**: MA

1860 CENSUS
Paine, Chester (Gen. VII, No 143)   **Brother to David Kingsley Paine**
  Son of Jonathan & Sally (Hayden) Paine
  Page 74 of the Paine Shepard Genealogy
              Age 41 **Birthplac**e: MA
              Farmer
Wife: Hannah Whittemore
              Age 40 **Birthplace**: MA
<u>**Home: Ludlow, Hampden, MA**</u>

<u>Children at Home</u>
Elvine   Age 17 **Birthplace**: MA

I believe **Elvine is Rosetta E.** listed in the 1850 census as 7 years old.
Found her in Paine Shepard Gen listed as R. Elvira b. Jan 29, 1843 p .91

Hannah L.   Age 1 born abt 1859 **Birthplace**: MA

Author's Note: In looking at the original handwritten census for 1860 it appears that Jonathan along with sons David K. and Chester resided on the same street next door to one another, perhaps all running the farm?

<u>**1870 CENSUS**</u>
Paine, Jonathan (Gen. VI, No 112)
  Son of David & Abigail (Shepard) Paine
  Page 60 of the Paine Shepard Genealogy
                    Age 86 **Birthplace**: MA
                    No Occupation
Housekeeper: Harriet Alexander
                    Age 39 **Birthplace**: MA
<u>**Home: Ludlow, Hampden, MA**</u>

<u>**1870 CENSUS**</u>
Paine, David K. (Gen. VII, No. 142)
  Son of Jonathan & Sally (Hayden) Paine
  Page 142 of the Paine Shepard Genealogy
                    Age 53 **Birthplace**: MA
                    Farmer
Wife: Marcia Fuller
                    Age 47 **Birthplace**: MA
<u>**Home: Ludlow, Hampden, MA**</u>

<u>Children at Home</u>
Alice A.   Age 19 **Birthplace**: MA
Herbert N   Age 17 **Birthplace**: MA
Alfred K.   Age 14 **Birthplace**: MA
Isabell T.   Age 8 **Birthplace**: MA

<u>**1870 CENSUS**</u>
Paine, Henry A. (Gen. VIII, No. 223)
  Son of David K. & Marcia (Fuller) Paine
  Page 91 of the Paine Shepard Genealogy
                    Age 24 Birthplace: MA
                    Farmer
Wife: Louisa L. (Stockwell)
                    Age 21 Birthplace: MA
<u>**Home: Belchertown, Hampshire, MA**</u>

1870 CENSUS
Paine, Chester (Gen. VII (Gen. VII, No. 143)   **Brother of David Kingsley Paine**
  Son of Jonathan & Sally (Hayden) Paine
  Page 74 of the Paine Shepard Genealogy
                    Age 51 **Birthplace:** MA
                    Farmer
Wife: Hannah Whittemore
                    Age 50 **Birthplace**: MA
Home Ludlow, Hampden, MA

1870 CENSUS
Rhodes, George D.
                    Age 25 **Birthplace**: MA
                    Farm Laborer
Wife: Rosetta E. Paine (Gen. VIII, No. 228)
  Daughter of Chester & Hannah (Whittemore) Paine
  Page 91 of the Paine Shepard Genealogy
                    Age 27 **Birthplace**: MA
Sister: Hannah L. Paine (Gen. VII, No 229)   **Sister of Rosetta E.**
                    Age 11 **Birthplace**: MA
Home: Ludlow, Hampden, MA

Child at Home
Martha A.   Age 4 mos. **Birthplace**: MA

1880 CENSUS
Paine, David K. (Gen. VII, No. 142)
  Son of Jonathan & Sally (Hayden) Paine
  Page 74 Paine Shepard Genealogy
                    Age 63 **Birthplace**: MA
                    Farmer
Wife: Marcia Fuller
                    Age 56 **Birthplace**: MA
Home: Ludlow, Hampden, MA

Children at Home
Herbert N.   Age 27 **Birthplace**: MA
Alfred J.   Age 24 **Birthplace**: MA
Arabell T.   Age 18 **Birthplace**: MA

1880 CENSUS
Paine, Henry A. (Gen. VIII, No. 223)
                    Age 34 **Birthplace**: MA
                    Farmer
Wife: Louise L. (Stockwell)
                    Age 31 **Birthplace**: MA
Home: Belchertown, Hampshire, MA

Children at Home

Marton K.	Age 9 **Birthplace**: MA (correct spelling of name Merton)	
George A.	Age 7 **Birthplace**: MA	
Herbert D.	Age 4 **Birthplace**: MA	

1880 CENSUS
George D. Rhodes

Age 35 **Birthplace**: MA
Boarding House Owner

Wife: Rosetta (Gen. VIII, No 228)
 Daughter of Chester & Hannah (Whittemore) Paine
 Page 91 of the Paine Shepard Genealogy

Age 36 **Birthplace**: MA

Home: Belchertown, Hampshire, MA

Children at Home

Martha A.	Age 10 **Birthplace**: MA
Albert C.	Age 6 **Birthplace**: MA

1890 CENSUS Nothing.
**The 1890 census records were destroyed by a fire in DC and only spotty records exist in various states.

1900 CENSUS
Paine, Henry A. (Gen. VIII, No. 223)
 Son of David K. & Marcia (Fuller) Paine
 Page 91 of the Paine Shepard Genealogy

Age 54 **Birthplace**: MA
Farmer

Wife: Louise Stockwell

Age 51 **Birthplace**: MA

Home: Belchertown, Hampshire, MA

Census also lists four children ages 6 through 22 as boarders.

1900 CENSUS
Paine, Marton K. (Gen. X, No 407)
 Son of Henry A. & Louise (Stockwell) Paine
 Page 117 of the Paine Shepard Genealogy

Age 29 **Birthplace**: MA

Wife: Ella G. French

Age 31 **Birthplace:** District of Columbia

Home: Westfield, Hampden, MA

Paine, Herbert D. Gen X, No 408).   **Brother of Merton K.**

Age 24 **Birthplace**: MA

Children at Home

Mildred L.	Age 8 **Birthplace**: MA
Irving A.	Age 4 Birthplace: MA
Madeline	Age 5 mos. **Birthplace**: MA

1900 CENSUS
Paine, Herbert (Gen. VIII, No 225)   **Brother of Henry A. Paine**
  Son of David K. & Marcia (Fuller) Paine
  Page 91 of the Paine Shepard Genealogy
                Age 47 **Birthplace**: MA
                Gave no occupation
Wife: Henrietta C. Boutelle
                Age 45 **Birthplace**: CT
Home: Ludlow, Hampden, MA

Children at Home

Arthur G.	Age 17	**Birthplace**: MA
Emma L.	Age 13	**Birthplace**: MA
Blanche A.	Age 9	**Birthplace**: MA
Albert H.	Age 7	**Birthplace**: MA
Archer M.	Age 7	**Birthplace**: MA
Warren D.	Age 1	**Birthplace**: MA

Border: Mary E. Norton   Age 46 **Birthplace**: MA

1900 CENSUS
Paine, Alfred (Gen. VIII, No. 226)   **Brother of Henry A. Paine**
  Son of David K. & Marcia (Fuller) Paine
  Page 91 of the Paine Shepard Genealogy
                Age 44 **Birthplace**: MA
                Farmer
Wife: Minnie E. Olds
                Age 35 **Birthplace**: MA
Home: Ludlow, Hampden, MA

Children at Home

Ralph D.	Age 11	**Birthplace**: MA
Ernest N	Age 8	**Birthplace**: MA
Lora M.	Age 6	**Birthplace**: MA
Herman C	Age 4	**Birthplace**: MA
Olive G.	Age 3	**Birthplace**: MA
Walter E.	Age 8 mos.	**Birthplace**: MA

Mother: Marcia A. (Fuller) Paine
                Age 75 **Birthplace**: MA
David Kingsley Paine, husband of Marcia, passed away Dec. 16, 1886

1910 CENSUS
Paine, Henry D. (Gen. VIII, No. 223) Middle **initial should be A**
  Son of David K. & Marcia (Fuller) Paine
  Page 91 of the Paine Shepard Genealogy
                Age 64 **Birthplace**: MA
                Farmer
Wife: Louise Stockwell
                Age 62 **Birthplace**: MA

Home: Belchertown, Hampshire, MA
Child at Home

Herbert D.	Age 34 Birthplace: MA

Note: Census also listed 2 Foster children

1910 CENSUS
Paine, Merton K. (Gen. IX, No. 407)
  Son of Henry A. & Louise (Stockwell) Paine
  Page 117 of the Paine Shepard Genealogy
                Age 38 born **Birthplace**: MA
                Farmer
Wife: Ella G. (French)
                Age 41 **Birthplace**: Washington, DC

Home: Simsbury, Hartford, CT

Children at Home

Mildred L	Age 18 **Birthplace**: MA
Albert E.	Age 14 **Birthplace**: MA
Madelaine (sp.)	Age 10 **Birthplace**: MA
Mable (sp)	Age 7 **Birthplace**: CT
Mattie	Age 7 **Birthplace**: CT
Archie	Age 5 **Birthplace**: CT

1910 CENSUS
Paine, Herbert (Gen. VIII, No. 225)   **Brother of Henry A. Paine**
  Son of David K. & Marcia (Fuller) Paine
  Page 91 of the Paine Shepard Genealogy
                Age 56 **Birthplace**: MA
                Farmer
Wife: Hattie (Henrietta) Boutelle
                Age 54 **Birthplace**: MA

Home: Ludlow, Hampden, MA

Children at Home

Anna E	Age 23 **Birthplace**: MA
Albert H.	Age 17 **Birthplace**: MA
Archer M.	Age 17 **Birthplace**: MA
Warren D.	Age 11 **Birthplace**: MA

Mother-in-Law: Johanna Boutilte (Bontelle) Actual last name is **Boutelle**

1910 CENSUS
Paine, Alfred K. (Gen. VIII, No. 226)   **Brother of Henry A. Paine**
  Son of David Kingsley & Marcia (Fuller) Paine
  Page 91 of the Paine Shepard Genealogy
                Age 55 **Birthplace**: MA
                Farmer

Wife: Minnie Olds
                Age 46 **Birthplace**: MA

Home: Ludlow, Hampden, MA

Children at Home

Ralph D.	Age 21	**Birthplace**: MA
Ernest	Age 19	**Birthplace**: MA
Herman	Age 14	**Birthplace**: MA
Olive	Age 13	**Birthplace**: MA
Walter	Age 10	**Birthplace**: MA
Alice	Age 8	**Birthplace**: MA
Milton	Age 5	**Birthplace**: MA
Morris	Age 1	**Birthplace**: MA

1920 CENSUS
Paine, Alfred (Gen. VIII, No. 226)   **Brother of Henry A. Paine**
  Son of David Kingsley & Marcia (Fuller) Paine
  Page 91 of the Paine Shepard Genealogy
                Age 64 **Birthplace**: MA

Wife: Minnie Olds
                Age 55 **Birthplace**: MA

Home: Ludlow, Hampden, MA

Children at Home

Ernest	Age 29	**Birthplace**: MA
Herman	Age 24	**Birthplace**: MA
Alice	Age 18	**Birthplace**: MA
Milton	Age 15	**Birthplace**: MA

1920 CENSUS
Paine, Murton (Marton) (Should be **Merton) (Gen IX, No. 407)**
  Son of Henry A. & Louise (Stockwell) Paine
  Page 117 of the Paine Shepard Genealogy
                Age 49 **Birthplace**: MA
                Farmer

Wife: Ella G. French
                Age 51 Birthplace: Washington (D. C.)

Home: Sinsbury(sp), Hartford, CT

Children at Home

Madaline (sp)	Age 20	**Birthplace**: MA
Mabel	Age 16	**Birthplace**: CT
Mattie	Age 16	**Birthplace**: CT
Archie	Age 14	**Birthplace**: CT

1920 CENSUS
Paine, Herbert D. (Gen. IX, No. 408)   **Brother of Merton K. Paine**
  Son of Henry A. & Louise (Stockwell) Paine
  Page 117 of the Paine Shepard Genealogy
                        Age 43 **Birthplace**: MA
                        Farmer
Wife: Harriet J. Alexander
                        Age 26 **Birthplace**: MA
Home: Enfield, Hampshire, MA

Child at Home
Harriet M.   Age 2 yrs 11 mos. **Birthplace**: MA

Mother: Louise Stockwell.
                        Age 71 **Birthplace**: MA
Henry A. Paine, husband of Louise, died **Jan 13, 1919**

Mother-in-Law: Martha J. Alexander
                        Age 64 **Birthplace**: MA

1920 CENSUS
Paine, Albert H. (Gen. Vol. No. 418)   **Cousin of Merton K. Paine**
  Son of Herbert N. & Henrietta (Boutelle) Paine
  Page 118 of the Paine Shepard Genealogy
                        Age 27 **Birthplace**: MA
                        Farmer
Home: Ludlow, Hampden, MA

Others in Household
Anher M.   Age 27 **Birthplace**: MA   **Albert's Twin Brother**
  (Name should be Archer)
Emma L.   Age 33 **Birthplace**: MA

1920 CENSUS
Ferdinand August
                        Age 27 **Birthplace**: CT
                        Farmer
Wife: Mildred Paine (Gen. X, No 626)
  Daughter of Merton K. & Ella G. (French) Paine
  Page 156 of the Paine Shepard Genealogy
                        Age 28 **Birthplace**: MA
Home: Sinsbury, Hartford, CT   (Simsbury)

Children at Home
Ferdinand   Age 2 **Birthplace** CT
Albert   Age 1 **Birthplace**: CT
Dorothy   Age 1 mo. **Birthplace**: CT

1930 CENSUS
Paine, Alfred R (should be K)   **Brother of Henry A. Paine**
  Son of David K. & Marcia (Fuller) Paine   **Uncle of Merton K. Paine**
  Page 91 of the Paine Shepard Genealogy
                    Age 74 **Birthplace**: MA
                    Farmer
Wife: Minnie Olds
                    Age 65 **Birthplace**: MA
Home: Ludlow, Hampden, MA

Children at Home
Ernest   Age 38 **Birthplace**: MA
Alice Allen   Age 28 **Birthplace**: MA

Son-in-Law: Arthur L. Allen
                    Age 28 **Birthplace**: MA
                    Gardener

1930 CENSUS
Paine, Herman C. (Gen. IX, No. 423)
  Son of Alfred K. & Minnie (Olds) Paine   **Cousin of Merton K. Paine**
  Page 118 of the Paine Shepard Genealogy
Wife: Olive A
                    Age 31 **Birthplace**: MA
Home: Ludlow, Hampden, MA

Children at Home
Chester M.   Age 7 **Birthplace**: MA   **First Cousins once removed of**
Merrill B.   Age 6 **Birthplace**: MA   **Merton K. Paine**

Author's Note: <u>Merrill B. Paine</u> still lives on Paine Ave in Ludlow with his wife, Mary, on part of the large property once owned by the Paine Family. They still pasture cattle there. There is more information on the family in the Chapter on Cemeteries, which is where I met him and his wife when Nancy, Archie and I visited there in Sept 1997 with our cousin Eleanor Toole.

1930 CENSUS
Paine, Archer M. (Gen. IX, No. 417)   **Cousin of Merton K. Paine**
  Son of Herbert N. & Henrietta (Boutelle) Paine
  Page 118 of the Paine Shepard Genealogy
                    Age 37 **Birthplace**: MA
                    Farmer
Wife: Florence
                    Age 26 **Birthplace**: MA
Home: Ludlow, Hampden, MA

Child at Home
Madeleine F.   Age 2 **Birthplace**: MA

1930 CENSUS
Paine, Albert (Gen. IX, No. 418)   **Cousin of Merton K. Paine**
  Son of Herbert N. & Henrietta (Boutelle) Pain
  Page 118 of the Paine Shepard Genealogy
                    Age 37 **Birthplace**: MA
                    Farmer
Wife: Minnie
                Age 32
Home: Ludlow, Hampden, MA

Child at Home
Ruth   Age 3 11/12 **Birthplace**: MA

1930 CENSUS
Paine, Herbert B (D) (Gen. IX, No. 408)   **Brother of Merton K. Paine**
  Son of Henry A. & Louise (Stockwell) Paine
  Page 117 of the Paine Shepard Genealogy
                    Age 54 **Birthplace**: MA
                    Grocer
Wife: Harriet J. Alexander
                Age 37 **Birthplace**: MA
Home: Enfield, Hapshire, MA

Children at Home
Harriet M.   Age 13 **Birthplace:** MA
Dorathy M.   Age 7 **Birthplace**: MA (Probably Dorothy)
Herbert B   Age 2 yr 2 mos. **Birthplace**: MA

Mother-in-Law: Marta Alexander   Age 72 **Birthplace**: MA

1930 CENSUS
Paine, Merton (Gen IX, No. 407)
  Son of Henry A. & Louise (Stockwell) Paine
  Page 117 of the Paine Shepard Genealogy
                    Age 59 **Birthplace**: MA
Wife: Ella G. French
                Age 61 **Birthplace**: District of Columbia
Home: Simsbury, Hartford, CT

Border: Danforth, Alfred   Age 13 **Birthplace**: Connecticut

CENSUS OF MARRIED CHILDREN OF MERTON K. & ELLA G. (FRENCH) PAINE

1930 CENSUS
Paine, Albert I. (Gen. X, No. 628)
  Son of Merton K. & Ella G. (French) Paine
  Page 156 of the Paine Shepard Genealogy
                        Age 34 **Birthplace**: MA
                        Farmer
Wife: Mary Hadsell
                        Age 31 **Birthplace**: CT
Home: Simsbury, Hartford, CT

Children at Home
Arthur   Age 7 **Birthplace**: CT
Donald   Age 2 & 10/12 **Birthplace**: CT
Gladys   Age 1 & 4/12   **Birthplace**: MA

1930 CENSUS
Seibert, Harry K.
                        Age 28 **Birthplace**: CT
Wife: Madeline Paine
  Daughter of Merton K. & Ella G. (French) Paine
  Page 156 of the Paine Shepard Genealogy
                        Age 30 **Birthplace**: CT (Actual place of birth Westfield, MA)
Home: Cheshire, New Haven, CT

Children at Home
Elenor (sp)   Age 8 **Birthplace**: CT
Leonard   Age 5 **Birthplace**: CT
William   Age 3 **Birthplace**: CT
Merton   Age 1 **Birthplace**: CT

AUTHOR'S NOTE: In the **1920 census** I located a **William J. & Mabel (Jones) Seibert** living in Sinsbury (sp) CT with a son **Harry** age 15. I think this may have been Harry's parents, although there is an age difference.

1930 CENSUS
Weed, William
   Age 25 **Birthplace**: CT
 Wife: Mattie Paine (Gen. X, No. 630)
   Daughter of Merton K. & Ella G. (French) Paine
   Page 156 of the Paine Shepard Genealogy
                        Age 26 **Birthplace**: CT
Home: Bethel, Fairfield, CT

Children at Home
Bertha M.   Age 1   **Birthplace**: CT
Lois M.   Age 4 mos. **Birthplace**: CT

1930 CENSUS
Glazier, Dimock   Age 33 **Birthplace**: CT
Wife: Mabel Paine (Gen. X, No. 631)
   Daughter of Merton K. & Ella G. (French) Paine
   Page 156 of the Paine Shepard Genealogy
               Age 26 **Birthplace**: CT
Note: on the printout of Mabel's page of the census her age shows as 34 and est. birth 1896 However, in viewing the original handwritten census sheet her age shows as 26. This age is correct as the she and Mattie were twins born in 1903.

Home: Simsbury, Hartford, CT

Children at Home
Sherley (sp.)   Age 3 **Birthplace**: CT
Dimock, Jr.   Age 2 **Birthplace**: CT

1930 CENSUS
Paine, Archie (Gen. X, No. 632)
   Son of Merton K. & Ella G. (French) Paine
   Page 156 of the Paine Shepard Genealogy
               Age **25 Birthplace**: CT
               Patrolman
Wife: Eldora Stoutenburgh
               Age 32 **Birthplace**: NY
Home: Simsbury, Hartford, CT

Child at Home
Beverly   Age 1 3/12ths **Birthplace**: CT

FRENCH FAMILY

1850 CENSUS
French, John (Gen. l, No.1)
               Age 49 **Birthplace**: England
               Shoemaker
Wife: Sara French
               Age 50 Birthplace: England
Home: Philadelphia South Mulberry Ward, Philadelphia, PA

Children at Home
Ethelinda   Age 28 **Birthplace:** England
Charissa W.   Age 18 **Birthplace:** England   (sp. Shld. Be Clarissa)
Thomas J.   Age 16 **Birthplace:** Philadelphia
               (believe he was born in Lansingburgh, NY)
William Henry   Age 14 **Birthplace:** New Jersey
Sarah Elizabeth   Age 8 **Birthplace:** Philadelphia, PA
John Edward   Age 5 **Birthplace:** Philadelphia, PA

1870 CENSUS
French, Frederic(k) (Gen. II, No. 2)
Age 50 **Birthplace:** England
Bootmaker
Wife: Abigail French Age 59 **Birthplace: MA**
Home: Boston Ward 11, Suffolk, Massachusetts

French, John (Gen. II, No 11)   **Believe he was brother to William H.**
Age 25 **Birthplace: PA**

Children of Frederic(k) & Abigail French
Clara   Age 22 **Birthplace:** PA
Joseph B   Age 16 **Birthplace:** MA

Also listed in household
Lydia L. Craft   Age 22 **Birthplace:** New Brunswick
Dressmaker

1880 CENSUS
French, Frederick   Age 60 **Birthplac**e: England
Boat Cutter (Believe this was Boot Cutter)
Wife: Abigal French (Abigail)
Age 69 **Birthplace**: MA
Home: Boston, Suffolk, MA

Child of Frederick & Abigail French
Clarasin   Age 32 **Birthplace**: MA
Cook Cutter (Believe this might be Book Cutter)
1870 Census listed her as Clara and as being born in PA
See original hand written Census for 1880

1880 CENSUS
French, William H. (Gen. II, No. 9)
Age 43 **Birthplace:** New Jersey
Merchant/Grocery
Wife: Mary H. French
Age 41 **Birthplace:** West Virginia
Home: Jefferson County, Bolivar Mag. Dist., West Virginia

Children at Home
Wilberta Fryer   Age 18 **Birthplace:** West Virginia-Stepdaughter
(believe she was born in Richmond, VA)
Thomas J.   Age 14 **Birthplace:** Washington, DC
Ella G.   Age 12 **Birthplace:** Washington, DC
Alice L.   Age 11 **Birthplace:** Nebraska
George W.   Age 9 **Birthplace:** Washington, DC
Clara   Age 7 **Birthplace:** Washington, DC
Julia   Age 4 **Birthplace:** West Virginia

1890 CENSUS unavailable due to fire in Washington, DC

1900 CENSUS
French, William H.   Age 63 **Birthplace:** New Jersey

Wife: Mary H. French
                Age 61 **Birthplace:** West Virginia
Home: Springfield, Ward 4, Hamden County, Mass.

Children at Home
Julia R. (French) Waterman
                Age23 **Birthplace:** West Virginia
William H. Waterman
                Age 21 **Birthplace: MA**
                Son-in-Law
Avis Waterman   Age 5/12ths yr. **Birthplace: MA**
                Niece

1910 CENSUS
French, William
                Age 73 **Birthplace**: New Jersey
Home: Simsbury, Hartford County, CT

Keith, Mary   Age 67
                Widowed
Keith, James   Age 13
                Son of Mary
Apparently housekeeping and boarding with **William French**.

1920 CENSUS
French, William   Age 83 **Birthplace:** New Jersey
                Lodger
Home: Springfield Ward 3, Hamden, MA

Author's Note: Whoever interpreted the last name spelled it Frerick. Handwritten census is pretty clearly French

Did not find William in 1930 Census. He was living with Merton K. & his daughter, Ella G. Paine on Bushy Hill Rd., in Simsbury, CT when he passed away January 7, 1932

DUGAN FAMILY

1840 Census
Dugan, George

Wife: Rebecca Dugan
Home: Harpers Ferry, VA (Jefferson County)

Lists:
Free White Male over 20 and under 30   1   probably **George**
Free White Female over 20 and under 30   1   probably **Rebecca**
Free White Female under 5   1   probably **Mary H.** about 2
This census only listed head of household by name.

1850 CENSUS
Dugan, George   Age 37 **Birthplace:** Maryland
                         Armorer
Wife: Rebecca Dugan
                         Age 29 **Birthplace:** VA
Home: Harpers Ferry, VA (Jefferson County)

Children of George & Rebecca Dugan
Henry   Age 18 **Birthplace:** VA
Elizabeth Dugan   Age 17 **Birthplace:** VA
                         (Was she a daughter of George or the wife of Henry?)
Mary H.   Age 12 **Birthplace:** VA
Frances   Age 10 **Birthplace:** VA
Sopheria   Age 8 **Birthplace:** VA
Ellen M.   Age 4 **Birthplace:** VA
George W.   Age 2 **Birthplace:** VA

1850 CENSUS
Fryer, James   Age 43 **Birthplace: VA**
                         Miller
Wife: Sarah Fryer   Age 33 **Birthplace:** VA
Home: District 28, VA (Jefferson County)

Children of James & Sarah Fryer
William N.   Age 16 **Birthplace:** VA*
John J.   Age 13 **Birthplace:** VA
Rachel E.   Age 10 **Birthplace:** VA
Ford   Age 7 **Birthplace:** VA
George T.   Age 3 **Birthplace:** VA

Author's Note: *Believe this is the William N. Fryer who was Mary H. Dugan's first husband.

1860 CENSUS
Dugan, George W.
                         Age 45 **Birthplace**: MD
                         Armorer
Wife: Rebecca Dugan
                         Age 42 **Birthplace:** VA
Home: Bolivar, VA (Jefferson County)

Children of George & Rebecca Dugan
Suphroma sp.   Age 17 **Birthplace:** VA   (Listed as **Sopheria** in **1850** Census)
Ellen   Age 14 **Birthplace:** VA
George   Age 10 **Birthplace:** VA
Emma S.   Age 4 **Birthplace:** VA
Sarah J.   Age 2 **Birthplace:** VA

Mary H. was not listed in the Dugan 1860 Census Report. I believe she was married to **William N. Fryer** prior to the census taking and had moved away from home.

1860 CENSUS
Storm, John C.

     Age 43 **Birthplace**: VA
     Armorer
Wife: Frances R. (Dugan) Storm
     Age 18 **Birthplace**, VA
Home: Bolivar, VA (Jefferson County)

1870 CENSUS
Dugan, George

     Age 59 **Birthplace**: VA (1860 Census says **Birthplace**: MD)
     Pattern Maker
Wife: Rebecca Dugan

     Age 52, **Birthplace**: VA

Home: Washington Ward 1, Washington, D.C.

Children of George & Rebecca Dugan
 George   Age 20 **Birthplace**: VA
 Emma   Age 14 **Birthplace**: VA

Mary Potts   Age 40 **Birthplace**: VA
     Tailorer

Rebecca Dugan

1870 CENSUS
Sarah Dugan*   Age 12 **Birthplace**: VA
     Domestic Service
 *Believe she was the sister of **Mary H.** & daughter of George & Rebecca.
Home: Parkersburg Ward 3, Wood, W. VA

The above address was the home of John & Louisa Brown and their children Effie & Ada
Would George & Rebecca have gone to D.C. and left Sarah behind?
Was Louisa related to George & Rebecca in some way?

1870 CENSUS
Storm, John C.   Age 50 **Birthplace**: MD
     Carpenter
Wife: Frances R. (Dugan) Storm   **Sister of Mary H.**
     Age 28 **Birthplace**: W.VA **Daughter of George & Rebecca**
Home: Bolivar, W.VA (Jefferson County)

Children of John C. & Frances R. Storm
George R.   Age 14 **Birthplace**: W.VA
Mary L.   Age 11 **Birthplace**: W. VA
Leo D.   Age 6 **Birthplace**: W. VA
Ellen R.   Age 3 **Birthplace**: W. VA

Some of the **Storm** children were probably **John Storm's** by a previous marriage. **Frances** died at the age of 31 during a confinement. The death records list her parents as **George & Rebecca Dugan** and her husband as **John C. Storm**

1870 CENSUS
Dugan, Henry   Age 38 **Birthplace**: MD
Wife: Susan   Age 37 **Birthplace**: VA
Home: Northern Division, Loudoun, VA

Children of Henry and Susan Dugan
Anna   Age 13 **Birthplace**
George   Age 11 **Birthplace**
Henry   Age 8   **Birthplace**

1880 CENSUS
Dugan George W.   Age 29 **Birthplace**: VA   **Son-in-law to Mr. Greens**
                        Machinist

Edward Greens   Age 69 **Birthplace**: MD   **Father-in-law/Head of Household**
                        Wheel Wright
Home: Washington, D.C.

Children of George W. Dugan
Richard   Age 6   **Birthplace**: Washington, D. C
Virlinda   Age 2   **Birthplace**: Washington, D. C.

I feel this is **George & Rebecca's** son because their son **George W.** lived with them in D.C. at the time of the **1870 Census**. It's probable that he married during the interim between 1870-1880 and that his wife probably passed away since he appears to be left with two children as shown in the 1880 census.

No information on 1890 Census due to D.C. Fire

1900 CENSUS
Dugan, G. W.
                Age 50 **Birthplace: W.VA**   **Brother of Mary H.**
                Marine Engr.   **Son of George & Rebecca**
Wife: Addelaide Dugan
                Age 49 **Birthplace** MD
Home: Washington, D. C.

Children of G.W. Dugan
Richard E.   Age 25 **Birthplace**: D. C.
Verlindia (sp)   Age 22 **Birthplace**: D. C.

ADDENDUM TO CIVIL WAR SERVICE OF WILLIAM H. FRENCH

Letter Recommending Employment Written by Ulysses S. Grant, Gen. Aug. 14, 1886

The following is a typewritten copy of a handwritten letter from Ulysses S. Grant, General to our great grandfather William H. French. I hope to be able to include a copy of the original handwritten letter in this book.

As you will note I have not been able to ascertain all the wording as over time with the letter being folded some of the writing on the fold has been lost.

Head Quarters Armies of the United States
Washington DC Aug. 14th,1866

B. B. French, Esq.
   Commissioner of Public Buildings
     Sir:
         Permit me to recommend to your favorable notice for employment as "   "
Wm. H. French, an honorably discharged soldier who served through the War of Rebellion and is now out of employment.

If (wording illegible) can be made I will be much pleased.

Very respectfully
Your obedient servant
U. S. Grant
General

This letter was written
Aug 14-1866
At Army Head Quarters
In Washington D C
   W. H. French

The following is also a letter of recommendation for employment.
Sept. 16, 1867:
From the War Dept. Signed by F. T. Smith to a General Michliss (?) The Gen Comdg as Sec. of War(?)   to call your attention to this written recommendation and to ask you to give him employment if you have a vacancy.

Since it was in great grandfather's possession I assume it was for him that the recommendation was written.

Both these letters were mounted on the front and back of a board.

The original of these letters may be seen at the Simsbury Historical Society, Inc. It is now a part of their archives, donated by Donald Paine in March 2004.

Author's Note: These letters would seem to bear out a report from our cousin William Cole, who in talking with Great Grandfather W. H. French, discovered that he had worked on the Capitol Building when the House and Senate wings were added.

The Capitol was burned in August 1814 at the time of the War of 1812 and took many years to rebuild. The wings for Senate and House and the Dome were built during the 1850's and 1860's, and brought the structure to the form we see today.

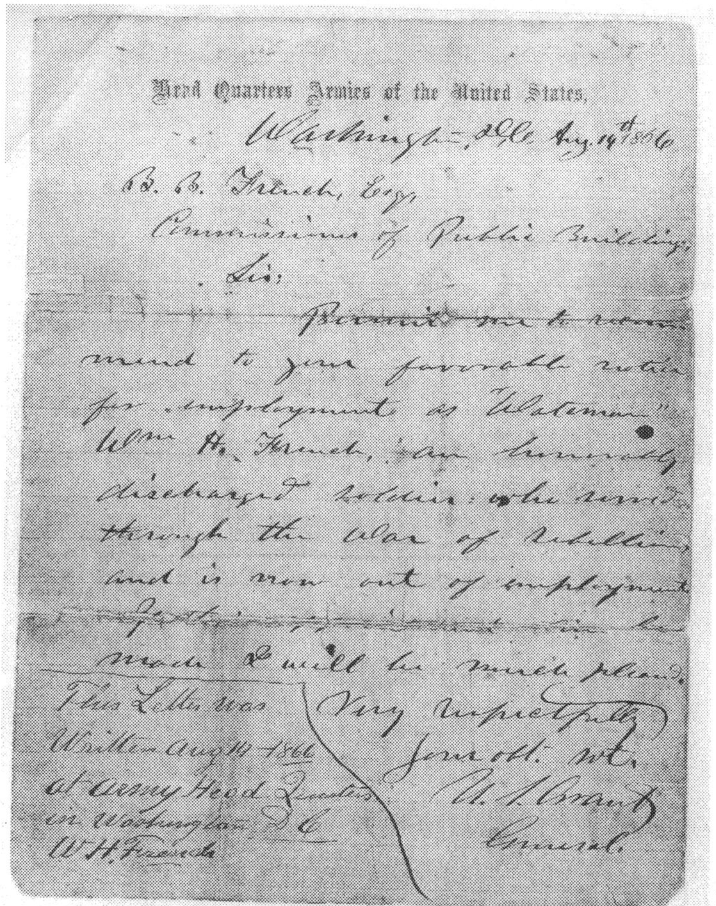

Handwritten copies of recommendation for employment

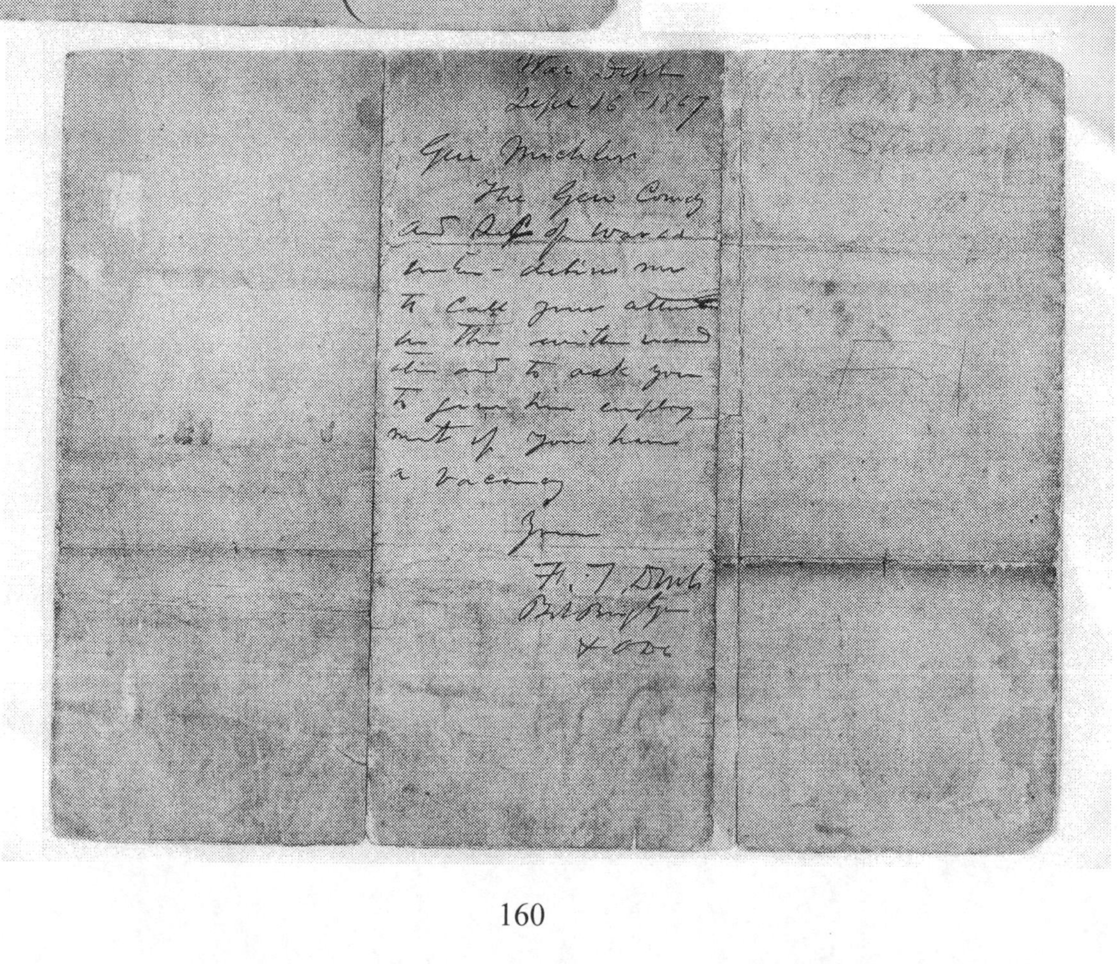

NOTE: Descendants of Robert B. August (Gen. XII, Paine Family) &
Gladys E. (Thompson) August
(continued from page 55)

MARNIE LOUISE AUGUST (GEN. XII, Paine Family)
   b. Dec. 30, 1964 at Hartford, CT
   m. July 19, 1997 at Avon, CT to
JEFFERSON RAY BERDEEN
   b. Jan. 6, 1964 at Westerly, RI

GENERATION XIII
Children of Marnie L. (August) Berdeen & Jefferson R. Berdeen
   Leah Kathryn   b. Jul. 6, 2003 at Farmington, CT
   Peter Jefferson   b. Feb.18, 2005 at Farmington, CT

POSTCRIPT

It's time to bring this volume of our family history to a close. I hope that all who choose to obtain a copy will find it informative, and that those reading the book will find what is recorded here as interesting as I have found it in researching the family over the past twenty years. Perhaps in years to come some member of our clan will decide to carry on from here.

I found researching the William H. French family most intriguing and I am sure there is more to be found on his life and travels. His try at homesteading in Omaha Territory with his family and Dugan in-laws and his family was chronicled to some extent in correspondence from our cousin William R. Cole, which I have included. According to birthdates recorded in the 1880 census, George W. French was born in Washington, D. C. and 9 years of age. I think it safe to assume the family was back in DC by 1871. Alice Landon French was born in Omaha on Dec. 13, 1869. It would appear that William H. certainly had great interest in seeing much of the world even after he married, taking the family with him. I was unable to locate a census report for them in 1870, perhaps because they were traveling home and somewhere in between Nebraska and D. C. My understanding is that the Dugan family who went up with them, chose to remain in Omaha.

One has to admire Grandpa French's wife, Mary Dugan French for following along so faithfully. I'll bet she heaved a sigh of relief when he finally settled in Massachusetts to run a restaurant for the better part of 30 years. She must have missed her Virginia and West Virginia Family. Bear in mind that most of the Dugan's were born in Virginia, and although living in the same place during the Civil War, the western part of Virginia where they resided, became West Virginia on June 20, 1863, due I believe to the western part of the state wishing to remain loyal to the Union.

It is possible that you will find some discrepancies in family information as to names and dates, however I have endeavored to report them as accurately as possible. Sometimes census reports differ as to age from one ten year period to another, as well as name spellings. The fact that the 1890 census all burned up in D.C. does not help at all in carrying on a genealogical search.

As indicated previously the Paine Ancestors arrived in this country in 1638. The French Ancestors came over in 1832. I have been unable to find the year the Dugan's arrived, and in their case can only show you what I discovered in the Census Records, as vital records did not give me too much information on their early days. The information may be there and perhaps some family member will be encouraged to delve into the history and find it. Be forewarned that genealogy research can become addicting!

This book has been prepared with love and gratitude. I'm proud to be a member of the Paine-French family who settled here in America and who have contributed so much to this great country over the generations.

INDEX

Emily Louise 96
George 95
John E. Dr. 94, 95
Jonathan L. 94, 95
Louise 94
Lovina Achsah 131
Oscar (V.) 94
Otis 94
Susan M. 95
William B. 95

Quagliaroli
Harold 57
Rosemary (Kelly) 57

Quance
Edna 118

Rau
Elizabeth Marie 121

Reid
Beverly A. (Chastain) 125
Melanie Rae 68, 125
Robert C. 125

Rhodes
Albert C. 145
George D. 144, 145
Martha A. 144, 145
Rosetta E. (Paine) 144, 145

Rice
Floy L. (Markham) 120
James Robert 120
Sharon Ann (A.) 62, 120

Richards
Bryce Andrew 61
Glen David (D.) 61
Hayley Catherine 61
Jared David 61
Kelsey Leigh 61
Kim Amelia (A.) (Seibert) 61

Riddell
Jackie Lee 63

Rider
Cora Belle Eaton 113

Rolligoom
Anneke A. 101

Rooney
Agnes Lillian (L.) (Pitts/Pettipas) 125
James Murray (M.) 125
Marian Ellen (E.) 68, 74, 125

Ross
Col. And Lady 80

Roth
Betty 121

Rowsom
Chris 5

Ruckinger
Frank 63
Karen Louise (L.) (Ferlingere) 63

St. Pierre
Albert Joseph 29, 30, 53
Barry Joseph (J.) 30, 53
Deborah Jean (J.) 30, 53
Dorothy (August) 29, 30, 53
Roberta (Kone) 53

Sainte Aldegonde
Marnix of 101

Scafani
Christi Irene 121

Scanelli/Schnelli
Joseph Dominic 109
Lena 109, 110
Mary (Ferari) 109

Schaub
Catherin Jane 45

Schmidt
Daniel Louis 55

Schnelli/Scanelli
Joseph Dominic 109
Lena 109, 110
Mary (Ferari) 109

Schrijn
James Udo 70, 126, 127
Jean Eugene 126

Storm
Ellen R. 157
Frances R. (Dugan) 157
George R. 157
John C. 157
Leo D. 157
Mary L. 157

Stoutenburgh/Stoutenburg
Aefje (Eva) (vanTienhoven) 101
Caroline (Allen) 102
Celeste (vanNess) 102
Deliana vonWeed 100
Eldora vanNess 24, 99, 103, 153
George Alfred (A.) 102, 103
Ida M. (Kendall) 102, 103
Jacobus 101, 102
Jason Lucas (L.) 102
Johan van Olden Barneveldt
(Lord of Stoutenburg) 100
Lucas (Luke) 102
Lydia (Zortman) 102
Margaret (Teller) 101, 102
Pieter 101
Rachel (Teller) 102
Sarah (Morris) 102
Tobias 101
Willem, Lord of Stoutenburg 99, 100, 101
William Isaac 102
William Jackson, Rev. 102
Wouter
(Lord of Stoutenburg) 99

Strong
Theona 29

Sullins
Karen Elizabeth (E.) (Cato) 121
Lloyd William 121

Summers
Jamie Lee 63

Sutherland
Dana Marie (M.) 40, 64
Dawn Terri (T.) 40, 65, 120, 121
Karen Lee (L.) (Fisher) 63, 64
Jaime Lee (L.) (Summers)) 63, 64
Jackie Lee (L.) (Ridell) 63, 64
Lois Mattie(M.) (Weed) 40, 63, 106
Mack Horice (H.) 40, 63, 106

Pearl R. (Trudell) 106
Renee Michelle (M.) 40, 64
Richard Thomas 64
Sean Michael 64
Spencer Matthew 64
Thomas 106
Thomas Lee 64
William Bradley 64
William Thomas (T.) 40, 63, 64

Sweeney
Paul 5, 139

Symonds
Mary Patricia (P.) (Keane) 126
Patricia 69, 70, 126
William 126

Taylor
Andrew Monty 107
Capt. 82
Clarence H. 77, 130
Deborah Lynn 107
Dennis Roy 107
Evelyn B. (Lowe) 106, 107
Frank Monte 107
Frederick Neal 40, 65
Lois Mattie (M.) (Weed) 40, 65, 107
Patricia A. (Trigoning) 107
Rebecca Christine 107
Ronald Anthony 107
Ronald Leo (L.) 40, 65, 107
Roy 77, 130
Tina M. (Hudson) 65
Wilberta (Fryer) 76, 77, 87, 92, 130

Teller
Margaret 101, 102
Rachel 102

Tellier
Jacqueline Yvette 52, 115
Raymond Adrien 115
Simone (Lavigne) 115

Tennett
Harriet Pauline (P.) (Houle) 124, 125
Karen Linda (L.) 68, 125
Ronald Eugene (E.) 124, 125

Wallace
Alice Louise 105

Ward
Lisa Ann (Nardi) 67

Waterman
Avis 88, 155
Julia (French) 89, 155
Mrs. W. H. (Julia) 87, 88
William H. 88, 89, 155

Webber
Sarah 75

Weed
Ada L. Boerum) 98
Alberta Ruth (R.) (Berry) 43, 65 108
Ammon 98
Ashley Cherie 66
Bertha Mae (M.) 5, 23, 37, 106, 152
Cara Lynne (L.) (Edwards) 65, 66
Daniel Patrick 43, 65, 66
Ebenezer 97
Elizabeth M. (Benedict) 98
Frederick Augustus 98
Frederick Davis 98, 99
Frederick Davis II 5, 23, 43, 108
James 97, 98
Jo Donna (Berry) 5, 43, 108
Keturah (Weed) 98
Lacy Danielle 66
Lois Mattie 5, 23, 40, 106, 107, 152
Mary A. (Davis) 98
Mattie (Paine) 23, 37, 41, 99, 152
Michael Davis 43
Rachael (Dibble) 98
Rosemarie Nina (N.) 43, 65, 121
Ruth E. (Long) 5, 43
Solomon 98
Tiffany Lynne 66
William Boerum (B.) 23, 37, 99, 152
William Boerum (B.), Jr. 23, 43, 65, 108

Welch
Dorothy Elizabeth 117

Wheeler
Alice Landon (French, Cole) 75, 87, 89, 92
Clarence 88, 89

White
Abial, Abiel 93, 95
Asa 95
Azubah 93, 95
Calvin 93
Daniel 93
John 93, 94, 95
Lavina 93, 94, 95
Levine 95
Lovina 93, 95
Lucy 95
Mary 93, 94
Mary (Grover) 94
Matthew 94
Nicholas 94
Otis 93
Peregrine 4, 93, 94
Rachel 93, 94, 95
Susanna, Susannah 93, 94, 95
Sybil 93
Ursula (Macomber) 94
William 93

Whittemore
Hannah 142, 144,

Wilbank
Caroline 76
Clarissa (Caroline?) (French 76, 90
John 75, 87, 90
John, Mrs. 91

Wilder
Ahlene (Gibbons) 116
Frank Earl 116
Joyce 116

Willey
Ann Luise 127